Important Information

EMERGENCY PHONE NUMBERS

Emergency Medical Service (EMS) _____

Hospital emergency room _____

Ambulance _____

Fire department _____

Police _____

Poison Control Center _____ 24-hour taxi service _____

Gas company _____ Electric company _____

Father's work # _____ Pager or cellular phone # _____

Mother's work # _____ Pager or cellular phone # _____

School # _____

Other _____

INFORMATION TO PROVIDE WHEN CALLING FOR EMERGENCY HELP

Your name / Type of emergency (poison, broken bone, loss of consciousness, gaping wound, etc.)

Your address _____ Apartment # _____

Major intersection or notable landmarks nearby _____

Phone # you're calling from _____

PHYSICIANS

Family physician _____

Phone # _____ Office hours _____

Dentist _____

Phone # _____ Office hours _____

Other physicians

Dr. _____ Phone # _____

Dr. _____ Phone # _____

Dr. _____ Phone # _____

Dr. _____ Phone # _____

RELATIVES

Name _____ Phone # _____

Name _____ Phone # _____

Name _____ Phone # _____

Name _____ Phone # _____

Name _____ Phone # _____

Name _____ Phone # _____

PASTORS, COUNSELORS, ATTORNEYS

Name _____ Phone # _____

Name _____ Phone # _____

Name _____ Phone # _____

Name _____ Phone # _____

MEDICATIONS AND PRESCRIPTIONS

All-night pharmacy phone # _____

Prescription-service phone # _____

Frequently used medications _____

_____

_____

_____

HEALTH INSURANCE

Health insurance agent _____

   Health insurance phone # _____ Policy # _____

   Phone # for verification of coverage _____

   Address for sending claims _____

   _____

Health insurance agent _____

   Health insurance phone # _____ Policy # _____

   Phone # for verification of coverage _____

   Address for sending claims _____

   _____

Focus on the Family®
The First Two Years

FOCUS
ON THE
FAMILY®

The First Two Years

THE
FOCUS ON
THE FAMILY
PHYSICIANS RESOURCE
COUNCIL, U.S.A.

PRIMARY AUTHOR:
Paul C. Reisser, M.D.

MANAGING EDITOR:
Melissa R. Cox

EDITOR:
Vinita Hampton Wright

Tyndale House Publishers, Inc.
WHEATON, ILLINOIS

The information contained in this book provides a general overview of many health-related topics.
It is not intended to substitute for advice that you might receive from your child's physician,
whether by telephone or during a direct medical evaluation. Furthermore, health-care practices
are continually updated as a result of medical research and advances in technology.
You should therefore check with your child's doctor if there is any question about
current recommendations for a specific problem.
No book can substitute for a direct assessment of your child by a qualified health-care professional.

Visit Tyndale's exciting Web site at www.tyndale.com

ISBN 0-8423-0894-6

Printed in the United States of America

05   04   03   02   01   00   99
10   9   8   7   6   5   4   3   2

To the children of this and future generations.

Table of Contents

Foreword
by Dr. James Dobson

If you've picked up this book, it is likely that you are a parent, soon to be one, or know someone who is. Maybe you and your spouse are expecting your first child. Pregnancy has been an experience more precious and indescribable than you could ever have imagined. Ultrasound photos, despite their blurry resolution, provide incontrovertible evidence of your baby's developing hands and feet, the shape of his or her head, the not-yet-seeing eyes. As this fragile life takes shape, you can't help being filled with wonder at the intricate, unfolding miracle of God's handiwork.

Perhaps your scenario is not so idyllic. Maybe you are not yet out of high school. The father of your baby conveniently excused himself when he learned of your condition. You've lived at home with your mom and dad throughout your pregnancy, or perhaps in a halfway house with other girls in crisis pregnancies.

Or your grown daughter has rejected her own baby, and now you're being asked to bring up your grandchild. Or you're a single dad trying to find your way in a world that fails to recognize that sometimes daddies have to be mommies too. This book was written with you in mind too.

Under the best of circumstances, rearing kids is a challenging assignment. As a parent, you will be called on to don a variety of hats, among them teacher, doctor, psychologist, friend, and pharmacist. As you contemplate the challenges ahead, you may feel overwhelmed by the responsibility. How can you nurture healthy self-esteem in your children? How can you teach them to protect themselves from unhealthy ideas, attitudes, habits, and associations? How can you build within them discernment and self-discipline? How can you develop in them, day by day, the values that are so basic to their well-being? And—one of the toughest questions of all—how can you guide them into independence until they themselves are walking with God in wisdom and truth, rather than simply following you?

The most discerning, vigilant, and competent parents ultimately find themselves feeling inadequate to accomplish these important tasks. A parent must have support, guidance, and encouragement—from other parents, from friends and family, from physicians and pastors. And we believe that, ultimately, each child must be entrusted to the care, love, and protection of Jesus Christ. I urge you not to shortchange your children by underestimating the importance of biblical precepts—either in the values you teach or in the way you conduct your own life. The stakes are simply too high.

Here at Focus on the Family, we recognize that parenting a child involves the care and nurture of the whole person—body, mind, *and* soul. That's why I'm particularly excited to be able to introduce to you this wonderful new offering from Tyndale House Publishers, *Focus on the Family The First Two Years.* This comprehensive, well-researched volume offers detailed advice from more than fifty of the country's most highly respected physicians and medical authorities. Some have appeared as guests on the *Focus on the Family* broadcast, and many are members of Focus's prestigious Physicians Resource Council. This book is full of practical, specific guidance on the child rearing process—from infancy through the toddler years.

And what truly sets this book apart is the spiritual guidance and encouragement woven throughout its pages. You will find countless helpful hints for instilling in your little ones the timeless truths of Scripture—and the foundation of faith upon which rest our ultimate hope and salvation.

You yourself may have gotten a rough start in life. You may not have received the nurturing and encouragement you deserved as a child. Maybe you've struggled with issues of low self-esteem and feelings of rejection from your own parents. If that's your story, I have good news for you: Starting here, you *can* do better by your own child. It begins with dedicating yourself and your baby to the care of the only truly perfect parent—the Lord Jesus Christ.

Whatever your parenting situation—be it by choice or by chance, whether the circumstances are ideal or heartbreaking, whether yours is a background of poverty or privilege—it matters not. What does matter is that you have been charged by God with a profound and sacred trust: that of shaping and nurturing a human life. Handle it with care. God bless you!

James Dobson

Acknowledgments

In many ways, the preparation of this book has resembled the process of parenting a child from infancy to adulthood. Our "baby" was born in enthusiastic brainstorming sessions, during which exciting and formidable proposals were set in motion. During the book's infancy, as the first chapters and reference topics were written, we slowly began to appreciate the amount of time, effort, and patience that would be required before our "young adult" would be ready to meet the world.

But there was no turning back. We eventually hit our stride over a period of months as more chapters and topics were written, reviewed, debated, revised, and reviewed again—often as many as nine or ten times over the course of several months. Our "child" grew and matured and received ongoing prayer, loving attention, and correction until another rite of passage arrived: an "adolescence" of sorts, when hundreds of pages of manuscript were presented to Tyndale House Publishers. More questions, suggestions, and insights from Tyndale's team led to further refinements, sometimes after spirited (but inevitably fruitful) discussions.

Finally graduation day has arrived, and our offspring is now vacating the nest and beginning an independent life, one that we pray will enhance and assist your family.

This project is the result of a diligent and cooperative effort of many talented individuals over a period of nearly three years. To all of them we are deeply indebted. While we cannot fully acknowledge the full length and breadth of their contributions, the following is our attempt to give credit where it is most certainly due.

First of all, a standing ovation is due to the members of the Physicians Resource Council review team, who spent endless hours in conference calls and many days in sometimes cramped quarters reviewing literally every letter of the manuscript. We thank you for your dedication, perseverance, patience, professionalism, and commitment.

THE FOCUS ON THE FAMILY
PHYSICIANS RESOURCE COUNCIL REVIEW TEAM
AND CONTRIBUTING EDITORS

Marilyn Maxwell Billingsly, M.D.
INTERNAL MEDICINE/PEDIATRICS—ST. LOUIS, MISSOURI

Douglas O. W. Eaton, M.D.
INTERNAL MEDICINE—SAN BERNARDINO, CALIFORNIA

J. Thomas Fitch, M.D.
PEDIATRICS—SAN ANTONIO, TEXAS

Patricia O. Francis, M.D.
PEDIATRICS—MORAGA, CALIFORNIA

Gaylen M. Kelton, M.D.
FAMILY MEDICINE—INDIANAPOLIS, INDIANA

Richard D. Kiovsky, M.D.
FAMILY MEDICINE—INDIANAPOLIS, INDIANA

Robert W. Mann, M.D.
PEDIATRICS—ARLINGTON, TEXAS

Paul Meier, M.D.
PSYCHIATRY—RICHARDSON, TEXAS

Mary Anne Nelson, M.D.
FAMILY MEDICINE—CEDAR RAPIDS, IOWA

The remaining members of the Focus on the Family Physicians Resource Council, in both the United States and Canada, also contributed to this project in a variety of ways.

UNITED STATES

John P. Livoni, M.D. (chair)
RADIOLOGY—SACRAMENTO, CALIFORNIA

Peter F. Armstrong, M.D.
ORTHOPEDICS—SALT LAKE CITY, UTAH

Reed Bell, M.D.
PEDIATRICS—GULF BREEZE, FLORIDA

Robb Blackwood, M.D.
FAMILY MEDICINE—CHESAPEAKE, VIRGINIA

Eugene Diamond, M.D.
PEDIATRICS—CHICAGO, ILLINOIS

Thomas E. Elkins, M.D.
OBSTETRICS/GYNECOLOGY—BALTIMORE, MARYLAND

W. David Hager, M.D.
OBSTETRICS/GYNECOLOGY—LEXINGTON, KENTUCKY

Walter Larimore, M.D.
FAMILY MEDICINE—KISSIMMEE, FLORIDA

Alan A. Nelson, M.D.
PSYCHIATRY—REDSTONE, COLORADO

Claudia Nelson, M.D.
PEDIATRICS—REDSTONE, COLORADO

Donald Nelson, M.D.
FAMILY MEDICINE—CEDAR RAPIDS, IOWA

Jeffrey B. Satinover, M.D.
PSYCHIATRY—WESTON, CONNECTICUT

Curtis Stine, M.D.
FAMILY MEDICINE—DENVER, COLORADO

Morton Woolley, M.D.
GENERAL SURGEON—LOS ANGELES, CALIFORNIA

CANADA

Margaret Cottle, M.D. (chair)
PALLIATIVE CARE—VANCOUVER, BRITISH COLUMBIA

Ron Calderisi, M.D.
GENERAL SURGEON—VANCOUVER, BRITISH COLUMBIA

Stephen Genuis, M.D.
OBSTETRICS/GYNECOLOGY—EDMONTON, ALBERTA

Jim Gilbert, M.D.
GENERAL SURGEON—PEMBROKE, ONTARIO

Rosemarie Gilbert, M.D.
FAMILY MEDICINE—PEMBROKE, ONTARIO

Ron Jarvis, M.D.
FAMILY MEDICINE—DUNCAN, BRITISH COLUMBIA

Tim Kelton, M.D.
FAMILY MEDICINE—NORTH YORK, ONTARIO

Peter Nieman, M.D.
PEDIATRICS—CALGARY, ALBERTA

Dickson Vinden, M.D.
FAMILY MEDICINE—CANNINGTON, ONTARIO

Peter Webster, M.D.
RESPIRATORY MEDICINE—TORONTO, ONTARIO

In addition to the members of the Physicians Resource Council, we would like to thank the many contributors who provided research, written material, and reviews of topics in their fields of expertise:

Jane Anderson, M.D.
PEDIATRICS—SAN FRANCISCO, CALIFORNIA

Karl Anderson, M.D.
UROLOGY—SAN FRANCISCO, CALIFORNIA

Brian L. Burke Jr., M.D.
PEDIATRICS—GRAND RAPIDS, MICHIGAN

Robin Cottle, M.D.
OPHTHALMOLOGY—VANCOUVER, BRITISH COLUMBIA

Sarah Chandler, M.D.
FAMILY MEDICINE—LUBBOCK, TEXAS

M. C. Culbertson Jr., M.D.
PEDIATRIC OTOLARYNGOLOGY—DALLAS, TEXAS

William G. Culver, M.D.
ALLERGY-IMMUNOLOGY—LOVELAND, COLORADO

Joyce Fischer, M.D.
PEDIATRICS—BLUFFTON, INDIANA

Russell Engevik, M.D.
EMERGENCY MEDICINE—JULIAN, CALIFORNIA

Linda Flower, M.D.
FAMILY MEDICINE—TOMBALL, TEXAS

Lawrence P. Frick, M.D.
FAMILY MEDICINE—CHILLICOTHE, OHIO

Stanley Hand, M.D.
OPHTHALMOLOGY—ORLANDO, FLORIDA

John Hartman, M.D.
FAMILY MEDICINE—KISSIMMEE, FLORIDA

Gerald Hough, M.D.
PEDIATRICS—BRANDON, FLORIDA

Duke Johnson, M.D.
FAMILY MEDICINE—TUSTIN, CALIFORNIA

W. Kip Johnson, M.D.
FAMILY MEDICINE—IRVINE, CALIFORNIA

Ronald Jones, M.D.
PEDIATRICS—SPRINGFIELD, MISSOURI

Paul Liu, M.D.
PEDIATRICS—PHOENIX, ARIZONA

Margaret Meeker, M.D.
PEDIATRICS—TRAVERSE CITY, MICHIGAN

Carl Meyer, D.O.
PEDIATRICS—GREENVILLE, PENNSYLVANIA

Michael C. Misko, M.D.
FAMILY MEDICINE—HOLDEN, MISSOURI

D. Brett Mitchell, M.D.
FAMILY MEDICINE—DENISON, TEXAS

John Moyer, M.D.
PEDIATRICS—DENVER, COLORADO

Steve Parnell, M.D.
FAMILY MEDICINE—FAIRMONT, MINNESOTA

Jan Payne, M.D.
PATHOLOGY—ST. PAUL, ALASKA

John C. Rhodes, M.D.
FAMILY MEDICINE—LAS VEGAS, NEVADA

David Sadowitz, M.D.
PEDIATRIC HEMATOLOGY/ONCOLOGY—CAMINUS, NEW YORK

Bodo Treu, M.D.
FAMILY MEDICINE—OMAHA, NEBRASKA

G. Scott Voorman, M.D.
OTOLARYNGOLOGY—THOUSAND OAKS, CALIFORNIA

James C. Wilkes, M.D.
PEDIATRICS/PEDIATRIC NEPHROLOGY—LEXINGTON, KENTUCKY

Franklin D. Wilson, M.D.
ORTHOPEDICS—INDIANAPOLIS, INDIANA

Gentry Yeatman, M.D.
ADOLESCENT MEDICINE—TACOMA, WASHINGTON

We would like to thank the following individuals for reviewing segments of the completed manuscript for accuracy:

Mary Beth Adam, M.D.
ADOLESCENT MEDICINE—TUCSON, ARIZONA

Stephen Apaliski, M.D.
PEDIATRIC ALLERGY—FORT WORTH, TEXAS

Sarah Blumenschein, M.D.
PEDIATRIC CARDIOLOGY—FORT WORTH, TEXAS

Paul Bowman, M.D.
PEDIATRIC HEMATOLOGY/ONCOLOGY—FORT WORTH, TEXAS

Preston W. Campbell, M.D.
PEDIATRIC PULMONOLOGY—NASHVILLE, TENNESSEE

James Cunningham, M.D.
PEDIATRIC PULMONOLOGY—FORT WORTH, TEXAS

Mary Davenport, M.D.
OBSTETRICS/GYNECOLOGY—BERKELEY, CALIFORNIA

Mary A. Eyanson, M.D.
PEDIATRICS—CEDAR RAPIDS, IOWA

David Michael Foulds, M.D.
PEDIATRICS—SAN ANTONIO, TEXAS

Roni Grad, M.D.
PEDIATRIC PULMONOLOGY—SAN ANTONIO, TEXAS

W. Wayne Grant, M.D.
PEDIATRICS—SAN ANTONIO, TEXAS

David Gregory, D.Ph.
PHARMACOLOGY—NASHVILLE, TENNESSEE

Lyn Hunt, M.D.
PEDIATRIC GASTROENTEROLOGY—FORT WORTH, TEXAS

Vernon L. James, M.D.
DEVELOPMENTAL MEDICINE—SAN ANTONIO, TEXAS

Cheryl Kissling, R.N.
LACTATION CONSULTANT—CEDAR RAPIDS, IOWA

Mary Kukolich, M.D.
GENETICS—FORT WORTH, TEXAS

Risé L. Lyman, D.D.S.
GENERAL DENTISTRY—SAN ANTONIO, TEXAS

Everett Moody, M.D.
PEDIATRIC OPHTHALMOLOGY—ARLINGTON, TEXAS

Britt Nelson, M.D.
PEDIATRIC INTENSIVE CARE—ARLINGTON, TEXAS

Amil Ortiz, M.D.
NEONATOLOGY—SAN ANTONIO, TEXAS

Steve Phillips, M.D.
PEDIATRIC NEUROLOGY—SACRAMENTO, CALIFORNIA

Judith L. Pugh, M.D.
PEDIATRIC NEPHROLOGY—SAN ANTONIO, TEXAS

S. DuBose Ravenel, M.D.
PEDIATRICS—HIGH POINT, NORTH CAROLINA

Brian Riedel, M.D.
PEDIATRIC GASTROENTEROLOGY—NASHVILLE, TENNESSEE

James Roach, M.D.
PEDIATRIC ORTHOPEDICS—FORT WORTH, TEXAS

Mark Shelton, M.D.
INFECTIOUS DISEASES—FORT WORTH, TEXAS

Glaze Vaughn, M.D.
PEDIATRIC SURGERY/UROLOGY—FORT WORTH, TEXAS

Teri Walter
PHYSICAL THERAPY—ARLINGTON, TEXAS

Paul Warren, M.D.
BEHAVIORAL PEDIATRICS—PLANO, TEXAS

Rick Weiser, M.D.
ADOLESCENT MEDICINE—PLEASANTON, CALIFORNIA

Also, this project would not have been possible without the immeasurable support of our loving spouses, Alan Cox and Teri Reisser. Your love, patience, and endurance literally kept us going. This project is not only ours but yours. We appreciate and love you!—Melissa R. Cox, Paul C. Reisser, M.D.

xiv

EDITORIAL STAFF

PRIMARY AUTHOR: Paul C. Reisser, M.D.
MANAGING EDITOR: Melissa R. Cox
TYNDALE EDITOR: Vinita Hampton Wright

FOCUS ON THE FAMILY

Bradley G. Beck, M.D. MEDICAL ISSUES ADVISOR
Lianne Belote, ADMINISTRATIVE ASSISTANT
Lisa D. Brock, RESEARCH EDITOR
Bob Chuvala, RESEARCH EDITOR
Kathleen M. Gowler, ADMINISTRATIVE SUPPORT
Karen Sagahon, ADMINISTRATIVE SUPPORT
Keith Wall, RESEARCH EDITOR

Special thanks to:

Glenn Bethany   Mark Maddox
Kurt Bruner   Dean Merrill
Charmé Fletcher   Craig Osten
Anita Fuglaar   Mike Yorkey
Al Janssen   Rolf Zettersten

TYNDALE HOUSE PUBLISHERS:
EDITORIAL

Meg Diehl, PROJECT MANAGER
Vinita Hampton Wright, EDITOR
Peter Bodnar, PROOFREADING SUPERVISOR
Jan Pigott, COPY EDITOR
Anisa Baker, ADMINISTRATIVE SUPPORT

Special thanks to: Ron Beers

TYNDALE HOUSE PUBLISHERS:
PRODUCTION

Julee Schwarzburg, PROJECT MANAGER
Annette Taroli, PROJECT MANAGER
Catherine Bergstrom, ART DIRECTOR
Ann Gjeldum, DESIGNER
Gloria Keibler, DESIGNER
Judy Wireman, TYPESETTER/DESKTOP PUBLISHER
Linda Walz, PRINT BUYER

GRAPHICS/ILLUSTRATIONS

BOOK DESIGN: Catherine Bergstrom
ASSIGNMENT EDITOR: Melissa R. Cox

MEDICAL ILLUSTRATIONS:
Jeff Lane, pages 15, 30, 37

NONMEDICAL ILLUSTRATIONS:
Alan Flinn, pages 211–212
Rick Johnson, pages 16–19, 28, 46, 48, 51,
199–205, 207–209

ART REVIEWERS:
Bradley G. Beck, M.D.
John Livoni, M.D.
Curtis Stine, M.D.

COVER PHOTOS:
Susan Andrews

CHAPTER PHOTOS:
Blaine Harrington, page 129
Mark Kozlowski, page 75
James McLoughlin, pages 1, 99
Camille Tokenrud, page 43

PHOTO BUYER:
Kristen Mapstone

BACK COVER TEXT:
Alan G. Cox

Introduction

Focus on the Family The First Two Years has been designed to assist you throughout the course of the most rewarding and challenging job of your life: parenting. Whether you are expecting your first baby in the near future or have years of parenting experience, we hope that you will find this book helpful—not only as a useful resource but also as a source of inspiration, especially when the going gets a little tough (or extremely difficult).

This book is divided into two major sections:

The first section is a detailed chronological tour of a child's life from infancy through toddlerhood. Chapters in this section are intended to be read in their entirety, but you may also benefit from reviewing specific topics contained within them. The chapters include:

- ◆ details about physical, mental, and emotional development through two years of age
- ◆ practical information about basic topics such as feeding, sleep, safety, and common illnesses
- ◆ suggestions for building strong bonds with your child, providing appropriate discipline through a balance of love and limits, and instilling moral and spiritual values
- ◆ encouragement for strengthening marriage, meeting the special challenges of single parenting, avoiding burnout, and managing conflicts

The second major section deals with special concerns including:

- ◆ when your child has a fever
- ◆ choosing a caregiver
- ◆ principles of discipline and training

This book contains a number of additional features:
- ◆ sidebars highlighting helpful tips on everything from parenting to keeping your marriage strong
- ◆ a section devoted to **emergency care** and **first aid**
- ◆ a topical index

As you begin to use *Focus on the Family The First Two Years,* it is important that you keep these cautionary points in mind:

- This book is intended to serve as a road map to help orient and guide you through your parenting journey. It does not provide detailed directions for every conceivable situation you might encounter along the way, nor is the advice it contains cast in concrete. The basic principles set forth in this book must be molded and adjusted to fit you and your own child.

- This book is not intended to serve as a substitute for specific input that you will receive from your child's physician. You will be encouraged many times throughout these pages to contact a doctor or (if the situation is urgent) to take your child directly to a medical facility, for a variety of specific problems. *No book can substitute for a direct assessment of your child by a qualified health-care professional.*

- Despite our best efforts to include the most up-to-date information, in the field of health care the "current wisdom" changes continuously, especially in areas such as immunization guidelines. What was hot news when this book went to press may be outdated in a matter of months. This is another reason to check with your child's doctor if you have any questions about a particular situation you might encounter.

For the physicians who serve on the Focus on the Family Physicians Resource Council, this book has indeed been a labor of love. Having spent countless hours over the past three years preparing the information and advice contained within this book, our heartfelt desire is that it will be a valuable resource for you while enhancing the life of your child(ren) for many years to come.

May you find joy in your parenting journey,
JOHN P. LIVONI, M.D., M.P.H., Chair
Focus on the Family Physicians Resource Council

The First Three Months, Part One

We are born helpless.
As soon as we are fully
conscious, we discover loneliness.
We need others physically,
emotionally, intellectually;
we need them if we are to know
anything, even ourselves.
C. S. LEWIS

The First Three Months, Part One: Family Adjustments, Feeding the New Arrival, and Dealing with Basic Health Concerns

Now that the efforts of labor and delivery are over, within a few hours or a few days after your baby's birth (with rare exception), you will be bringing your son or daughter home. If this is your first child, you will most likely have some apprehensions about the coming weeks—or, for that matter, about the first night. Will he get enough nourishment? How often should he be fed? Where should he sleep? Will *we* get any sleep? What if he starts crying—and won't stop? If there are other children at home, how will they respond to the new arrival?

Many of these questions have already been addressed in a childbirth- or parenting-preparation class. And if you have older children at home, you have already dealt with most of these concerns before and may not feel the need for any further "basic training." But just in case you didn't get all the bases covered, the following two chapters will cover the ABCs of new baby care.

Before we begin, remember:

- The information in this book assumes that your baby is full-term, has been examined, and is basically healthy. If he was born prematurely or has medical problems that require special care, you should follow the specific directions of your physician.
- In the coming months you will be getting all sorts of advice from friends, relatives, and other resources. Much of it will be helpful and appropriate, at least for most babies. But if something you read or hear doesn't make sense or doesn't work, don't be afraid to get a second opinion. And if you get conflicting advice, don't panic. Newborns are much

more sturdy and resilient than you might think, and there are very few mistakes that loving, attentive parents might make that cannot be straightened out later on.

♦ While it is normal to feel some anxiety over the responsibility of full-time care for a new baby, the process of parenting a newborn should not be dominated by fear and uncertainty. Be confident that you and your baby can and will survive and thrive, even while all of you are learning. Since every parent-child combination is unique, some adjusting and improvising will be a necessary part of the process. But it is neither necessary nor wise to wade through the first months or years purely on blind instinct.

FIRST THINGS FIRST FOR COUPLES: MOM AND DAD'S PARTNERSHIP

With all the excitement and changes that come with the role of parenting, whether for the first time or with a new addition, *it is extremely important that mother and father continuously reaffirm the importance of their own relationship.* For many reasons, it is common for a new baby to take center stage and for parents, especially new ones, to put the maintenance of their marriage at the bottom of the daily priority list. Remember that the two of you became a family with the exchange of vows, before children were in the picture. You will remain a family after the children have grown and left your home. While they are under your roof, a rock-solid partnership, continually renewed and refreshed, will be the foundation for the security of any and all children you add to your original family of two. Your new baby is to be loved and cherished, but he must not, for his own sake, become the permanent center of gravity around which everything else in your home revolves.

Preventing turmoil in the nest

You might assume that the awe and wonder of having a newborn at home would automatically forge a powerful bond between the proud parents. But it is also quite possible for the new demands of baby care to generate some unexpected friction, resentment, or jealousy in the marriage.

If the new baby is breast-fed rather than bottle-fed, much of a young mother's time and energy will be occupied with feeding, not to mention the many other details of infant care. (This can also occur, of course, when a baby is bottle-fed, although in this case others can take turns with feeding sessions.) As a result, a father might begin to feel left out and could even resent a nursing child who seems to have displaced him from his wife's affections.

This may be aggravated by unspoken assumptions about mothers' and fathers' roles, especially with newborns. If one parent believes that tending to a baby is "women's work" and that Dad need not report for duty until his son can throw a ball or his daughter is ready to ride a bike, a wedge can develop between mother and father. He may become weary of seeing her attention directed toward meeting the newborn's seemingly endless needs. She may become irritated if he isn't pulling his weight at home, especially if he seems to expect her to meet a lot of his needs when she is thoroughly exhausted.

How can you prevent a newborn nest from becoming a "house divided"?

Hot tips for Mom: Make sure your husband knows that he hasn't been relegated to the back burner of your affection and interest. Beware of total and absolute preoccupation with your new baby, as normal as that desire might seem to you. If you nurse, carry, rock, caress, and sleep with your baby twenty-four hours a day without offering some attention to your mate, before long your marriage may be a shadow of its former self.

Whenever possible, try to freshen up if you haven't seen your spouse for several hours—even if you're pooped. It's important that you take care of yourself even in these early days of motherhood, because from now on it will be tempting to neglect yourself when there are so many needs and tasks surrounding you. Certainly your husband will appreciate seeing you take steps to maintain your health and appearance. But for your own sake it is important to cultivate good feelings about who *you* are by giving some priority to your personal needs and interests. Taking care of yourself, even in small ways, can help you avoid baby-care burnout—not only now but also in the days and seasons to come.

Hot tips for Dad: Pay lots of attention to your newborn, for whom you can do all sorts of things (such as cuddling, rocking, and changing). Wives tend to become very enamored with husbands who clearly cherish their babies. Don't expect to be treated like another child at home, waiting for a weary housekeeper to fix your meals, do your laundry, and clean up your messes. Roll up your sleeves and pitch in. Your commitment to "love, honor, and cherish" has no expiration date.

Patterns you establish now in your marriage may well continue as your new baby and other children at home grow to maturity. Ultimately their sense of security will rise or fall with the visible evidence of stability, mutual respect, and ongoing love of their mother and father for one another. Overt demonstrations of affection not only fulfill deep and abiding needs between husband and wife, but they also provide a strong, daily reassurance for children that their world will remain intact. The same can be said of time set aside by parents for quiet conversation with one another *before* the children have gone to bed.

Equally significant is a regular date night for Mom and Dad, which should be instituted as soon as possible and maintained even after the kids are grown and gone. These time-outs need not be expensive, but they may require some ongoing creativity, planning, and dedication. Dedication is necessary because child-care needs, pangs of guilt, and complicated calendars will conspire to prevent those dates from happening. But the romance, renewal, and vitality they generate are well worth the effort.

Special note to single parents

Taking care of a new baby is a major project for a couple in a stable marriage. For a single parent—who usually, but not always, is the mother—the twenty-four-hour care of a newborn may seem overwhelming from the first day. But even without a committed partner, you *can* take care of your baby and do it well. The job will be less difficult if you have some help.

Hopefully, before the baby was born you found a few people who would be willing members of your support team. These might be your parents, other relatives, friends, members of your church, or volunteers from a local crisis pregnancy center (CPC). By all means, don't hesitate to seek their help, especially during the early weeks when you are getting acquainted with your new baby. If your parents offer room, board, and child-care assistance, and you are on good terms with them, you would be wise to accept. Or if a helpful and mature family member or friend offers to stay with you for a while after the birth, give the idea careful consideration. (Obviously, you should avoid situations in which there is likely to be more conflict than help.)

Even after you have a few weeks or months of parenting under your belt, at some point you may need a brief time-out to walk around the block, or advice on calming a crying episode. But no one will know unless you ask. Many churches and CPCs have ongoing single-parent groups in which you can relax for a few hours on a regular basis, swap ideas, and talk with others who know first-hand the challenges you face.

Preparing other children for the new arrival

Parents often worry about how the arrival of a new baby will affect other children in the family. Children's responses are as different as the children themselves. Some siblings will struggle with jealousy for a while; others welcome the new baby excitedly, eager to be "big sister" or "big brother." But most children, especially if they are younger than age six or seven, will experience a range of emotions: happiness, jealousy, possessiveness toward the baby, protectiveness, fear of being forgotten by the parents, fear that there won't be enough love in the family to go around. While parents can't prevent the onset of these emotions, they can do much to prepare children for an additional person in the family.

Talk about the baby's coming well in advance. When Mom's stomach begins to grow, the other children may ask about it; this is a good time to begin talking about the new sister or brother to come. Allow your other children to enjoy the anticipation along with you.

Include your other children in discussions about the baby. Let big brother or sister join in the conversations about names for the baby and preparations for the nursery. Involve them in as much of the process as you can.

Be careful about how much the arrangements for the baby will impinge on other children's space in the house and schedule. Be sure to prepare children if they are going to get moved out of a bedroom or if their possessions are going to be displaced. Don't disturb their routine any more than necessary, both in preparation for the new baby and after the baby has come home.

Make plans for other relatives to pay attention to the other children. Since Mom and Dad are going to have their hands extra full the first several weeks after the baby comes home, arrange for Grandma or some other relative to do some special things with the other children. And make sure Mom and Dad are relieved of baby duty part of the time so they can spend time with the other children.

Pay attention to signs of jealousy or other forms of upset. Don't take lightly difficult emotions your children may be experiencing. Respond to them, talk to them, let them know they are still important, and continually assure them of your love for them.

Small children are quite capable of harming infants, often without realizing the seriousness of their actions. If a child is acting angry or jealous toward the new baby, don't leave them alone together.

Direct visitors' attention to the other children. Visitors will ooh and aah over the new baby and often neglect siblings. Bring big brother or sister into the circle. Praise their accomplishments. Talk about how well they help you with the baby.

Remember that much of the negative emotion young children feel toward a new baby is rooted in their own fear of being forgotten or not loved by you. As long as you continually express your love for them and their importance to your family, most of their jealousy will subside with time.

LIFE WITH A NEWBORN: WHAT CAN YOU EXPECT?

If you are bringing home a new baby for the very first time, you have probably been wondering what your life will be like on a day-to-day basis. Perhaps you have envisioned your new parenthood as a tranquil scene from a greeting card or a TV commercial: a contented mother and father sitting by the fireside, smiling softly at the tiny cherub who sweetly coos her love in return. Or you may have heard tales of misery from family or friends, describing endless sleepless nights, relentless fatigue, and no life at all away from the seven-pound tyrant who demands attention every moment. Some young mothers arrive at parenthood believing that caring for their new baby will be like bringing a puppy home from the pet store. If you already have children, you know that none of these visions accurately encompass the breadth and depth of caring for a newborn.

In one sense, a newborn has a relatively simple agenda: eating, sleeping, crying, being quietly alert, and eliminating urine and stool, repeated over and over each day. Therefore, it wouldn't seem all that difficult or complicated to care for her. After all, she won't be feverishly exploring every cupboard in the house, struggling with overdue homework assignments, or arguing with you over rights to the car.

But there are countless variations on these basic activities and some unpredictability in the way each baby behaves from day to day. If you have had two or more children, you are already aware that, as unique human beings, each of your offspring has displayed various differences from the others since day one, or even *before* day one.

Furthermore, the first few days of life at home may seem unsettled for both you and your baby. You may be coping for the first time with the profound reality of being responsible for a tiny, helpless human twenty-four hours a day and wondering if you will ever "have a life" again. It may take several character-building days for both baby and parents to establish a predictable pattern of eating and sleeping—or to become used to the absence of a predictable pattern. In response to her new surroundings, your baby may also be more fussy or sleepy after she first arrives home.

For all these reasons, cookbook approaches to baby care, with step-by-step directions for every situation, are unrealistic. Instead, as we look at the elements of your new baby's daily routine, we will outline some basic facts and principles that you can then adapt and fine-tune to your family's unique circumstances. Above all, try your best to relax and trust that you and your baby will in fact eventually settle in (and settle down) together.

FEEDING YOUR NEWBORN

For a new baby and her parents, feeding time represents far more than "open mouth, insert milk." In the course of receiving life-sustaining calories, nutrients, and fluids from multiple feedings every day, your baby is also having a series of important multisensory experiences. The receptors of sight, hearing, touch, taste, and smell are all actively gathering information during feedings. More important, emotional bonds are forming as the discomfort of hunger is repeatedly ended by a loving parent. As you become more familiar with your baby and more relaxed, you can look forward to each feeding as a special, satisfying, and relaxing event rather than a time-consuming chore or a source of anxiety. Like so many other aspects of parenting, how you approach and prepare for this activity will have a major impact on its success.

The vast majority of newborn babies are ready, willing, and able to take in the milk offered to them. They come equipped with rooting, sucking, and swallowing reflexes that are quite efficient at transporting milk from nipple to stomach. While babies may show differences in feeding styles and some may seem more adept than others at the outset, you should assume from the beginning that you and your baby are very capable of working together to accomplish this important goal.

Breast or formula?

Over the past few decades a mountain of scientific evidence has validated what is, in fact, a very straightforward observation: Human mothers are beautifully designed to feed their own babies. Breast milk, with extremely rare exception, is the best—and should normally be the complete—source of nutrition during the first months of a child's life, without additional water, juice, cereal, or other foods.

While there is clear medical consensus that breast feeding is the preferred source of fuel for the newborn, it should not be viewed as a sacred rite. If you need or choose to bottle-feed, you can do so with assurance that your baby will do well physically and emotionally. There are a variety of formulas available that will meet a baby's nutritional needs quite adequately, and both Mom and Dad or a single parent can provide a warm, nurturing experience while feeding an infant from a bottle.

Whether you feed your baby breast milk or formula (or a combination of the two), it is important to understand that *she does not need other types of food or fluids during the first three to four months.* Juice, cow's milk from the dairy case, cereal, fruit, and other solids are all unnecessary and/or inappropriate for your baby at this stage of her life.

Details about formula feeding begin on page 27. However, if you are planning to use formula but have the option to breast-feed or if you are not sure which approach to use, take time to consider carefully the following information before you make your final decision.

What are the advantages of breast feeding?

Human milk is uniquely suited to human babies. It is not only nutritionally complete and properly balanced, but it is also constantly changing to meet the needs of a growing infant. The fat content of breast milk increases as a feeding progresses, creating a sense of satisfied fullness that tends to prevent overeating. Furthermore, the fat and cholesterol content of breast milk is higher in the early months, when these compounds are most needed in a baby's rapidly growing brain and nervous system. The primary proteins in all forms of milk are whey and casein, but in human milk, whey, which is easier to absorb, predominates. Compared to cow's milk, the carbohydrate component of breast milk contains a higher percentage of lactose, which appears to play an important role in both brain development and calcium absorption.

Vitamins and minerals are adequately supplied in mother's milk. No supplements are needed for the normal breast-fed infant, although additional vitamin D may be recommended by your baby's physician if you live in a climate or geographical area where sunshine is rare. Trace elements, such as copper and zinc, are present in the right amounts, and iron is present in breast milk in a form that is easier to absorb than in any other type of milk.

Breast milk is absorbed extremely efficiently, with little undigested material passing into stool. Experienced diaper changers are well aware that formula-fed infants tend to have smellier stools, a by-product of the nutritional odds and ends (especially certain fats and proteins) that are not thoroughly absorbed on their trip through the bowel.

From day one, breast milk contains antibodies that help protect babies from infections. The first product of the breast after birth, known as **colostrum,** is particularly rich in antibodies known as **immunoglobulin A,** which help protect the lining of the intestine from microscopic invaders. As the mother comes in contact with new viruses and bacteria, her immune system generates the appropriate microbe-fighting antibodies and passes them on to her baby, thus reducing—but by no means eliminating—the newborn's risk of becoming infected. This is particularly important in the first several months of life, when the newborn's immune system is less effective at mounting a defense against microscopic invaders. While formula manufacturers have labored mightily to duplicate the nutritional mixture of breast milk, they cannot hope to supply any of these complex immune factors. Breast-fed infants thus tend to have fewer infections (including ear and intestinal infections) as long as they are given breast milk than their formula-fed counterparts.

Breast milk is free. It is clean, fresh, warm, and ready to feed, anytime and virtually anyplace. It does not need to be purchased, stored (although it can be expressed into bottles and frozen for later use), mixed, or heated.

Stimulation of a mother's nipples by a nursing infant releases a hormone called oxytocin, which helps her uterus contract toward what will become its nonpregnant size. The hormonal response to nursing also postpones the onset of ovulation and the menstrual cycle, providing a natural—though not foolproof—spacing of children. Nursing mothers also tend to reach their prepregnancy weight more quickly.

Breast feeding lends itself to a sense of closeness, intimacy, and mutual satisfaction. The skin-to-skin contact, the increased sensory input for the baby, and the mother's satisfaction in being able to provide her child's most basic needs can help establish strong bonds between them.

Are there any reasons not to breast-feed?

There are a few medical situations in which breast feeding poses a risk for the baby. HIV, the virus responsible for AIDS, has been reported to be transmitted from infected mother to noninfected infant through breast feeding. A mother with ac-

As a mother comforts her child, so will I comfort you; and you will be comforted over Jerusalem.

ISAIAH 66:12-13

tive hepatitis B or tuberculosis should not nurse her baby. Obviously, a serious illness in the mother may make breast feeding extremely difficult or even unsafe for both mother and child. Furthermore, virtually all medications show up to some degree in breast milk, and some are potentially harmful for infants. If one or more drugs that may be unsafe for a baby are needed to preserve the mother's life and health, formula feeding should be used. Careful consultation with both mother's and baby's physicians is in order when making this decision.

Previous breast surgery may affect a mother's ability to nurse. A biopsy or local lump removal in the past normally will not cause difficulty. Even after a mastectomy it is possible to feed a baby adequately using the remaining breast. Breast-reduction surgery, however, may result in an inadequate milk supply if the majority of milk-producing tissue has been removed. Previous breast-enhancement/implant surgery should not cause a problem for nursing unless the ducts that carry milk to the nipple were cut during the procedure.

Infants born with phenylketonuria (PKU) or galactosemia, rare metabolic disorders that are detected by routine screening tests after birth, must be fed special formulas to prevent a variety of serious consequences. Congenital problems such as a cleft lip or palate, heart disease, and Down syndrome can create special challenges for nursing. However, the benefits of mother's milk for these infants are usually well worth the extra effort needed to provide it for them, even if they cannot obtain milk directly from the breast. A team effort involving parents, physicians, and a lactation consultant will be necessary.

A number of nonmedical concerns might cause a woman to be reluctant to breast-feed or to consider abandoning it too quickly. These are worth some review and reflection.

A previous bad experience. "I had a baby who wouldn't nurse/couldn't nurse/didn't want to nurse. She wouldn't stop crying until we gave her a bottle. After days of frustration, tears, and sore nipples, I felt like a total failure."

If you had difficulty nursing a baby in the past, remember that each newborn is different. There is no rule that says history must repeat itself, and there are, in fact, very few women who simply are unable to supply enough milk to sustain their offspring.

Physical problems. "My breasts are too small/too big. My nipples are flat/dimpled/inverted."

Your milk is supplied by **mammary** (milk-producing) **glands** whose function is not related to breast size. In response to large amounts of hormones circulating during pregnancy—especially prolactin (literally, "for milk"), estrogen, progesterone, and human placental lactogen (which, as its name indicates, is secreted by the placenta)—the mammary glands enlarge, mature, and become capable of producing milk. However, the actual process of creating milk is held in check during pregnancy by these same elevated hormone levels. When your baby is born and the placenta delivered, the abrupt loss of placental hormones allows milk production to begin in earnest—whether you plan to nurse or not. This interplay between multiple hormones and structures within the body is intricately designed, and you can assume that it will function as intended.

Nipples may vary in shape, and some may be easier for infants to grasp and suck than others. Those that clearly protrude may look like better nursing candidates than those that are flat, dimpled, or inverted. What matters most, however, is what happens when the infant attempts to latch on and suck. To get a preview, gently squeeze *behind* the nipple using thumb and index finger.

When properly attached, a baby will grasp the entire **areola** (the dark area surrounding the nipple) and not just the nipple itself. If your nipple clearly extends outward in response to this squeeze, your baby should have little difficulty. If your nipple flattens or inverts further, however, you may have tiny adhesions under the skin that are preventing it from extending outward. Normally, changes in the breast related to pregnancy will help correct this problem. However, if the squeeze test is still yielding a flat or inverted nipple by the last trimester of pregnancy, a **breast shell** may help. This is a simple plastic device, worn inside the bra, that exerts constant gentle pressure on the areola and gradually helps the nipple protrude. If help is needed after birth, shells can be worn between feedings.

Don't try to toughen up your nipples by pulling or rubbing them before or during pregnancy. Not only will this fail to prevent any soreness during nursing, but it might stimulate the release of hormones that can cause the uterus to contract or even begin labor prematurely. (Nursing an older child may also cause premature contractions. If this happens, the child must be weaned immediately.)

Lifestyle issues. "I don't want to be the only one who can feed the baby. I've seen women whose babies are like appendages stuck permanently on their chests. They have no life—they can't go anywhere or do anything without their baby."

Breast feeding does take more of Mom's time, but it need not be a ball-and-chain experience. After nursing has become a well-established routine, milk can be expressed into a bottle and stored for Dad, grandparents, or baby-sitters to use at a later date. And if you need to get away for a long evening or even overnight, it won't harm your baby to have a formula feeding or two if you don't have enough of your own milk in the freezer. Don't forget that nursing means being free from the hassle of buying formula; preparing it; and dealing with nipples, bottles, bottle liners, and other items.

Keep in mind that it is hardly a major setback if nursing slows your life down for a while. Your body needs time for rest and restoration after accomplishing the formidable tasks of completing pregnancy and childbirth. Do you really need to accelerate immediately back into the fast lane of your prepregnant lifestyle? This very dependent season of your child's life—whether she is breast- or bottle-fed— is relatively short, and it would be beneficial for both of you if you could settle back and enjoy it as much as you can. (This applies whether or not you need to return to a full- or part-time job outside the home or have other children making demands on your time.)

Returning to work. "I need to return to my job in two months, and I don't see how I can spend eight or ten hours in the office at the same time I'm trying to nurse."

Even one or two months of nursing are worth doing, and believe it or not, with some planning, creativity, and assistance on the home front, it is possible for a breast-feeding mother to return to work. The adjustments will vary considerably with the age of the baby, the location of the job, and the hours involved.

BREAST-FEEDING BASICS

Your new baby may be nursed for the first time immediately after delivery or some time later if you or the baby has medical needs that require immediate attention. A newborn is alert and most ready to nurse during the first two hours after birth; therefore many physicians recommend that a mother offer the breast during that time if at all possible. However, even if your first feeding must be delayed several hours or even days, you can still get off to a good start.

Whenever you begin, you and your baby should be able to find a position that not only is comfortable but also allows him to latch on to the breast properly. This occurs when his mouth closes over the areola and forms a seal with his gums. His tongue should be positioned against the underside of the nipple and then with wavelike motions, compress it, emptying the milk-containing ducts just below the areola.

If he repeatedly clamps down on the nipple only and not the areola, you will probably develop some major pain and cracking in the nipple before long—and have a frustrated baby as well because he won't get much milk this way. Some babies at first seem more interested in licking or nibbling than in grasping the breast properly. While it is a good idea in general to avoid bottle feedings during the first several days unless absolutely necessary, it is particularly important that these "lick and chew" newborns stay away from formula and pacifiers until they catch on to latching on.

If you nurse immediately after delivery, it will usually be easiest to lie on your side with the baby's entire body facing you, stomach to stomach. This position will also be very useful in the days following a cesarean delivery, in order to prevent the weight of the baby from pressing on your sore abdomen. In this position you will need to lift your breast with the opposite hand to move the areola next to his mouth. More common is the sitting cuddle position, in which the infant's head is cradled in the bend of your elbow with your forearm supporting his back and your hand holding his bottom or upper leg. An alternative sitting position, called the football hold, places your baby's body at your side supported by your arm with your hand holding his head. This is another helpful position if you have had a cesarean birth, since it minimizes pressure on your incision site. It is also useful for mothers of twins who wish to nurse both babies simultaneously.

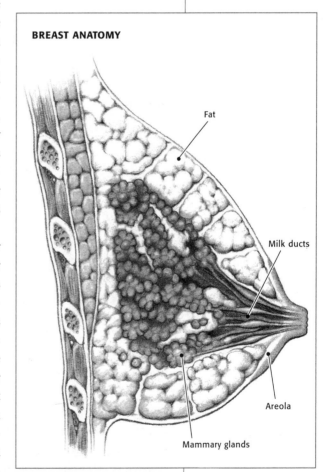

BREAST ANATOMY

Fat

Milk ducts

Areola

Mammary glands

Once you are positioned comfortably, gently lift your breast and stroke your baby's cheek or lower lip with your nipple. This will provoke his rooting reflex. When his mouth opens wide, gently pull him to you so that your areola enters his mouth. You will need to make this move relatively quickly before his mouth closes. Be sure not to "meet him halfway" by leaning forward, or else you will have a very sore back before long. It helps to compress your breast slightly between thumb and palm or between two fingers in a scissorlike position, using your free hand, but stay a couple inches behind the areola when you do so.

When your baby begins sucking, nerve endings in the nipple send a message to the pituitary gland at the base of your brain. The pituitary in turn secretes the hormone prolactin, which stimulates more milk production, and **oxytocin,** which causes tiny muscles that surround the milk ducts to squeeze milk toward the areola. This event is called the **let-down reflex,** which you will probably feel as a change of pressure or, less commonly, as a tingling within the breasts. Some women, however, can't feel the let-down reflex at all. Once your milk has come in, you may notice anything from a slow drip of milk to a full-blown spray during let-down. Many women will experience let-down not only in response to their baby's sucking but also when their baby—or someone else's—begins to cry. During the first days after delivery, you will also feel contractions of the uterus in response to the oxytocin released by the pituitary gland. While these might be uncomfortable, they are carrying out the important function of reducing the size of your uterus.

The let-down reflex may be inhibited by certain drugs, as well as by smoking. Let-down also may not function as well if you are upset or tense. It is therefore important that your nursing times be as relaxed and calm as possible. You might consider setting up a comfortable "nursing corner" at home, where your favorite chair (very often a rocker) and a table with soft light, a few key supplies, soft music, and even something to read are within easy reach. A small stash of healthy snack food and some water or juice may be a welcome addition as well. If you live in a multistory setting, you may want to set up one of these "nursing stations" on each floor. Take the phone off the hook and savor these moments, not worrying about whatever else you think you should be doing. Watch your baby, caress him, talk or sing softly to him, or take some time to pray quietly. These can be sweet times of reflection and meditation during otherwise busy days.

**NURSING POSITION—
SIDE**

Remember that for the first three or four days you will be producing **colostrum,** the yellowish, high-protein liquid full of antibodies and white cells. With rare exception, this is all your baby will need, since he was born with extra fluid in his system that compensates for the relatively low fluid volume of colostrum. When your milk supply begins to arrive, you will notice some increased fullness, warmth, and probably tenderness. During this process your breasts are said to be **engorged,** and they may actually swell so much that your baby will have trouble latching on to them. Should this occur, you can gently ex-

press some milk from each breast, softening it so your baby can grasp more easily. To express milk, grasp the edge of the areola between thumb and fingers and
then repeatedly squeeze while pushing gently toward your chest. (A warm compress or hot shower may be needed to get the milk flowing.) Engorgement typically lasts only a day or two (see page 21).

Nursing patterns

Each baby has a unique style of nursing, and yours may mesh easily with your
milk supply and lifestyle or may require that you make some adjustments. Some
infants get right down to business, sucking vigor-
ously and efficiently without much hesitation.
These "barracudas" contrast sharply with the
"gourmet" nursers, who take their sweet time,
playing with the nipple at first, sampling their
meal, and then eventually getting started. Some
babies vary the gourmet approach by resting every few minutes, as if savoring their feeding, or
even falling asleep one or more times during the
nursing session. The "suck and snooze" types may
exasperate a mother who feels that she doesn't
have all day to nurse. While it's all right to provide
a little mild stimulation (such as undressing him)
to get Sleepy back on task and complete his feeding, some downsizing of your expectations for
the day's activities may be necessary to prevent
ongoing frustration.

NURSING POSITION—
CUDDLE

Newborns also vary in the frequency with which they need to nurse. A typical span between feedings will be two to three hours or eight to twelve times per
day, but during the first days after birth, the interval may be longer, with only six
to eight feedings in a twenty-four-hour period. The baby will feed more often
than usual during growth spurts. The time involved in a feeding will also vary,
but a typical feeding will take ten to fifteen minutes per breast.

As with nearly every aspect of life, what is said to be "typical" may not match
with what happens in reality—especially with newborns. For example, your first
nursing experiences in a hospital setting may be somewhat confusing, especially if
you are not rooming in. Many hospital nurseries still adhere to the tradition of
bringing out all the babies to their mothers for feeding on a fixed schedule. But
most babies don't automatically synchronize to Nursery Standard Time and may
be sound asleep for these nursing "appointments." The result is repeated frustra-

tion for mothers whose zonked-out newborns seem to have little interest in latching on, let alone sucking, during the first few days after birth. In a worst-case scenario, a baby who hasn't been ready to nurse with Mom might wake up and sound off when he's parked in the nursery, only to have his crying ignored or answered with a bottle. Many hospital nurseries now bring newborns to their mothers when they're hungry rather than in fixed shifts. Overall, however, rooming in gives everyone a better chance to get acquainted and, more important, nurse when the baby is awake and hungry.

Don't worry if your baby doesn't seem terribly interested in frequent nursing during the first few days. That will change, often just after you bring him home. The early phase of sleepiness that occurs as he adjusts to the outside world will usually give way to more active crying and nursing—sometimes every few hours—after the first week. Some parents are aghast when this happens. The mellow baby they enjoyed in the hospital suddenly seems wired and insatiable just a few days later. Don't panic. Instead, look at this as a time to hone your nursing skills with a very willing partner.

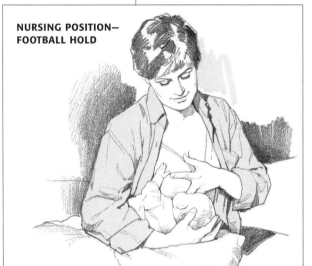

**NURSING POSITION—
FOOTBALL HOLD**

The newborn baby normally will announce his desire for milk very clearly, with some insistent crying every two to four hours. When this occurs, it is appropriate to tend to him promptly, change him if necessary, and then settle in for a feeding. Some infants make sucking movements or fuss for a while before overtly sounding off. There's no point in waiting for full-blown crying before offering the breast. For five to ten minutes you will notice him swallowing after every few sucks, and then he will shift gears to a more relaxed mode or even seem to lose interest.

At that point he can be burped, either by lifting him and placing his head over your shoulder, or by sitting him up with your hand under his jaw and gently patting him on the back. You can also place him face down across your lap, with head supported and chest a little higher than abdomen, and gently pat his back.

Once he burps, he may show interest in the other breast. (If he doesn't burp and yet he appears comfortable, you can still proceed with the feeding.) Since the first side may be more completely emptied during the feeding, it is wise to alternate the breast from which he starts. (A small pin or clip that you move from one side of your nursing bra to the other can help remind you where to begin next time.)

Relatively frequent nursing is typical after the first days of life, and it will help stimulate your milk production and let-down reflex. A newborn who seems to be very content with infrequent feedings (more than four hours apart) should probably be checked by your physician to confirm that his activity level is satisfactory. He may in fact need to be awakened to feed every three hours to ensure adequate weight gain during the first two or three weeks.

Problems and concerns with nursing

"How do I know if she's getting enough?" During the first few days after birth, this concern often prods new mothers toward bottle feeding, where they have the security of seeing exactly how much the baby is consuming. Remember that the quantity of milk you produce during a feeding will start with as little as half an ounce (15 ml) of colostrum during the first day or two and increase to an ounce (30 ml) as the milk supply arrives by the fourth or fifth day. After the first week, your milk output will range from two to six ounces per feeding. Obviously, there is no direct way for you to measure how much your baby is sucking from your breast, but other signs will indicate how the two of you are doing:

- When the room is quiet, you will hear your baby swallowing.
- Once your milk has arrived, you may notice that your breasts soften during a feeding as they are emptied of milk.
- After the first four or five days, you should be changing six to eight wet diapers each day. In addition, you will notice one or several small, dark

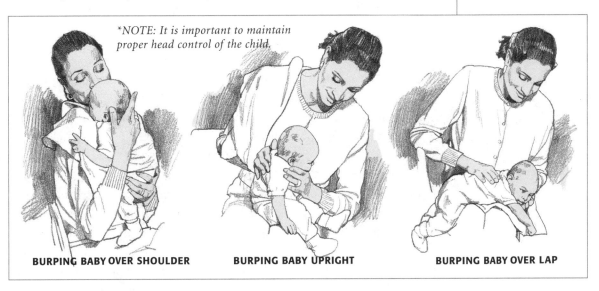

NOTE: It is important to maintain proper head control of the child.

BURPING BABY OVER SHOULDER   **BURPING BABY UPRIGHT**   **BURPING BABY OVER LAP**

green stools—sometimes one after every feeding—that become lighter after the first (meconium) stools are passed. As your milk supply becomes well established, your baby's stools will take on a yellowish color and a soft or runny consistency. Later on, stools typically become less frequent.

♦ Tracking your baby's weight will give you specific and important information. *It is normal for a baby to drop nearly 10 percent of her birth weight (about eleven or twelve ounces, for example, for a seven-pound baby) during the first week.* Usually she will have returned to her birth weight by two weeks of age, and thereafter she should gain about two-thirds to one ounce per day. Obviously you can't track these small changes at home on the bathroom scale. Instead, it is common to have a checkup during the first week or two after birth, during which your baby will be weighed on a scale that can detect smaller changes. If there is any question about appropriate weight gain, your doctor will ask you to return every week (or more often, if needed) to follow her progress.

One of the most important—and hardest—things to remember if you are concerned about the adequacy of your nursing is to *relax*. If you approach every feeding with fear and trembling, you may have difficulty with your let-down reflex. Furthermore, newborns seem to have an uncanny sense of Mom's anxiety, and their jittery response may interfere with smooth latching on and sucking. Remember that for many women, breast feeding requires time, effort, and learning. Even if your first few feedings seem awkward or your baby doesn't seem to be getting the hang of it immediately, you should be able to make this process work. Take a deep breath, take your time, and don't be afraid to ask for help if you are truly having trouble getting started.

"It hurts when I nurse!" No one wants to spend a good portion of the day in misery, and a strong dose of pain with every feeding can demoralize even the most dedicated breast-feeding mother. Some tenderness during the baby's first few sucks of each feeding is not unusual for a few days after birth while a callus is being formed.

Many mothers also feel aching during the let-down reflex, and some may even notice a brief shooting pain deeper in the breast after nursing as the milk supply is refilling. For some women the engorgement of the breasts prior to each nursing session can be very painful. It is possible, in fact, to have intense pain with engorgement even when your nursing technique is correct and nothing specific is wrong with your breasts. Some mothers who are unprepared for such severe discomfort may give up on nursing too soon. But becoming comfortable with nursing may, in fact, take a few days or even a few weeks as your baby learns and your body adjusts to this new function.

In most cases, pain serves as a warning that should not be ignored. If you have significant, ongoing pain with nursing, you should review this with your doctor and attempt to identify one of the causes that can and should be treated.

Intense discomfort can arise from traumatized, cracked, or inflamed nipples, which, of course, are sensitive areas to begin with. If the nipple is irritated at the tip, it is probably entering your baby's mouth at an upward angle and rubbing on her palate. During the latching-on process, try holding your breast so the nipple points downward. This is often easier if you are sitting, using the cuddle or football hold.

If the nipple is more tender at the base, it is more likely being chewed during feedings. Remember that your baby needs to take the entire areola into her mouth when she latches on, so your nipple lies against her tongue. If she won't open her mouth fully or slides off the areola after latching on, your nipple will be gummed continually while you nurse. To add insult to injury, your baby may not get enough milk when this occurs. The combination of miserable mom and crying newborn is often enough to send Dad out into the night in search of formula.

To help your baby latch on to the whole areola (and not just your nipple), wait for her to open her mouth wide enough and then gently pull her to the breast. If you are engorged and she is having difficulty forming a seal around the areola, you can express or pump some milk so that area will be softer. You may have to utilize the football hold (see page 15) to give your hand better control of her head and thus keep her from sliding off the areola. If she seems to lose her position during the feeding, don't be afraid to pull her gently from the breast and then reattach. If she has a strong hold, you should first loosen it by pulling downward gently on her chin or inserting a finger into the corner of her mouth to release the vacuum seal formed by her gums.

Other causes of painful irritation of one or both nipples, or even full-blown inflammation known as **dermatitis,** include:

- Overzealous use of soap and water that can remove the skin's own moisturizers. Rinse your breasts during your normal shower or bath but keep soap away from your nipples.
- Continuous moisture on the skin surface. This can occur when the breast is not allowed to dry off after a feeding or when the pads of a nursing bra are moist. Air drying for a few minutes after nursing is the

simplest solution, while making certain that your nursing bra is dry as well.

- An allergic reaction to breast creams or oils. Paradoxically, traditional remedies for breast soreness such as vitamin E preparations or impure lanolin may make the problem worse if they provoke an allergic dermatitis. If your nipple develops redness, swelling, and a burning sensation, stop using any nipple cream. If the problem persists or worsens, see your doctor. You may have to use a mild anti-inflammatory prescription cream for a few days to calm this problem down more quickly.

- An infection with the yeast organism known as **Candida albicans,** which will also be present in the baby's mouth. In this case the irritation may not only burn but also itch. Candida may appear sometime after you have been nursing without any problems. A tip-off is the presence of small, white patches inside your baby's cheeks. Candida infection in the baby's mouth (also known as **thrush**) is not a dangerous condition, but it can be a persistent annoyance.

  Candida infections usually respond to treatment with an antifungal cream (check with your doctor). At the same time, your baby should be given antifungal drops by mouth. If both of you are not treated concurrently for several days, the infection may bounce back and forth between you. Furthermore, in order to prevent reinfection, you will need to change nursing pads after every feeding. If your baby is receiving any feedings from a bottle or is using a pacifier, you will need to boil the rubber nipples and pacifiers every day until the infection clears.

- Rarely an ongoing **eczema** problem that has appeared on other parts of your body will erupt on the breast during nursing. You will want to consult with your doctor about appropriate treatment, which may involve the short-term use of a mild anti-inflammatory cream.

- A potentially more serious cause of pain is **mastitis,** an infection caused by bacteria that gain entry into breast tissue, usually through a cracked nipple. Symptoms include pain, swelling, heat, redness, and tenderness in a localized area of one breast, accompanied by generalized aching and fever. If there is no fever, it probably is a plugged duct and does not require antibiotics. Should this problem develop, it is important to contact your physician. Antibiotics that are safe for both mother and baby will normally be prescribed, and acetaminophen may be used to reduce both pain and temperature. The use of warm, moist compresses can assist in the treatment. *In addition, it is important to continue nurs-*

ing, although you may be more comfortable with more frequent, shorter sessions. Your baby will not become ill by nursing from an infected breast, and emptying the breast of milk helps clear the infection. Ice cubes can be applied directly to the breast (at first in quick, short strokes) above and below the infected area. This can help reduce pain and swelling.

Aside from some of these specific treatments for breast and nipple pain, how else do you spell *relief* until the cracking or irritation heals?

- Don't attempt to toughen your nipples, either before or after the birth, by rubbing, stretching, or pinching them.
- Acetaminophen (or ibuprofen) may be taken thirty to sixty minutes before you nurse. Of course, it is wise to take medications only when necessary while nursing, but a short-term pain reliever that helps you continue nursing will be a worthwhile exception.
- Take some measures to "move things along" during your feedings. Express a little milk before your baby latches on and then gently massage your breasts while nursing to help them empty more quickly. Think in terms of shorter but more frequent feeding times.
- Air dry your nipples for several minutes after you nurse. Some mothers find that ice applied to the nipple just before nursing may reduce pain when the baby latches on. Many traditional remedies such as breast creams, oils, vitamin E capsules, or even tea bags have fallen out of favor, especially since some may actually increase the irritation. However, a *pure* lanolin preparation applied after nursing may help restore normal skin moisture and decrease pain.
- If your baby forms a strong suction with her gums, be sure to release her grip before you pull her from your breast.
- If all else fails, consider pumping your breasts and allowing your baby to accept your milk from a bottle while your nipples are healing, especially if they have been bleeding. This is less desirable during the first several days while she is still learning the ropes, but it's better than giving up on nursing altogether.

Remember that a temporary time-out from breast feeding to allow for healing or for any other reason (for example, an illness affecting either mother or baby) does not mean that you cannot resume nursing when things calm down. Pumping your breasts at feeding time will help you maintain your supply.

Furthermore, even if your baby has spent a fair amount of time with a bottle, she can learn (or relearn) to obtain nourishment successfully from your breast.

"My baby wants to nurse all the time. I'm getting sick of being a human pacifier." All babies derive comfort and satisfaction from sucking, but some are true enthusiasts who would be more than happy to turn every nursing session into a ninety-minute marathon. You may be happy with this arrangement, but more likely it can lead to sore nipples and a gnawing concern that your entire existence has been reduced to being a mobile restaurant. Fortunately, you are not without options.

A healthy newborn, properly attached to the breast and sucking continuously, will empty about 90 percent of the milk available on each side within ten

PUMPING AND STORING BREAST MILK

There will likely be at least a few, if not many, times during your breast feeding when you will not be able to nurse your baby for several hours (or days) at a time. These occasions might involve anything from an evening out for dinner, an unexpected trip, a time-out to allow irritated nipples to heal, or even the desire to supply breast milk to a premature infant who must be fed by tube. Nursing mothers who begin or resume work outside the home may have to contend with daily absences of several hours from their babies. While formula can be a satisfactory substitute in these situations, it is also possible to maintain your baby's nourishment with your own milk.

GUIDELINES FOR EXPRESSING MILK—FOR
IMMEDIATE OR FUTURE USE
- First, hands should be thoroughly washed with soap and water each time you collect milk. (The breasts do not need to be washed, however, but should be free of any lotions or creams.)
- Next, before any milk is expressed, each breast should be gently massaged. Using the palm of the hand, stroke several times from below, above, and sides of the breast toward the nipple, applying gentle pressure.
- After massaging, milk can be expressed from each breast, either by hand or with the assistance of a breast pump. Either method is acceptable, and the choice of one or the other approach can be based on effectiveness, convenience, and cost.

- As with the first days of nursing, you may find it easier to begin expressing milk for three to five minutes at a time and then gradually progress to ten- or fifteen-minute sessions if you are collecting milk on a regular basis.

To express by hand. Sit in a comfortable position and lean over the container into which you will be collecting the milk. Place the thumb and index finger of one hand about an inch to either side of the nipple and then press toward your chest while gently squeezing the fingers toward one another. At first, you may see a few drops, a literal spurt, or nothing at all.

When the milk stops flowing, release your fingers, rotate to another position around the nipple, and squeeze again. If you don't see much milk, keep trying and don't give up—becoming adept at expressing milk may take practice. You may find that massaging again improves your flow. It may also be helpful to alternate between breasts, rather than expressing all the milk from one before moving to the other.

To express using a breast pump. Breast pumps utilize a funnel or bicycle-horn-shaped apparatus that is placed against the breast. A vacuum is created, either by manually moving a piston or by an electrically powered device, and milk is sucked into an appropriate container. Electrical pumps are more expensive but may be more efficient, especially for a mother who needs to express minutes. You can usually hear and feel the transition from intense sucking and swallowing to a more relaxed, pacifying sucking after five to ten minutes on each side, at which point you can decide how long you want to continue. If you're both feeling snugly and comfortable, relax and enjoy it. But if it's the middle of the night and you need sleep, or other children need your attention, or you're getting sore, you won't destroy your baby's personality by gently detaching her.

A problem can arise, however, if your baby sounds terribly unhappy and indignant when you decide enough's enough. How do you respond? The answer depends on how far along and how well established you are in your nursing relationship. In the earliest days when milk is just arriving or you're not sure whether she is truly swallowing an adequate volume, it is probably better to give

---

(continued)

milk on a regular basis. (Some models can pump from both breasts simultaneously.) It is usually possible to rent one from a medical-supply company, hospital, or other local resource in order to confirm its usefulness before actually buying one.

To make an airtight seal between the pump and your breast, a little water or milk can be applied to the skin where contact is made. The apparatus should be applied snugly enough to make a good seal but not pressed so tightly to restrict the flow of milk. Pumping can continue until after the milk has stopped flowing for a minute or so. After you are finished, use soap and water to wash whatever components of the pump came in contact with the milk and then allow them to air dry. (Check the manufacturer's directions for specific details about cleaning and proper handling of the equipment you are using.)

COLLECTING AND STORING MILK
Your milk can be collected in a clean baby bottle or a nurser bag that attaches directly to a nipple assembly. Your baby can immediately drink what you have just expressed (which would be the case, for example, if you are expressing milk while sore nipples are healing), but you can also store milk for future use.

Remember that breast milk is a perishable food. Here are some guidelines for handling it so it will maintain its nutritional value and not become contaminated:

- If you plan to refrigerate or freeze milk, do so as soon as you have finished collecting it. Label and date it.
- You may feed a baby fresh breast milk that has been left at room temperature for up to six hours, after which the milk should be discarded.
- Breast milk that has just been expressed may be kept in the refrigerator for seventy-two hours, but any that is thawed from the freezer must be used within twenty-four hours.
- Various time limits for safe storage of breast milk in the freezer have been recommended; they range from two weeks to six months. A reasonable guideline would be to store milk no longer than one month. Mark each bottle or plastic bottle liner with the date you collected it and use the oldest milk first.
- You can combine the milk from both breasts into a single bottle or plastic bottle liner. If a particular pumping session has not yielded enough milk, you can freeze it and then add more cooled milk to the same container later—but don't change the date on your label.
- When you want to feed your baby expressed milk, thaw it by placing the bottle or bottle liner in warm water. Heating milk in a microwave is not recommended because of the potential formation of hot spots in the milk that could burn the baby's mouth.

her the benefit of the doubt and continue for a while longer. This is especially true if you are blessed with a casual "gourmet" or "suck and snooze" baby who may not empty your breast very quickly.

But watch the various indicators of your progress: good swallowing sounds, frequent wet diapers, weight gain, and softening of your breast after feeding. If these are going well and you feel you have developed a smooth nursing routine after two or three weeks, you can consider other calming maneuvers, including the use of a pacifier (see sidebar). *If your soothing maneuvers aren't working, however, or your baby doesn't seem to be gaining weight, contact your baby's doctor for further evaluation and recommendations.*

Some mothers make the mistake of assuming that every sound from a baby should be answered with nursing, when something else (or nothing in particular) may be bothering her. If, for example, she has just finished a good feeding thirty minutes ago and begins to fuss after being put down for a nap, it is reasonable to wait and listen for a while, since she may settle down on her own, rather than trying to nurse her again. Otherwise you may find yourself spending nearly every minute of the day and night with your baby attached to your breast.

PACIFIER POINTERS

Some parents say they could not have survived their baby's infancy without these gadgets, while others (and some breast-feeding advisers) see them as an abomination. While they are not exactly a threat to world peace, pacifiers can be overused. They are definitely not good for very young infants who have not established stable and efficient nursing patterns. The feel, texture, taste, and smell of a pacifier are clearly different from that of Mom's nipples, and sucking a pacifier too soon may interfere with a baby's learning the real thing. But after two weeks or more, assuming nursing is going well, a pacifier can help calm a baby who

- is already fed and full, but still wants to suck;
- doesn't have anything else, such as a wet diaper, bothering him; and
- will suck on it with apparent satisfaction.

Inserting a pacifier in an infant's mouth must not be a substitute for normal feeding, parental nurturing, or checking to see if something is wrong.

If you decide to use a pacifier, make sure you get a one-piece model with a soft nipple—either the straight bottle shape or the angled "orthodontic" type. Never use the nipple assembly from a feeding bottle as a pacifier because the nipple can come loose and choke your baby. Make sure you have the right size for babies younger than six months and that it is designed to survive boiling or trips through the dishwasher. For the first six months, you will need to clean pacifiers frequently in this way to reduce the risk of infection.

Babies are unable to replace pacifiers that fall out of their mouth, so you will have to do this for them. *Do not, under any circumstances, tie a pacifier to a string or ribbon around a baby's neck to keep it in place. Your solution to the wandering pacifier could strangle your baby.*

If you find a pacifier that your baby likes, buy several. They have a knack for disappearing into the sofa, under the car seat, or into the bottom of the diaper bag, so lots of backups are a good idea.

As the days pass, you will become more discerning about the meaning of your baby's various crying messages.

A final note: If you are having a significant problem with breast feeding—whether it be latching on, anatomy problems, sore nipples, sluggish nursers, slow weight gain, or anything else—seek out a **lactation consultant** for some additional help. This is a health-care professional whose wealth of knowledge and practical suggestions can help both mother and baby succeed at breast feeding, even when the going gets very tough. Your baby's doctor or a local hospital should be able to give you a referral.

BOTTLE-FEEDING BASICS

Choosing a formula

First things first: *For the first year, do not feed your baby cow's milk from the dairy section at the store.* Cow's milk that has not been specifically modified for use in infant formulas is not digested well by human infants; it contains significant loads of protein that your baby's kidneys will have difficulty processing, and it contains inadequate amounts of vitamin C and iron. It also contains inadequate amounts of fat, which provides 50 percent of the calories in human milk and formula. Furthermore, the new baby's intestine may be irritated by cow's milk, resulting in a gradual but potentially significant loss of red blood cells. Finally, some of the protein in cow's milk may be absorbed through the baby's intestine in a way that can lead to allergy problems later in life.

The vast majority of bottle-fed infants are given commercial formulas, whose manufacturers have gone to great lengths to match mother's milk as closely as possible. The most commonly used formulas are based on cow's milk that has been *significantly* altered for human consumption. Among other things, the protein is made more digestible and less allergenic, lactose is added to match that of human milk, and butterfat is removed and replaced with a combination of other fats more readily absorbed by infants.

Soy formulas, which are based on soy protein, do not contain lactose, which is the main carbohydrate in cow's milk. These are used for the small percentage of infants who cannot digest lactose and who develop excessive gas, cramps, and diarrhea when they consume regular formula. In addition, bottle-fed infants who have diarrhea resulting from a viral or bacterial infection may develop a temporary difficulty processing lactose. During their recovery, these babies often tolerate soy formulas better than cow's milk formulas. Infants from families with a strong history of cow's milk allergy have traditionally been started on soy formulas as a precautionary measure, but many of these may be allergic to soy formula as well.

There is a variety of formulas that have been designed for special needs. Infants who are allergic to both cow's milk and soy formulas may use what are called **protein hydrolysate** formulas, in which the proteins are essentially predigested. Special formulas are also available for babies with phenylketonuria (PKU) and for premature infants.

Check with your baby's physician regarding the type(s) of formula he or she recommends. Once you have made your choice, you can stock up with one or more of the three forms in which they are normally sold:

BOTTLE-FEEDING BABY

- **Ready-to-feed** is just that. Put it into a bottle if it isn't already packaged in one, make sure the temperature is right, and you're all set. While extremely convenient, this format is also the most expensive.
- **Concentrate** must be mixed with water in the exact amount recommended by the manufacturer. If it is too diluted (mixed with too much water), your baby will be shortchanged on nutrients. But if it is too concentrated (mixed with too little water), diarrhea and dehydration may result. The unused portion of an opened can of concentrate may be sealed and stored in the refrigerator for twenty-four hours, after which it should be discarded.
- **Powdered formula** is the least expensive form and must be mixed exactly as recommended, using the measuring scoop provided.

If you cannot afford formula and do not have access to community resources, it is possible to mix your own using evaporated (*not* condensed) milk, corn syrup, and sterile water. However, you must talk to your doctor about the specific combination of ingredients as well as additional vitamin supplementation.

You can prepare a day's worth of bottles at one time, storing the ones you don't immediately need in the refrigerator for up to twenty-four hours. The good news for today's bottle-feeding parents is that the laborious process of boiling water and sterilizing bottles, which consumed a great deal of time and energy in previous generations, is (with a few exceptions) usually not necessary to prepare formula safely today. However, these basic precautions will prevent your baby's formula from being contaminated by potentially harmful bacteria:

- Wash your hands before you begin handling formula, water, bottles, and nipples.
- If the formula you are using comes from a can, wipe the top before you open it. Use a separate can opener specifically designated for this purpose, and clean it on a regular basis.
- Unless there has been a recent flood, earthquake, outbreak of bacterial infection, or other local calamity, tap water is usually safe to use in mixing formula. (Check with your baby's doctor for a recommendation regarding whether your water should be boiled first.) Running the cold-water tap for a minute or two will decrease the amount of lead or other impurities that might have collected within the pipes. *Well water should be checked for bacterial contamination or excessive mineral content and should always be boiled before you use it.* If you have any doubts or concerns, use bottled water.
- After each use, bottles and nipple assemblies can be washed in the dishwasher or by hand with hot, soapy water, using a bottle brush to clean the inside thoroughly. Follow with a good rinse.

It's not necessary to warm a bottle, although younger babies prefer tepid or room-temperature formula. To warm a bottle you've stored in the refrigerator, let it sit for a few minutes in hot water. Warming the bottle in a microwave is *not* recommended because uneven heating may cause pockets of milk hot enough to scald a baby's mouth. Before feeding, shake the bottle well and let a drop or two fall on your hand. It should be barely warm and definitely not hot. Also check the flow rate from the nipple. An ideal flow is about one drop per second when the bottle is held upside down. If the nipple allows milk to flow too quickly, your baby may choke on it. If it flows too slowly, he may swallow air while he tries to suck out his meal.

You can use four- or eight-ounce bottles made from plastic or glass. (Later on, however, when he can hold his own bottle, glass bottles should be replaced with plastic.) Many parents prefer the nurser style in which formula is poured into a plastic bag that attaches to a plastic shell and nipple assembly. Babies tend to swallow less air from the bags, but they cost more in the long run. It is important not to use the bags to mix concentrate or powder because you cannot measure accurately with them.

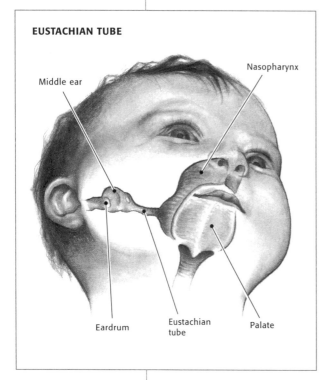

EUSTACHIAN TUBE

Middle ear

Nasopharynx

Eardrum

Eustachian tube

Palate

As with breast feeding, bottle feeding should be relaxed and unhurried, preferably in a comfortable and quiet area of your home. Hold your baby across your lap with his upper body slightly raised and his head supported. A flat position during feedings not only increases the risk of choking but also allows milk to flow into the passageways, called **eustachian tubes,** that lead into the middle ears. Frequent ear infections may result. Stroke the nipple across his cheek or lower lip to start the rooting reflex, and be sure to keep the bottle elevated enough so the milk completely covers the inside of the nipple. Otherwise, he may start sucking air.

The fact that milk is flowing from a bottle does not mean that the feeding should switch to autopilot. Take time to lock eyes with your infant, talk or sing softly to him, gently caress him, and pray about this new life with which you've been entrusted. Your baby should not be left unattended with a bottle propped in his mouth. This practice puts your baby at an unnecessary risk for ear infections or choking.

Formula-fed newborns typically will consume two or three ounces every three or four hours, gradually increasing to a routine of taking about four ounces every four hours by the end of the first month. A general rule of thumb is that a normal baby will need between two and two and one-half ounces of formula per pound of body weight each day (up to fifteen pounds). Normally he will give crying or fussing cues when he is hungry and turn his head away or push the nipple out of his mouth with his tongue when he is full. If the bottle isn't empty, don't force the issue. However, during the first few weeks it is wise to awaken him to feed if he is sleeping for stretches of more than four hours during the day.

When (if ever) should the baby's formula be changed?

Most doctors will recommend that bottle-fed infants begin with an iron-fortified cow's milk formula, and if doing well with it, use it through the first year of life. (Iron is not absorbed as efficiently from formula as from breast milk, and the amount added to iron-fortified formula ensures that your baby will get what he needs.) Like their breast-fed counterparts, babies in this age-group do not need other vitamin supplementation.

One of the headaches that most bottle-feeding parents eventually face is figuring out whether irritability, especially if accompanied by gas or loose stools, means that baby and formula are not getting along. There are no clear-cut answers to this dilemma.

If you think your baby might be having a problem with the current formula, discuss it with his physician. It may be appropriate to try another brand, or even a different form of the same brand, and observe the results. Sometimes persistent crying, irritability, and poor sleep at night—definitely one of the most disturbing situations for new parents—will provoke a switch to soy-based formula. If it seems to help, stay with it. Beware of making changes too quickly or attributing every one of your baby's problems to his current formula, because you won't be able to sort out cause and effect, and you may overlook some other cause of his discomfort. Occasionally there may be such frustration and expense associated with finding a tolerated formula, that relactation may be considered. A lactation consultant can assist even if several weeks without nursing have passed.

HEALTH AND SAFETY CONCERNS: CHECKUPS AND IMMUNIZATIONS

Your pediatrician or family physician will ask that you follow a specific routine of well-baby visits; there is a definite purpose to this plan that involves monitoring the baby's progress and administering immunizations that are very important to her health. If you have been sent home from the hospital within twenty-four hours of your baby's birth, your baby should be checked within the next twenty-four to forty-eight hours. If all is going smoothly, you can expect to take your baby back for a checkup between two and four weeks of age and then again at two months.

During these visits, the baby will be weighed and measured and the results plotted on a standardized growth chart, which allows the health-care provider to track her progress over time. You will be asked how she is feeding, sleeping, and eliminating urine and stool. At the one- and two-month visits, specific behavioral milestones such as smiling and head control will probably be discussed. The baby will be examined from head to toe, so be sure to put her in an outfit that can be removed easily.

It is important that you bring up any problems or concerns you have, no matter how minor they seem. If you have a number of questions, write them down and present them at the beginning of the visit so the practitioner can see what's on your mind. Don't suddenly pull them out as a list of by-the-way items after everything else is done. If the examiner seems rushed and uneasy about taking time to deal with your concerns, find out how and when you can go over them. Some large practices have well-trained nurses or other health educators who can answer most of the questions you might have.

Your baby will most likely receive her first **hepatitis B** immunization either at birth or during the first two months of life. The second dose will be given one month after the first. At the two-month visit, it is customary for babies to receive their **DTaP (diphtheria/tetanus/pertussis)**, **OPV (oral polio)** or **IPV (inactivated polio)**, and **hemophilus B** immunizations.

Many parents are anxious about the prospect of their tiny baby receiving these vaccines, and some have read literature suggesting that they are dangerous or ineffective. But the overwhelming evidence indicates that these shots do indeed drastically reduce the risk of these terrible diseases and that the odds of having a problem from any of the vaccines are far less than the odds of contracting the disease if no vaccine is given.

All the infections that vaccines guard us against can be very serious or even lethal. Some, such as diphtheria and polio, terrorized entire communities a century ago but have become extremely uncommon through widespread vaccination efforts. On the other hand, the bacteria that cause whooping cough and tetanus are still very prevalent, and quite ready, willing, and able to infect those who have not been adequately vaccinated. These illnesses can be prevented for a very modest amount of discomfort and cost and with an extremely low risk of any significant complications. Unfortunately, because of concerns over the expense, risks, or appropriateness of vaccines, some parents neglect, avoid, or even actively oppose immunization programs. This is unwise and places children in needless peril. If you have any concerns over the safety or effectiveness of any vaccine recommended for your child, be sure to discuss them with her physician.

What about side effects of immunizations?

Of these routine immunizations, pertussis (the *P* in DTaP) traditionally has caused the most side effects when given in the original DPT format. Now most children are receiving the so-called "acellular" form of pertussis (abbreviated *aP*), which causes far fewer problems. Local soreness and fussiness after the injection, if present, may be treated with a dose of acetaminophen infant drops. These can be given at the time of the immunization or shortly thereafter in order to relieve discomfort. For babies weighing less than twelve pounds, the appropriate amount is one-half a dropper (or 0.4 ml) of the standard infant solution (which contains 80 mg per 0.8 ml). For infants who are heavier than twelve pounds, a full dropper (or 0.8 ml) may be used. Fewer than one in one hundred infants will

WHAT DO DTAP, OPV/IPV, HEMOPHILUS B, AND HEPATITIS B VACCINES PREVENT?

Diphtheria is a serious bacterial infection that causes a thick membrane to form in the nose, throat, or airway. The membrane is attached to underlying tissues, so that attempting to remove it causes bleeding. Diphtheria bacteria within the membrane produce a toxin that can damage heart, liver, kidney, and nerve tissue. Paralysis and death may result. Because of widespread vaccinations, fewer than five cases occur in the U.S. each year.

Pertussis (whooping cough) causes severe coughing, often to the point of choking; it can last for months. It is particularly rough on infants and small children and can lead to pneumonia, seizures, and death. This disease is highly contagious and much more common than diphtheria. About four thousand cases are reported each year, half of which involve children less than a year old.

Tetanus results from a toxin produced by bacteria that enter the body through contaminated wounds. The toxin causes painful, spasmodic contractions of muscles (which gave rise to the colloquial term *lockjaw* for this disease) and can lead to death.

Polio is a viral infection that damages the central nervous system; it can cause mild or serious paralysis and results in death in 5 to 10 percent of the cases.

Hemophilus B is a type of bacteria that can cause, among other things, pneumonia and meningitis (an infection of the membranes that enclose the brain and spinal cord). Since the introduction of hemophilus B vaccines during the past decade, the number of cases of meningitis in young children caused by this bacteria has fallen dramatically.

Hepatitis B is an infection of the liver caused by a virus that is most commonly transmitted in three ways: from an infected mother to her infant, (later in life) through sexual contact with an infected person, or by exposure to infected blood. However, a large number of cases occur without a history of any of these events, which is one reason health officials recommend universal vaccination against this virus.

Fortunately, most people infected with hepatitis B recover without any long-term effects. In a small percentage of cases, however, the immediate illness can be severe enough to cause death. In others, prolonged active infection with the virus occurs, a process that can lead eventually to cirrhosis and cancer of the liver. While hepatitis B is not a common childhood disease, children are at a higher risk for developing long-term complications if they should become infected. Immunization of all children has been recommended as the most effective means to reduce the total number of cases of this disease over the next several years.

develop a persistent cry (lasting longer than three hours); about one in three hundred may get a high fever (ranging as high as 105°F); while about one in one thousand may develop an unusual, high-pitched cry. *More severe neurologic complications following the DTaP vaccine, such as a prolonged seizure or change in consciousness, are extremely rare—and may not be directly related to the vaccine at all.* All things considered, these are reasonable risks to take in exchange for protection against a very disruptive and potentially lethal illness.

Oral polio vaccine (OPV) contains live virus, which can very rarely cause the disease in someone receiving it. According to the Centers for Disease Control (CDC), the odds of this occurring are practically infinitesimal: one case in 1.5 million first doses, and one case in 30 million subsequent doses. Some virus may be excreted in the baby's stool after the vaccine is given, and this could cause an infection in someone whose immune system is defective (for example, a person receiving cancer chemotherapy or an individual with AIDS). People with these conditions should avoid close contact with a baby who has just received OPV vaccine, or as an alternative, the baby may be given the inactivated polio vaccine (IPV). Although it is permissable to use all oral or all injectable polio immunization, many physicians are now choosing to use a sequential schedule of IPV/OPV in hope of reducing the number of cases of vaccine associated paralytic polio (VAPP). This would consist of two doses of IPV followed by two doses of OPV.

If your baby is ill at the time of the visit, the vaccines will usually be postponed, because it may be difficult to determine afterwards whether a problem, especially a fever, has been caused by the illness or by the vaccine. If your baby has only a minor case of sniffles, the vaccines will usually be given. If you have any doubt or questions about vaccinations, be sure to get all your questions answered before any immunization is given to your baby.

What if the baby becomes ill?

Because newborns normally receive a healthy donation of Mom's antibodies through the umbilical cord blood supply prior to birth, they usually escape common illnesses such as colds and flu during the first several weeks, as long as they are well nourished and their environment is kept reasonably clean. Nursing infants have the added advantage of ingesting their mother's antibodies at every feeding.

This is indeed providential, because an illness in a baby younger than three months of age is a completely different situation from one in an older baby. For one thing, your new baby has very few ways to notify you that something is wrong. You will not have the luxury of language and specific complaints ("My ear hurts" or "I have a headache") to guide you. You won't have months or years of experience with this particular child—or, if this is your first baby, perhaps with any child—to sense what is "normal" for her.

In addition, your baby's defense system is still under construction, and her ability to fight off microscopic invaders will not be fully operational for a number of months. As a result, a seemingly minor infection acquired during the first several weeks can turn into a major biological war.

Also—and this is the most unsettling reality of all—an illness can go sour much more rapidly in a newborn than in older children. If bacteria are on the move, they can spread like wildfire. If fluids are being lost through vomiting or diarrhea, dehydration can develop over several hours rather than days.

These warnings are not meant to generate undue anxiety but rather to encourage you to notify your baby's health-care provider if you think something is wrong, especially during the first three months of life. You can also reduce your newborn's risk of infection by keeping her out of crowded public places, preventing, if possible, direct contact with individuals who are ill with contagious infections, and minimizing group child-care situations, especially during the first few weeks after birth.

What are the signs that a baby might have a problem?

Some of the danger signals in infants are similar to those that will alert you to problems later in life. But in newborns, several of these signals are more critical and require a more immediate and detailed evaluation than in older babies and children. Here are some important newborn distress signals:

Fever. There will be many occasions in the coming months and years when your child will feel hot, and the thermometer will agree. In babies over three months of age, this may or may not be cause for alarm, depending on what else is going on. *Remember, in a baby under three months of age, a rectal temperature over 100.4°F should be considered cause for an immediate call to the doctor's office.*

(If your baby seems perfectly well, his temperature is slightly above 100.4°F, and there is a possibility that he was overdressed or in a hot environment, you can remove some clothing and try again in thirty to forty-five minutes. A temperature that is closer to normal will be reassuring—but you should run the story by your baby's physician anyway. Do not give the baby acetaminophen (Tylenol) or a tepid bath in this situation, because you need to know whether the fever will come down on its own. Besides, the fever itself is not dangerous. It is the possible causes of the fever that you need to worry about.)

If there is no doubt about the presence of fever, your baby needs to be evaluated right away, either by his own physician or at the emergency room. You may be surprised or even alarmed by the number of tests that may be requested after your baby is examined. The problem is that a newborn fever can indicate a serious bacterial infection that could involve the lungs, urinary tract, or the tissues that surround the brain and spinal cord (these tissues are called **meninges**). Bacteria could also be present in the bloodstream, in which case the baby is said to have **sepsis.**

It is not unusual for a doctor to recommend that a newborn with a fever undergo blood tests, an evaluation of the urine, and a lumbar puncture (or spinal tap), all of which obtain specimens to be cultured for bacteria. A chest X-ray may be ordered if there is any question about pneumonia. In addition, the baby may be admitted to the hospital for two or three days so antibiotics can be given intravenously (that is, through a vein) while the cultures are growing in the laboratory. If he is doing well and no bacteria are growing in the cultures, he will be sent home.

All of this may seem rather drastic in response to a simple fever, but babies in this age-group are more vulnerable to the spread of bacteria—especially into the bloodstream and meninges. If left untreated, the results could be disastrous.

TAKING AN ACCURATE TEMPERATURE

You cannot accurately judge your baby's temperature by placing your hand on her forehead or anywhere else. *Skin temperature strips are no better.* Furthermore, you cannot get an accurate reading using an oral thermometer in babies and small children because they can't cooperate in keeping the little bulb (whether mercury or electronic) under the tongue. Electronic ear thermometers will give you a ballpark number, but results may vary somewhat depending on your technique. Therefore, even in these days of slick and expensive electronic equipment, an old-fashioned, low-tech rectal mercury thermometer remains the standard when you need to know what's going on with a very young infant. (While mercury has been used in glass thermometers for decades, some now utilize a different silver-colored liquid that behaves the same way. We will use the term *mercury* to refer to the contents of all glass thermometers.)

You should get two or three of these at the drugstore, since they have a habit of breaking or disappearing just when you need one. A rectal thermometer has a short rounded mercury bulb at one end, while an oral thermometer has a longer straight bulb (see diagram on next page). If you're not experienced with a mercury thermometer, you may want to practice reading the temperature

before the moment of truth arrives. Hold the end opposite the mercury bulb between thumb and index finger and slowly rotate the thermometer back and forth. You should be able to see the squared-off end of the mercury column next to the temperature markers. When you read the result, be sure not to confuse numbers such as 100.2° (which lies just above 100°) with 102°, which is quite a bit higher.

Before taking the temperature, shake the thermometer until it reads below 98.6° by grasping the end opposite the bulb and snapping your wrist a few times. Make sure your fingers aren't slippery, and stay away from tables and counters.

Your baby should be lying tummy-down on a bed or crib, or across your knees if he is very small. Keep one hand firmly in control of his lower back and don't try to take the temperature while he is actively squirming or resisting you. Lubricate the mercury tip of the thermometer with petroleum jelly and put a little around the baby's anus as well. Then gently insert the thermometer into the child's rectum about one inch. *Do not force the thermometer into the rectum.* Hold it for about three minutes, then remove it and read the temperature. Afterwards cleanse and rinse the bulb end, shake it down, and put it in its case—which should be labeled as a rectal, not oral, thermometer.

Feeding poorly. Lack of interest in nursing, poor sucking, or failing to awaken for feeding well beyond the expected time could be an important indicator of a medical problem. If you contact a physician with a concern that your newborn is ill,

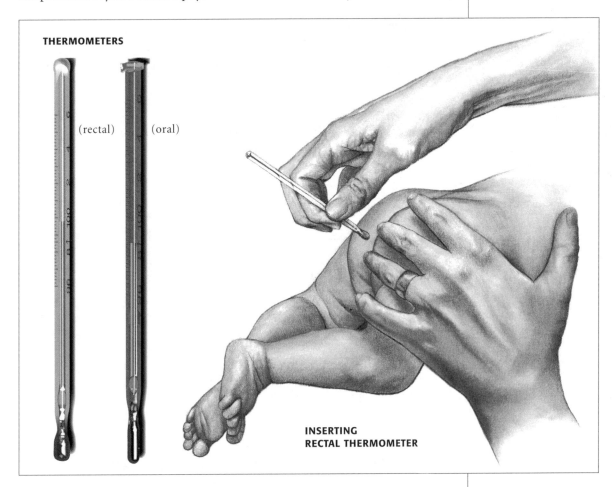

THERMOMETERS

(rectal) (oral)

**INSERTING
RECTAL THERMOMETER**

the physician will want to know, among other things, how the baby appears to be feeding.

Vomiting. As will be discussed later in this chapter, you will need to distinguish between spitting up and vomiting, since the latter is much more significant in a newborn (see page 41).

Decreased activity or alertness. A baby who is listless—with eyes open but little spontaneous movement, an indifferent response to stimulation, or very floppy muscle tone—may be quite sick. Believe it or not, a vigorous protest by a baby during an examination is a reassuring finding. At this age, remaining quiet and disinterested while being poked and prodded by the doctor is not a sign of being a "good" patient but rather an indication of probable illness.

Nonstop crying. As will be described in the next chapter, many babies enter a "crying season" between two weeks and three months of age, without any specific medical cause. But you can't assume that prolonged, inconsolable crying is normal until the baby has been evaluated by his physician.

Abnormal movements. Unusual jerking of arms, legs, or head, especially if sustained for several seconds, may represent a seizure or other significant problem affecting the nervous system. Contact your baby's doctor immediately for further advice if you observe this type of activity.

Unusual color. A pale or mottled color of the skin or bluish discoloration of the lips could indicate a change in normal circulation patterns.

HOME MEDICAL SUPPLIES
FOR BABY'S FIRST THREE MONTHS

- rectal thermometers
- bulb syringe for clearing nostrils
- cotton swabs, cotton balls
- acetaminophen infant drops
- topical ointment for diaper rash
- humidifier/vaporizer

COMMON MEDICAL PROBLEMS DURING THE FIRST THREE MONTHS

Jaundice is a yellow orange discoloration of skin caused by the buildup of a substance called **bilirubin** in the bloodstream. Bilirubin is a by-product of the breakdown of red blood cells, which normally circulate for about four months until they wear out. (New red cells are constantly produced within the bones in tissue called **marrow.**) Removing and recycling the contents of red cells require the liver to process bilirubin, which before birth is largely managed through the mother's circulation. After birth, the newborn's liver takes a few days to gear up for this job, and the level of bilirubin in the bloodstream will increase by a modest amount. If a significant backlog of bilirubin develops, the baby's skin will take on a yellow orange hue, beginning with the head and gradually spreading toward the legs.[1]

Whether or not jaundice is significant will depend upon several factors, including the level of bilirubin, how soon and how fast it has risen, the suspected cause, and whether the baby was full-term or premature. In some instances, extremely high bilirubin levels can damage the central nervous system, especially in the premature infant. *Therefore, if you notice that your new baby's skin color is changing to pumpkin orange, or the white area of the eyes is turning yellow and/or your baby is feeding poorly, see your doctor.*

If there is any concern, the doctor will order blood tests to check the bilirubin level, and other studies may be done to look for underlying causes. Normally the jaundice will resolve on its own, although some healthy babies will carry a slight yellow orange tint for weeks. Occasionally a little extra help is needed. This may involve five approaches, as directed by the baby's physician:

- Treat any underlying cause (such as an infection), if possible.
- Increase the baby's fluid intake by feeding him more often.
- Expose the baby to *indirect* sunlight—that is, undressed down to diapers in a room bright with sunlight *that does not directly shine on his sensitive skin.* Since indirect sunlight has only a modest effect on clearing bilirubin, don't use this approach unless you are sure that your baby won't become too hot or cold in the room you use.
- In some cases of jaundice, an enzyme found in mother's milk may interfere to a modest degree with the clearing of bilirubin. Occasionally your health-care provider may ask you to stop breast feeding briefly and use formula until the problem improves, after which nursing can resume. In such a case, it is important that you continue to express milk so your breasts will continue to produce it and will be ready when your baby is able to resume breast feeding. This should *not* be an occasion to stop nursing altogether.
- A treatment called **phototherapy** may be utilized if the bilirubin level needs to be treated more actively. Under a physician's direction, the baby, wearing protective eyewear, lies under a special intense blue light like a sunbather at the beach. In addition, or as an alternative, a baby can lie on a thin plastic light source called a **Bili Blanket.** Whether carried out at a hospital or at home (using equipment provided by a home-health agency), phototherapy usually reduces bilirubin gradually within two or three days, if not sooner.

Colds and other respiratory infections are relatively uncommon in this age-group. The breathing patterns in a newborn baby, however, may cause you some concern. He will at times move air in and out noisily, with snorting and sniffing sounds emanating from his small nasal passages, even when they are completely dry. Some sneezing now and then isn't uncommon, but watery or thick drainage from one or both nostrils is definitely abnormal. A call to the doctor's office and usually an exam are in order when this "goop" appears in a baby under three months.

If your newborn has picked up a cold, you can gently suction the excess nasal drainage with a rubber-bulb syringe, since a clogged nose will cause some difficulty breathing while he is feeding. *Do not give any decongestant or cold preparations to a baby this young unless given very specific directions—not only what kind, but exactly how much—from your baby's physician.* (In general, experimental evidence has suggested that such medications are not terribly effective in babies and young children.)

Even when his nose is clear, your baby's breathing rate may be somewhat erratic, varying with his activity and excitement level. A typical rate is thirty to forty times per minute, often with brief pauses, sighs, and then a quick succession of breaths. If he is quiet and consistently breathing fifty or more times per minute, however, he may have an infection or another problem with his lungs or heart. Flaring of the nostrils, an inward sucking motion of the spaces between the ribs, and exaggerated movement of the abdomen with each breath suggest that he may be working harder than usual to breathe. An occasional cough probably doesn't signal a major problem, but frequent or prolonged bouts of coughing should be investigated, especially if there are any other signs of illness.

Infections of the middle ear (known as **otitis media**) may complicate a cold in any baby, including a newborn. There are, however, no specific signs of this important problem in a young baby. (At this age, movement of the hands around the side of the head are random, and your baby cannot deliberately point to or try to touch any area that is bothering him.) Furthermore, an ear infection can be much more serious in this age-group. If he is acting ill, irritable, running a fever, or all of these, he will need to have his ears checked by his doctor.

Some babies always seem to be overflowing with tears in one eye. This is caused by a narrowing of the duct near the inner corner of each eye, which acts like a drain for the tears that are produced constantly to keep the eye moist. Aside from causing a nonstop trail of tears down one side of the face, this narrowing can lead to a local infection, manifested by goopy, discolored drainage, crusting, and if more widespread, a generalized redness of the eye known as **conjunctivitis**. The crusting and drainage will need to be removed gently using moist cotton balls, which should be promptly thrown away after being used, since they may be contaminated with bacteria. In addition, the baby's health-care provider will probably prescribe antibiotic eye drops or ointment for a few days. He or she may also suggest that you gently massage the area between the inner corner of the eye and the nose to help displace and move any mucous plug that might have formed.

Usually the clogged tear duct will eventually open on its own, but if it continues to be a problem after six months, talk to your baby's doctor, who may refer you to an ophthalmologist.

Spitting up breast milk or formula is not uncommon during the first weeks of life, and some babies return a little of their feedings for months, sometimes if they are not promptly burped. As long as he is otherwise doing well—gaining weight and making developmental progress—this can be considered a temporary annoyance that will correct itself. However, if a baby in this age-group begins **vomiting,** with stomach contents returning more forcefully, some prompt medical attention is in order.

If there is also a marked increase in the amount of stool (usually indicating that an infection in the intestinal tract has developed), the baby will need careful observation for signs of dehydration. These signs include poor feeding, a decrease in urine output (manifested by fewer wet diapers), sunken eyes, decreased tears or saliva, persistent fussiness or listlessness, and cool or mottled skin. A baby under three months of age with any of these problems should be evaluated immediately.

Projectile vomiting is an alarming event in which the stomach's contents fly an impressive distance. A young baby with this problem should be checked promptly. In a few cases forceful vomiting is caused by a thickening muscle in the portion of small intestine known as the **pylorus,** just past the stomach, which can begin to cause trouble after the second week of life. This condition, known as **pyloric stenosis,** has been traditionally considered a problem of firstborn males, but a baby of either gender or any birth-order position can be affected. In a young baby with forceful vomiting, a combination of an examination with an ultrasound or an X-ray study of the stomach will usually clarify the diagnosis. If pyloric stenosis is present, surgical correction is a must and should be carried out as soon as possible. The surgery is relatively simple, however, and is very well tolerated by the vast majority of infants.

Settling in at home and getting a good start with your baby's feeding are important accomplishments during the first few weeks of life. But there are other concerns to deal with and new learning curves to master as you and your baby become better acquainted. In the next chapter we will look at your baby's other important behaviors, especially sleeping and crying; a number of guidelines and ground rules for commonsense baby care; and some survival skills for new parents.

NOTES
1. Why jaundice progresses from the head downward rather than evenly over the entire body is unknown, but this peculiarity can give an examiner a rough idea of its severity.

The First Three Months, Part Two

Definition of a baby:
That which makes the home happier,
love stronger, patience greater, hands busier,
nights longer, days shorter, purses lighter,
clothes shabbier, the past forgotten,
the future brighter.
MARION LAWRENCE

The First Three Months, Part Two: Sleeping, Crying, and Other Newborn Pursuits (. . . and Survival Skills for New Parents)

From the moment you see, touch, and begin to live with your new baby, one basic reality will become abundantly clear: She can do nothing to meet her own needs. She can't feed herself, lift her head, change position, or scratch where she itches. She can—and will—let everyone know when she is unhappy, but she can't communicate exactly what is bothering her.

The fact that she is totally dependent on those who care for her may not sink in until your first day and night at home. Assuming that your baby was born in a hospital, it is likely that nurses and other health-care personnel provided some, if not most, of her care. Now you're on your own with this little person who needs you for everything. Don't feel strange if this thought creates a sense of mild anxiety or near panic. Almost every parent has felt the same sense of inadequacy.

For many young parents, a combination of grandparents, other relatives, and friends who are baby veterans is available to lend a hand, a few helpful hints, and a shoulder to lean on during these first weeks. Remember, however, that some of the advice you receive from others may not be medically accurate. Grandparents and other relatives may suggest—perhaps with considerable enthusiasm—approaches to baby care that differ from your own or even from your doctor's advice. Many of these are more a matter of style than substance, but if any differences of opinion seem significant, seek input from your baby's physician.

If you are isolated from your family or are a single parent, you may feel as if you're drowning in this new, nonstop responsibility. Most likely your discouragement won't last long, especially as you get used to the basic routines of baby care. *But don't be afraid to seek help if you feel that you are going under for the third time.* Your church, a local crisis pregnancy center, or even the social-services department of the nearest hospital should be able to provide both emotional and practical support.

Remember that your baby's need for total care has a time limit. Indeed, one of the most important tasks of your child's first two decades will be the gradual process of becoming completely independent of you. As she develops new skills, she will need and want you to do less and less for her—and she'll probably be quite vocal about telling you so. All too soon you will face the ultimate challenge of releasing her to live on her own. During those times of emerging independence, you will find yourself thinking back, perhaps misty-eyed, to the time when she needed you so much.

HOLDING A NEWBORN PROPERLY
Hold infant with your hand protecting the child's neck from sudden movement.

SPECIAL CONSIDERATIONS OF A NEWBORN'S TOTAL DEPENDENCE

Your baby's total dependence on you has a number of practical, as well as emotional, ramifications that should be kept in mind as you begin your first weeks of parenthood.

Controlling the head

Because a newborn's head is so large relative to his body size—more so than it will ever be in the future—and because his neck muscles are not strong enough to control it, his head must be constantly supported. Allowing it to flop freely in any direction could injure both his head and neck. Always pick him up with two hands, one of which should support and control the baby's head. Once you have picked him up, you can cradle him in one arm with his head resting in your hand. Never pick him up quickly, especially if you don't have control of his head, and *never shake him for any reason, because this can cause brain damage.*

Temperature and clothing

A newborn is less capable of regulating his body temperature than he will be in just a few months. This doesn't mean that he should be bundled in arctic gear twenty-four hours a day or that your thermostat at home should be set at greenhouse levels. Keep his environment at a temperature that's comfortable for you, and dress him in about the same number of clothing layers that you would want for yourself, with a light receiving blanket added during the first few weeks. Typically this will involve a diaper and an infant T-shirt covered by a gown or sleeper set. If the weather is hot and you don't have air-conditioning, you can dispense with everything but the diaper and T-shirt. In cold weather, extra layers will be needed if you take him outside. Because he can lose a considerable amount of heat from the surface of his head, keep it covered when he is outside in chilly weather.

When dressing or undressing your young baby, be careful with his head and hands. Don't pull a shirt or sweater over his head in a way that drags the material forcefully past his skin, ears, and nose. Instead, use your hand to spread the shirt's neck wide open, and then maneuver it over his head so there's little if any pressure of the garment against his skin. Once his head is through, don't try to push his hands through the narrow opening of the sleeves. Instead—one sleeve at a time—reach through the opening, gently grasp his hand, and carefully pull the sleeve over it. When removing a top, reverse the procedure, pulling the garment over the hands first and then his head.

DIAPER DUTY

Before your child passes her final exam in Toilet Training 101, you can look forward to changing about five thousand diapers. (Actually the number may seem more like about 43 trillion, especially if you have more than one baby in diapers at the same time.) Since your newborn will need to be changed eight to ten times a day, you'll have plenty of opportunities to practice this skill.

You'll need to decide whether your baby will spend most of her time in disposable or cloth diapers. You'll also need supplies to clean up dirty bottoms, either small washcloths that can be moistened with warm water or commercial baby wipes, which are convenient when you are away from home. Some babies' skin may be sensitive to fragrances or irritated by the alcohol contained in some wipes, but fragrance-free and alcohol-free varieties are also available. Baby powder isn't necessary and can be left out of the changing procedure altogether unless your baby's health-care provider recommends it for a moist rash. If you do need to use powder, shake a little into your hand and then apply it directly to the infant's skin. Don't shake out clouds of powder, which can be irritating if inhaled. And keep the powder can out of the reach of older babies and children.

DIAPERING STEPS
Place baby on diaper with tabs facing up.

Pull diaper between baby's legs.

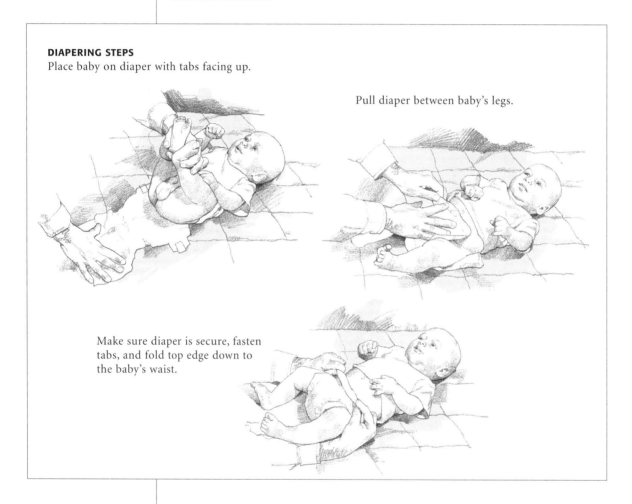

Make sure diaper is secure, fasten tabs, and fold top edge down to the baby's waist.

You'll want to check your baby's diaper for moisture or stool every two or three hours when she's awake. You don't need to rouse a sleeping baby if you notice a wet diaper unless you are trying to calm down a rash. Urine alone is normally not irritating, although stool left in contact with skin can provoke a rash because of its acidity.

When it's time to change a diaper, gather all your supplies before you begin. This is particularly important if you are using a changing table.

Remember—you must not walk away from a baby lying on a table or, for that matter, on any open surface above the floor. Unfasten the diaper while you gently grasp her feet by the ankles and pull them upward to expose the genital area. Use the diaper to remove the bulk of any stool that remains on the baby's skin and then use your washcloth or wipe to clean the skin. Be careful to cleanse the creases between legs and upper body, then lift up her ankles again to slide the new diaper under her bottom, and fasten it into place. A baby girl's bottom should be cleaned from front to back to avoid spreading bacteria from her rectal area to the vagina or urinary tract, and you don't need to wipe between the labia (the folds of skin that border the opening of the vagina) unless stool is present. If you are using diaper pins, keep your finger between the cloth and her skin. If the pin strays, you'll tolerate the point far better than your baby's sensitive abdomen will.

Changing diapers certainly isn't anyone's favorite activity, and the job shouldn't be left solely to Mom. Dad can and should learn to become adept at this task, along with any preadolescent or teenage children at home. Even if you're squeamish about cleaning up stool, avoid making a "yuck" face and groaning at every mess you find. As often as they occur during the day, diaper

DEALING WITH DIAPER RASH

Nearly every baby will develop diaper rash at some point. Causes can include:

- Prolonged exposure to urine or stool, especially after solid foods are started.
- Chemical or fragrance irritants in baby wipes, detergents used to wash diapers, or soaps used during bathing. Some babies will even react to the material used in a specific brand of disposable diaper.
- Infections with bacteria or, more commonly, yeast (candida). Yeast infections tend to cause a more intense irritation, often with small extensions or "satellites" around the edges of the rash.

Steps you can take to calm a diaper rash include:

- Change the diaper as soon as possible after it becomes wet or soiled. Once a rash develops, ongoing contact with urine and stool can irritate it further. Super-

absorbent diapers, while more convenient, tend to be changed less frequently, which may unintentionally increase contact of urine with skin.

- Try to eliminate other types of irritants. Change to fragrance- and alcohol-free wipes. If you are washing your own cloth diapers, use soap rather than detergent (this will be marked on the label) and double-rinse. If using disposable diapers, try another brand.
- Let your baby's bottom air dry after it is cleaned. If you feel particularly adventurous, leave it open to the air for a while before putting on a new diaper.
- Ointments such as Desitin or A&D may have a soothing effect. If the rash is severe, your baby's physician may prescribe a mild cortisone cream for a few days. If yeast appears to be involved, an antifungal cream, either alone or in a blend with cortisone, will usually calm the rash within a few days.

changes should be times when you communicate love and reassurance, not repulsion (even in fun). Some babies routinely put up a howl during these cleanup sessions, but with rare exception they eventually get used to the process. After two or three months, your baby may even coo at you during diaper changes.

BATHING YOUR BABY

Aside from daily cleansing of the diaper area, newborns and young babies don't need to be bathed more than two or three times a week. Before the umbilical remnant falls off, don't immerse your baby in water. Instead, give him a simple sponge bath, using a soft washcloth and a basin of warm water (comfortable to your touch) containing a small amount of a mild baby soap.

The remnant of your baby's umbilical cord may generate some goopy material, and for the first several days the area around the umbilical stump should be kept clean and dry. Use a cotton swab moistened with rubbing alcohol to wipe away any moist debris that accumulates until the cord falls off. The remnant of the cord will shrivel and fall off within two or three weeks. You may notice small spots of blood at the umbilical site for a few days.

Occasionally, local bacteria will get a foothold at the stump site, generating pus, tenderness, and redness. Contact your baby's physician if this occurs or if there is any persistent swelling and moisture several days after the stump is gone. This area will normally be examined during the first few routine checkups, but be sure to bring it to the practitioner's attention if you don't like the way it looks.

If your baby was circumcised, he may have a small dressing wrapped around the area from which the foreskin was removed. The dressing will normally fall off within a day or two, and it does not need to be replaced. If a Plastibell was used for the circumcision, it will begin to separate after a couple of days. Don't try to pull it off; let it come loose by itself. A small dab of lubricating jelly applied to any moist or raw surfaces will prevent them from sticking to the diaper. Later on, you can use a soft, warm, moist washcloth to remove (gently) any debris that remains on the penis.

You can sponge-bathe your baby while he lies on any surface that is adequately padded. To keep him from losing body heat, cover him with towels, except for the area you are washing. Start with the head, using water only (no soap) around the eyes and mouth. Then, using the washcloth dipped in soapy water, work your way down, saving the diaper area for last. Be sure to cleanse the skin creases of the neck, behind the ears, under the arms, in the groin, and beneath the scrotum in boys.

After the umbilical stump is dry, you can bathe your baby in a "bathinette" specifically designed for this purpose or even in the sink. As with the sponge bath, water should be comfortably warm but not hot (test with your elbow or wrist) and no more than a couple inches deep. Make sure you have all your supplies (washcloth, soap, shampoo, towel) ready before you undress your baby. If you have forgotten something you need or the phone rings, pick your baby up out of the water and take him with you. *Never leave a baby unattended in a bath, even with only one or two inches of water.*

BATHING NEWBORN

If he has a dirty diaper at the time you undress him, clean the area as you normally would *before* he goes into the water. You may choose to give him a sponge bath just as you did before the umbilical cord remnant fell off and then rinse him off in the bathwater. If you plan to use shampoo (not necessary with every bath, especially if he isn't endowed with a lot of hair), be sure to control his head so the shampoo and water used to rinse it don't get in his eyes, nose, or mouth.

Your baby will have no interest in rubber ducks or other bath toys at this age. Some babies fuss when put into water, but usually the sensation of warmth and rubbing by a pair of loving hands will have a calming effect. At this age, long baths are neither necessary nor wise, since the effect of prolonged contact with water may dry out his skin and cause rashes. (This is also the reason he should not be bathed every day.) In a few months, as he comes to enjoy splashing and playing in water, baths can extend beyond the time it takes to be cleaned.

Because he can lose body heat so quickly when he's wet, be ready to wrap him in a towel as soon you bring him out of the water. This will also improve the stability of your hold on him. The last thing you want is to have a wet, wiggly baby slip out of your hands.

A Newborn's Skin

A new baby's skin is so sensitive that at times looking at her cross-eyed may seem to provoke a new rash. You will see spots and splotches come and go, especially in the first several weeks, but most don't need special treatment.

During the first few weeks many babies develop pimples on the face, neck, and upper back, which in some cases look like acne. (A full-blown eruption is sometimes referred to as **neonatal acne.**) These pimples most likely are a response to some of mother's hormones acquired just before birth, and with rare exception they will resolve without treatment. If they become progressively worse, however, have them checked by your baby's health-care provider.

Another common skin problem in early infancy is **seborrheic dermatitis**, an inflammation of those areas of skin where the oil-producing sebaceous glands are most abundant: the scalp, behind the ears, and in the creases of the neck and armpits. The most striking form is **cradle cap,** a crusty, scaly, oily eruption of the scalp, which may persist for months. Fortunately, cradle cap is neither contagious nor uncomfortable, but you can help shorten its appearance with a few simple measures. Washing the hair with a gentle baby shampoo every two or three days, followed by gentle brushing, will remove much of the scaly material. Baby oil applied for a few minutes before shampooing may help soften more stubborn debris, but use it sparingly and be sure to wash all of it off. In more severe cases, your baby's doctor may recommend an antidandruff shampoo. A mild cortisone cream or lotion may also be prescribed, especially if there are patches of seborrhea on other parts of the body.

Another common rash appears on the chin and upper arms and is caused by excessive heat. **Heat rash** produces tiny red bumps rather than overt pimples and can usually be remedied by removing excess clothing.

A newborn's skin is easily dried out by excessive exposure to water, so if her skin seems dry or flaky, you may use a little baby lotion on the affected areas. Stay away from baby oil, which plugs pores and can actually provoke rashes. Keep your new baby completely out of direct sunlight because even very brief exposure can cause sunburn.

A Newborn's Behavior Patterns

As you settle into your routines with a new baby, you'll begin to notice patterns developing in a number of his behaviors. Although a newborn has only a few basic activities that occupy his first days and nights, he will carry them out in ways that are uniquely his. Mothers are often aware of differences between their children well before birth, as they feel the kicks and prods inside. The initial cry, the first waving of arms and legs, the attachment at the breast, and the willingness to cuddle will be some of the first strokes of a unique signature for this person you have brought into the world.

While every child is one of a kind, there are certain common threads and trends in behavior that have been observed in many newborns. Harvard pediatrician T. Berry Brazelton, M.D., who has studied and written extensively about newborn behavior, has described three basic types of babies, which he has dubbed "quiet," "active," and "average."

Quiet newborns sleep a lot—up to eighteen hours a day, even while nursing. They may sleep through the night very early and snooze through daytime feedings. They fuss or cry for about an hour each day and may communicate their needs quietly by sucking on their hands or wriggling in their cribs.

Active newborns behave quite differently. They sleep about twelve hours a day and spend half of what's left crying and fussing. They seem extremely sensitive to the environment, arouse easily, and may be slow to calm. When they're hungry, everyone will know about it. When it's time to nurse, they may clamp onto the breast or bottle frantically, gulping and swallowing air and then burping back a partial refund on whatever went down.

Average babies fall into the middle ground, sleeping fifteen hours or so each day, crying and fussing for about three hours a day. While more reactive to light and sound around them than quiet newborns are, they may calm themselves back to sleep if aroused. They'll let you know whenever they're hungry, but they usually settle fairly quickly when fed.

These are thumbnail sketches rather than detailed portraits, and no baby's behavior will fit precisely into one category or another. Furthermore, these characteristics are not necessarily previews of permanent coming attractions. During their first few days at home, many newborns go through a transition period that is marked either by seemingly endless sleeping or nonstop fussing. They may then shift gears after the first week, behaving quite differently as they adjust to their new surroundings. The newborn who is more active for the first weeks or longer may become much calmer later on, and vice versa.

What is most important for parents to know is that *these patterns are all inborn variations of normal behavior, not the result of child rearing techniques, the phase of the moon, or the virtues or sins of the parents.* Some newborn behaviors, however, may be altered if drugs or alcohol was used by the mother during pregnancy.

These characterizations of babies should not be taken as value judgments. Because the quiet baby may not seem very demanding, it could be tempting to think of him as "sweet," "good-natured," or "mellow." On the other hand, the active baby might bring to mind a different vocabulary: "a handful," "high-strung," "a real pistol," or "exhausting." In fact, the weary parents who were not prepared for an active baby may find themselves bleary-eyed at 3 A.M., wondering if their child is still under warranty and whether it's too late to trade for another model.

Parents should not waste too many hours gloating over their angelette who sleeps peacefully all the time or reminiscing about the good old days before their baby kept them up for hours every night. The quiet baby may become lost in the shuffle, especially in a house already busy with the activities of older children, unless parents deliberately take the time and effort to interact with him. Worse, his low-key nursing style could lead to an inadequate intake of calories and poor weight gain. If you have a quiet baby, you and the doctor will need to keep a close watch on his weight and possibly deliberately awaken him (at least during the day) to nurse at more frequent intervals. The active baby, on the other hand, for all of his intensity, will tend to be more social and interactive when he's not fussy. He may seem like a "taker" much of the time, especially during the first three months of life, but he will also give back quite a bit to those who hang in there with him.

"Sleeping like a Baby"

This timeworn phrase is reinforced whenever we behold a baby in deep, relaxed sleep. Wouldn't it be nice if we could sleep like that?

Well, not exactly.

During the first three months of life, a baby's sleeping patterns are quite different from those she will experience the rest of her life. A newborn sleeps anywhere from twelve to eighteen hours every day, but this is not unbroken slumber. Her small stomach capacity and her round-the-clock need for nutrients to fuel her rapid growth essentially guarantee that her life will consist of ongoing three- or four-hour cycles of feeding, wakefulness, and sleep. Like it or not, two or three feedings will be on the nighttime agenda for the first several weeks.

Furthermore, the patterns of brain activity during sleep are unique in a newborn. All of us experience cycles of two different types of sleep—rapid eye movement, or REM, and non-REM—throughout the night. During REM sleep, the brain is active with dreams, manifested by movements of the eyes and frequently other body parts as well. We may twitch, roll, or thrash, and we may be more easily awakened if the bed is cold, the bladder full, or the environment noisy. Non-REM sleep, during which little, if any, dreaming takes place, passes through phases of light, deep, and very deep sleep. There is less movement, deeper and slower breathing, and increasing relaxation of muscles when we pass through these stages in repeated cycles throughout the night. Adults spend about one-fourth of their sleep time in REM sleep and the rest in non-REM.

Babies also manifest these types of sleep but spend equal time in each, alternating about every thirty minutes. During non-REM, or quiet, sleep they will appear very relaxed, breathing regularly, and moving very little. During REM or active sleep, they seem to come to life, moving arms and legs, changing facial expressions, breathing less regularly, and perhaps making a variety of sounds. They may be experiencing their first dreams during these periods.

Adults and children older than about three months pass through the increasing depths of non-REM sleep before they enter a REM phase. *But newborns reverse this pattern,* starting with a period of REM sleep before moving into non-REM stages. As a result, the new baby who has just fallen asleep may be easily awakened for twenty minutes or more, until she moves into her non-REM phases.

This accounts for those character-building situations for some parents in which they feel they are dealing with a little time bomb with a short fuse. A fed, dry, and apparently tired baby fusses and resists but finally succumbs to sleep after prolonged cuddling and rocking. But when placed ever so gently into the cradle or crib, she suddenly startles and sounds off like a fire alarm. The cycle repeats over and over until everyone, baby included, is thoroughly exhausted and frustrated. The problem is that this baby isn't getting past her initial REM phase and happens to be one who is easily aroused out of it. If all else fails, the problem usually will resolve itself by the age of three months, when she shifts gears and enters non-REM sleep first.

Helping a new baby enter the slumber zone

For those parents who don't want to wait twelve weeks, there are two basic, but quite different, approaches to helping this baby—or, for that matter, any baby—fall asleep. Each approach has advocates who tend to view their ideas as vital to a happy, stable life for both parent and child, while seeing the other as producing troubled, insecure babies. In reality, both have something to offer, and neither will work for every baby-parent combination.

One method calls for parents to be intimately and directly involved in all phases of their baby's sleep. Proponents of this approach recommend that she

Ultimately, the key to competent parenting is being able to get behind the eyes of your child, seeing what he sees and feeling what he feels.

THE STRONG-
WILLED CHILD

be nursed, cuddled, rocked, and held continuously until she has fallen asleep for at least twenty minutes. She can then be put down in her customary sleeping place, which may be Mom and Dad's bed. The primary advantage of this approach is that it can help a baby navigate through drowsiness and REM sleep in the comfort and security of closeness to one or both parents. Those who favor this approach claim that a baby does best when she has more or less continuous contact with a warm body, having just exited from the inside of one. Those who challenge this approach argue that she may become so accustomed to being "manipulated" into sleep that she will not be able to fall asleep on her own for months or even years. Every bedtime or nap time will thus turn into a major project, and parents (or whoever is taking care of the baby) will be hostage to a prolonged routine of feeding and rocking well into the toddler years.

The other approach suggests that a baby can and should learn to "self-calm" and fall asleep on her own. Rather than nursing her to sleep, she can be fed thirty to sixty minutes before nap or bedtime and then put down before she is asleep. She may seem restless for fifteen or twenty minutes or even begin crying but will likely settle and fall asleep if left alone. Proponents of self-calming feel this approach frees Mom and Dad from hours of effort to settle their baby and allows the baby to become more flexible and independent, without her security being dependent on their immediate presence at all times. Critics argue that leaving her alone in a bassinet or crib represents cruel and unusual treatment at such a young age. Some even suggest that this repeated separation from parental closeness leads to sleep disorders (or worse) later in life.

You may be relieved to know that neither of these methods was carved in stone on Mount Sinai along with the Ten Commandments. You should tailor your approach to your baby's unique temperament and style and to your (and your family's) needs. Whatever you do will probably change over time as well. What works for your first baby may fail miserably for the second, and what helps this month may not the next. When dealing with newborns and very young infants, a fair amount of adjusting and pragmatism are not only wise but necessary. "Let's see if this works" is a much more useful approach than "We *have* to do it this way," except for a few ground rules dealing with safety.

Most babies give clues when they are ready to sleep—yawning, droopy eyelids, fussiness—and you will want to become familiar with your child's particular signals. If she is giving you these cues, lay her down in a quiet, dimly lit setting and see if she will fall asleep. If she is clearly unhappy after fifteen or twenty minutes, check on her. Assuming that she is fed and dry, comfort her for a while and try again. If your baby is having problems settling herself, especially during the first few weeks of life, do not attempt to "train" her to do so by letting her cry for long periods of time. *During the first few months of life, it is unwise, for many reasons, to let a baby cry indefinitely without tending to her. Babies at this stage of life cannot be "spoiled" by adults who are very attentive to their needs.*

If you need to help your new baby transition into quiet sleep, any of these time-honored methods may help:

- Nursing (or a bottle, if using formula) may help induce sleep, especially at the end of the day. However,

    (a) Don't overfeed with formula or, worse, introduce solids such as cereal at this age in hopes of inducing a long snooze. A stomach that is too full will interfere with sleep as much as an empty one. Solids are inappropriate at this age and will not lengthen sleep.

    (b) Never put a baby to bed with a bottle propped in her mouth. Not only can this lead to a choking accident, but it also allows milk to flow into her eustachian tubes (which lead into the middle ears), increasing her risk of ear infections.

- Rocking gently while you cuddle your baby can calm both of you. If this works for your baby, relax and enjoy it. A comfortable rocking chair is a good investment, by the way, if one hasn't been handed down from earlier generations of your family.

- One alternative to the rocking chair is a cradle—again, rocked smoothly and gently. Another alternative is a baby swing, but it must be one that is appropriately designed for this age-group.

- Many new babies settle more easily if they are swaddled—wrapped snugly in a light blanket.

- Quiet sounds such as the whirring of a small fan (not aimed toward the baby), a tape or CD recording of the ocean, or even small devices that generate monotonous "white noise" may help settle your baby and screen out other sounds in the home. For the musically inclined, there are several lovely anthologies of lullabies, quiet classical music, or gospel songs and hymns that might soothe a fussy baby.

- A gentle touch, pat, or massage may help settle a baby who is drowsy in your arms but squirmy in her bed.

- Many babies routinely fall asleep when they are continuously jostled during a car ride. Occasionally a frustrated parent who is dealing with a wakeful baby during the night may take her out for a 3 A.M. automobile trip—although this does not guarantee that she will stay asleep once the ride is over. Since staggering out into the night isn't much fun, especially in the dead of winter, some high-tech baby catalogues offer a device that attaches to a crib and simulates the motion of a car. Needless to say, both of these measures should be considered only as last-resort maneuvers for a very difficult sleeper.

All of the above, except for the white noise and the swaddling, involve ongoing parental activity to help settle a baby. In some situations, however, prolonged rocking, jostling, patting, and singing may be counterproductive, keeping a baby awake when she needs *less* stimulation in order to settle down. If a few weeks of heroic efforts to induce sleep don't seem to be working, it may be time to take another look at self-calming. Steps that may help the self-calming process when a baby has been put down but is not yet asleep include the following:

- Guide a baby's flailing hand toward her mouth. Many infants settle effectively by sucking on their hand or fingers.
- Identify a simple visual target for the baby's gaze such as a single-colored surface; a small, nonbreakable mirror in her crib; or a nearby window or night-light and place her in a position where she can see it. (Complex visual targets such as moving mobiles or busy patterns may not be as useful for settling during the earliest weeks, especially when a baby is very tired.)
- But make sure she is on her back before falling asleep.

What about sleeping through the night?

Newborns do not typically sleep in long stretches during the first several weeks of life, nor do they know the difference between day and night. By two months, however, they are capable of lasting for longer periods without a feeding. Most parents will go through the pulse-quickening experience of awakening at dawn and realizing that the baby didn't sound off in the middle of the night. "Is he okay?" is the first breathless concern, followed by both relief and quiet exultation: "He slept through the night!"

By three months of age, much to their parents' relief, a majority of babies have established a regular pattern of uninterrupted sleep for seven or eight hours each night. However, some will take longer to reach this milestone. A few actually drift in the wrong direction, sleeping peacefully through most of the day and then snapping wide-awake—often fidgeting and fussing—just when bleary-eyed parents are longing for some rest. If you have a baby who favors the wee hours, you will want to give him some gentle but definite nudges to use the night for sleeping:

- Make a specific effort to increase his awake time during the day. Don't let him fall asleep during or right after eating, but instead provide some gentle stimulation. Talk or sing to him, lock eyes, change his clothes, play with his hands and feet, rub his back, or let Grandma coo over him. Don't make loud noises to startle him, and do not under any circumstances shake him. (Sudden movements of a baby's head can cause physical damage to the brain.) Let him nap only after he has been awake for a while after nursing. This can also help prevent a baby from becoming dependent on a feeding to fall asleep.

- If your baby is sleeping for long periods during the day and fitfully at night, consider gently awakening him while he is in one of his active sleep phases when a nap has lasted more than three or four hours.

- By contrast, make nighttime interactions—especially those middle-of-the-night feedings—incredibly boring. Keep the lights low, the conversation minimal, and the diaper change (if needed) businesslike. This is not the time to party.

- Remember that babies frequently squirm, grunt, and even seem to awaken briefly during their REM sleep phases. Try to avoid intervening and interacting with him during these times, because you may unknowingly awaken your baby when he was just shifting gears into the next phase of sleep. This may require some adjusting of your sleeping arrangements.

- If your baby tends to awaken by the dawn's early light and you don't care to do likewise, try installing shades or blinds to block out the first rays of sunlight. Don't assume that his rustling around in bed necessarily means he is waking up for good. Wait for a while before tending to him, because he may go back to sleep. Sometimes, however, he will wake up with the local roosters no matter what you do, at which point you may want to consider adjusting your schedule to follow the famous "early to bed, early to rise" proverb until a few more months pass.

Where should your baby sleep?

By the time your baby arrives home for the first night, you will have had to address a basic question: Will she sleep in her own room, in a cradle or bassinet next to your bed, or in your bed right next to you? There are advocates for each of these arrangements.

Those who espouse sleeping with your baby point out that this is widely practiced throughout the world and that it gives the newborn a sense of security and comfort she won't feel in a crib. Critics of shared sleeping raise concerns about parents accidentally rolling over and crushing the baby; however, the risk of this is remote. The more immediate concern is the potential disruption of parental sleep, intimacy, and privacy.

New babies don't quietly nod off to sleep at 10 P.M. and wake up calmly eight hours later. They also don't typically sleep silently during the few hours between feedings. As they pass through their REM sleep phases, they tend to move around and make all sorts of noises, often sounding as if they're waking up. All of this activity isn't easy to ignore, especially for new parents who tend to be tuned in and concerned, if not downright worried, about how their new arrival is doing. Unless you learn to screen out these distractions and respond only when she is truly awake and in need of your attention, you may find yourself woefully short on sleep and patience within a few days.

SAFE SLEEP: REDUCING THE RISK OF SUDDEN INFANT DEATH SYNDROME (SIDS)

Sudden infant death syndrome (SIDS), also called **crib death,** has been the subject of intense research for a number of years. While the exact cause is uncertain, SIDS involves a disturbance of breathing regulation during sleep. It is relatively rare, occurring in two or three out of every thousand newborns, most often between the first and sixth months, with a peak incidence between the second and third months. It is more common in the winter months, the reason of which remains unknown.

SIDS is more common in males with low birth weight and in premature infants of both sexes. Breast-fed babies, on the other hand, may have a reduced risk. In addition, some potential contributing factors to SIDS can be minimized by taking a few basic preventive measures:

♦ *Stay completely away from cigarettes during pregnancy, and don't allow anyone to smoke in your home after your baby is born.*

♦ *Lay your baby down on his back.* For decades, childcare guidebooks recommended that new babies sleep on their stomachs, based on the assumption that this would prevent them from choking on any material they might unexpectedly spit up. However, recent evidence suggests that this position might be a risk factor for SIDS. *Therefore, it is now recommended that a newborn be positioned on his back to sleep.*

Exceptions to this guideline are made for premature infants, as well as for some infants with deformities of the face that might cause difficulty breathing when lying face up. In addition, your doctor may advise against the face up position if your baby spits up excessively. If you have any question about sleeping position, check with your baby's doctor. Sometime after four months of age, your baby will begin rolling

The other issue to consider is the effect on the mother and father's relationship. If Mom and Dad are equally enthused about having a new bedmate, great. But many young couples aren't prepared for the demands a new baby may place on them and especially on a mother who may have little energy left at the end of the day for maintaining her relationship with her husband. A father who feels that his wife's attention is already consumed by the baby's needs may begin to feel completely displaced if the baby is in his bed too.

Many parents prefer to have their baby sleep in another room but wonder whether they will hear her if she needs them. They need not worry. An infant who is truly awake, hungry, and crying during the night is difficult to ignore. And new parents, especially moms, are uniquely tuned in to their baby's nighttime vocalizing and will normally awaken at the first sounds of crying, even after sleeping through louder sounds such as the rumble of a passing truck.

The advantage of this arrangement is that parents will be less likely to be aroused repeatedly through the night by their baby's assorted movements and noises during sleep. They will also avoid intervening too quickly during a restless period, which can accidentally interrupt a baby's transition from active to quiet

---

(continued)

over on his own, at which point he will determine his own sleeping positions. By this age, fortunately, SIDS is extremely rare.

• *Put your baby to sleep on a safe surface.* Don't place pillows or any soft bedding material other than a fitted sheet under the baby. His head or face might become accidentally buried in the soft folds (especially if he happens to be face down), which could lead to suffocation. Sheepskin, down mattresses, and feather beds pose a similar risk. For similar reasons don't put your baby to sleep on a wavy waterbed or beanbag chair. Even on one of these plastic surfaces, a baby whose face shifts to the wrong position could suffocate.

• *Don't overbundle your baby.* Overcompensating for the cold of winter by turning up the thermostat and wrapping a baby in several layers of clothing should be avoided. If he looks or feels hot and sweaty, start peeling off layers until he appears more comfortable.

A few parents experience the terror of seeing their baby stop breathing, either momentarily or long enough to begin turning blue. It is obviously important in such cases to begin infant CPR and call 911 if he does not start breathing on his own (see Emergency Care, page 201). A careful evaluation by your doctor or at the emergency room is mandatory. It is also likely that this baby will be sent home with an **apnea monitor,** which will sound off if a breath is not taken after a specified number of seconds.

Parents who have suffered the loss of an infant for any reason must work through a profound grieving process. When SIDS is the cause, they may also feel a great sense of guilt as well as great anxiety over the safety of their other children. It is important that they obtain support from family, church, and if available, a local support group for families who have dealt with such a loss.

sleep. Having your baby sleep in another room may also increase her nighttime adaptability, allowing her to go to sleep in a variety of environments.

If you are truly concerned about hearing your baby when she first begins to cry, you can purchase an inexpensive electronic baby monitor, which will broadcast sounds from the baby's room into yours. However, you may find that you are hearing (and possibly being kept awake by) a lot of "false alarms" as your baby stirs and makes a variety of sounds without actually awakening. On the other hand, it would be unwise to leave your baby in a place where you would be totally unable to hear her and then rely on a monitor to be your electronic ears. If the monitor failed for some reason, your baby might lie uncomfortable, crying, and unattended for an extended period of time.

Many parents prefer to place their newborn in a cradle next to their bed. In order to get any sleep, however, they will have to filter out the baby's assorted nocturnal noises that do not need a response. Nevertheless, this arrangement may be useful with a newborn who has a difficult time settling during the night. If she is in another room, one or both parents may begin to feel like a yo-yo, circulating in and out of bed in response to repeated bouts of crying or fussing. These infants and their parents may have an easier time if they sleep in close proximity, so that Mom and Dad can offer nursing and comfort as often as needed without having to get up several times throughout the night.

As with the techniques you choose to help your baby settle down to sleep, you will need to determine which sleeping arrangements work best for your family and be flexible about the various possibilities. Moreover, it is important that parents keep their communications about this subject open with each other. If Mom is the one getting up to nurse a fussy baby and as a result spends more hours in the baby's room than in her own bed, Dad may need to assume a larger share of the nighttime duties. He could, for example, bring the baby to Mom for nursing and then return her to her crib when the feeding is done. Similarly, if Dad is feeling an increasing distance from Mom because of a baby in their bed, Mom may need to be willing to empty the nighttime nest of offspring.

One of the tricky issues for parents who share their bed with one or more children is deciding when and how to reclaim their bed for themselves. Most children are more than happy to sleep with Mom and Dad well into or beyond their toddler years, and making the transition to their own bed may be easier said than done. Parents who routinely allow one or more babies and children in bed with them for months or years should regularly take stock of the effect this custom is having on their marriage. Regaining sexual intimacy after the birth of a child normally requires some time and effort for both parents. It may be far more challenging if there are more than two bodies in the marriage bed.

Crybabies: What Happens When the Tears Won't Stop?

One of the greatest mental and emotional adjustments new parents must make is sorting out the meanings of, and their responses to, the new baby's crying. In most cases, crying is a clear signal that a stomach is empty or a diaper full, and the appropriate response will quiet it. Even in these routine circumstances, however, the newborn cry has distinct qualities—insistent, edgy, and downright irritating. Indeed, it can sound almost like an accusation—"I don't like the care you're giving me!"

If your new baby's cry gives you a twinge of discomfort or even annoyance, don't panic; your response is quite normal. If you're a mother acutely short on sleep and sore in body (especially if you've had a cesarean delivery), with hormones shifting in all directions, you may find yourself harboring some troubling thoughts about your crying newborn. These feelings can enter the minds of even the most dedicated parents.

How should you feel about and deal with your baby's crying? First of all, it's important to understand the function of crying. Remember that a newborn baby is totally helpless and cannot do *anything* for himself other than suck on a breast or bottle given to him (or one or two of his own fingers that have accidentally found their way into his mouth). Unless someone meets his most basic needs on an ongoing basis, he will not survive. Crying is his only means—but a most effective one—of provoking a parent into action. It's *designed* to be annoying and irritating, to create all sorts of unpleasant feelings, especially among those closest to him. The responses that usually stop the crying—food, clean diapers and clothing, cuddling and cooing—are what keep him alive.

During these first three months of your baby's life, assume that when he cries, it's for a good reason. His crying is definitely *not* a deliberate effort to irritate you, manipulate you, or test parental limits. Therefore, it is appropriate to take action in response to your baby's crying, as opposed to ignoring it and hoping it will go away. *You cannot spoil a baby at this young age,* and for now it is far better to err on the side of giving too much attention than too little. He needs comfort, open arms, and ongoing love from those around him, even though he cannot express any signs of gratitude or even pleasure in response to all you give him. This is not the time for any misguided attempts to "train, mold, and disci-

O Lord, you are our Father. We are the clay, you are the potter; we are all the work of your hand.

ISAIAH 64:8

pline" your child. (In several months you will begin to have plenty of opportunities to carry out that important assignment.)

What is your baby trying to tell you when he cries? Most likely, one of these things:

- He's hungry and wants to be fed.
- He has a wet or dirty diaper.
- He's wet, hot, cold, or uncomfortable in some other way.
- He wants to be held.

At some point, usually between two weeks and three months, there will be at least one occasion when you suspect that *something has gone terribly wrong*. Just a day or so ago you could comfort your baby regularly and predictably. A feeding every few hours, dry diapers, and a little rocking and cooing would end crying fairly quickly. Now, however, he starts fussing late in the afternoon or early in the evening, and nothing works for an hour . . . or two . . . or three. Or he suddenly lets out an ear-piercing wail or screams for no apparent reason in the middle of the night. What's going on? You may never know for sure. But it may help if you understand that many babies cry like this now and then, some do it every day, and a few seem determined to set a world's record for the longest crying episode in history.

Dealing with colic

According to a long-standing definition, if your baby cries three hours a day three days a week for three weeks, and he's between two weeks and three months of age, he has **colic.** A simpler definition, without counting hours and days (and more to the point), is "a whole lot of crying that doesn't calm down with the normal measures, and the doctor says there's nothing really wrong with him." True colicky episodes tend to occur around the same time each day, usually in the late afternoon or evening, and are marked by intense activity on the baby's part, such as flailing about or pulling his knees to his chest. From all appearances, he acts like he's feeling a lot of discomfort—and undoubtedly he is.

The classic theories about the cause of colic have assumed that the baby's intestinal tract is at fault—that it goes into uncontrollable spasms, perhaps because of immaturity or a reaction to something in Mom's milk or the current formula. Other proposed explanations include a problem interacting with parents, often assuming that Mother is tense or high-strung, and as a result the baby is also. But changing feeding patterns or formulas may or may not help, and colicky babies may land in families that are intact or disjointed, relaxed or uptight. Basically, a universal cause for colic has yet to be determined.

If your baby begins having long stretches of crying, you will need to address two basic concerns:

1. Does he have a medical problem?
2. How is everyone—baby included—going to get through this?

The first question needs to be answered relatively quickly, because a medical illness can be a much more serious problem during the first three months of life than when the baby is older. Some indicators of a disturbance that might need a physician's care include:

- Any fever over 100.4°F taken with a rectal thermometer (see sidebar, page 36)
- Poor sucking at the breast or bottle
- Change in color from normal pink to pale or bluish (called **cyanosis**) during feeding or crying
- Overt vomiting, as opposed to spitting up. (When a baby spits up, the partially digested food burps into his mouth and dribbles down his chin and clothes. When he vomits, this material becomes airborne.)
- A marked increase in the amount and looseness of bowel movements
- Unusual jerking movements of the head, eyes, or other muscles that you don't recall seeing before

If any of these occur, you should contact your physician, and your baby should be checked—especially if he has a fever. If he is crying up a storm but seems okay otherwise, he should still have a medical evaluation, either as part of a routine checkup or at an appointment specifically for this purpose. The more specific information you can give the doctor, the better. When did the crying start? How long does it last? Does anything seem to set it off? Is it improved or worsened after a feeding? Are there any other symptoms?

Assuming your baby is doing well otherwise (gaining weight, arriving at his developmental milestones more or less on time, showing no apparent signs of medical illness), your primary tasks during his crying episodes are to *be there* for him and to make ongoing efforts to comfort him. *You are not a failure, and you should not give up if your measures do not succeed in stopping the crying.* Eventually each crying episode will end, and the crying season overall will come to a close, in nearly all cases by the third to fourth month of age.

So what do you do for a colicky baby, assuming that he is fed, dry, and not sick? You can try any or all of the following, once or many times. If a particular measure helps one time but doesn't the next, don't panic. You may get impressive results today with something that failed miserably last week.

Soothing movements. Gentle rocking or swaying in someone's arms is a time-honored baby comforter. Unfortunately, when a baby is wailing at full volume, you may unconsciously begin moving faster or more forcefully—but you should *avoid rapid, jerky movements,* which not only make the problem worse but may even injure the baby. Cradles and baby swings that support the body and head can also provide this type of movement.

Soothing sounds. Provide humming, gentle singing, white noise, or pleasant recorded music.

Soothing positions. Some colicky babies respond to being held tummy-down against your forearm like a football or across your thigh. Others seem to calm down while being carried close to Mom's or Dad's body in a baby sling. Swaddling in a light blanket and resting on one side or the other might help.

Soothing environments. Spending time in a quiet, dimly lit room can help calm a baby who may be in sensory overload at the end of the day. Turn down the TV and unplug the phone if you have to.

Soothing trips. A ride in the car or a stroller may provide the right mix of gentle movement and sound to soothe the crying.

Soothing touch. Gentle touching or stroking of the back, stomach, or head may help.

Soothing sucking. Nursing may seem to calm the crying, even if he just had a feeding. A pacifier may also work. If your baby doesn't seem satisfied by *any* of your feedings, you should check with his physician and possibly a lactation consultant as well. This is particularly important if he's not gaining adequate weight, because the problem may be that his hunger is never satisfied. If your colicky baby is formula-fed, you may at some point want to try a different brand or a different type of formula—for example, switching from cow's milk to soy-based formula. (Check with your baby's health-care provider on this.) Sometimes a change will bring about some noticeable improvement.

Self-soothing. Sometimes all the rocking, singing, touching, and pacifying maneuvers unwittingly overload the baby's capacity to handle stimulation. The self-soothing measures mentioned in the previous section on sleep (page 58) may work wonders when everything else has failed.

What can you do for yourself while all of this is going on?

Keep reminding yourself that "this too will surely pass." You will deal with crying problems for only a short period of your child's life. Believe it or not, before you know it there will come a time when you'll wonder where all those baby years went.

If you find yourself reaching the end of your rope, *don't take it out on the baby.* Mounting frustration and anger are indications that you need a brief time-out. If that time arrives, don't allow yourself to become a martyr or a child abuser. Sounding off verbally at the baby will accomplish nothing, and *you must not carry out any physical act of anger*—picking him up or putting him down roughly, shaking him, hitting him, or anything else that inflicts pain or injury—no matter how upset you may feel. Instead, put him in his cradle or crib and *walk away* for fifteen or twenty minutes until you have a chance to collect your thoughts and calm down. It won't hurt him to cry by himself for that period of time, and you can then try comforting him again. He may have expended enough energy to become more responsive to calming efforts at this point. If necessary, call a friend or relative and get your frustration off your chest, or let someone else come look after your baby for a while (see sidebar, page 68).

If at all possible, husband and wife should pass the baton during a prolonged crying episode. Let Dad hold the baby while Mom takes a walk around the block and vice versa. Single moms—and for that matter, married ones—shouldn't be embarrassed to seek help from an experienced relative or friend. If Grandma wants to help you for a while during a rough evening, by all means let her do it. She may have a few tricks up her sleeve that aren't in any book.

Try to find some humor in all this to maintain your perspective. Pretend you are the next Erma Bombeck and jot down some of your observations. If you have one or more books that have made you laugh out loud, by all means keep them close at hand.

Try to maintain "self-preservation" activities as much as possible. A quiet time for reflection and prayer may have to occur during a feeding, but it will provide important perspective and strength. Having a world-class wailer is a humbling experience, and it is during these rough times that special intimacy with God often develops. The question to ask Him isn't "Why did You give me such a fussy baby?!" but "What do You want me to learn about myself and life in general through this experience?" You may be surprised at the answer.

If you have "gone the distance," repeatedly trying every measure listed here (and perhaps a few others as well) without success, check back with your baby's doctor. Be prepared to give specific information—for example, how many hours the baby has been crying, not just "He won't stop!" Depending upon your situation and the baby's crying pattern, another medical evaluation may be in order.

MILESTONES AND MEMORIES

Even though nursing, sleeping, and crying may dominate the landscape during the first several weeks, you'll be happy to know that your baby will also be taking in all kinds of information and learning new ways to respond to it. Young babies manifest six different levels of consciousness: quiet sleep, active sleep, drowsiness, quiet alertness, active alertness, and crying.

Quiet alertness occupies about 10 percent of your baby's time at first, but you will want to watch for these moments of calm attentiveness, during which you can begin to have some genuine interaction. Enjoy them, file them in your memory bank, and if you have time, you may want to jot your impressions in a personal journal. As the weeks pass, you will begin to notice that your baby is

---

TO GRANDPARENTS AND OTHER PARENT SUPPORTERS: THE GIFT OF TIME

If you have experience as a parent, whether recently or in the more distant past, one of the greatest gifts you can offer a relative or friend with a fussy baby is a brief respite. This is particularly important for single moms, but even a married mother may have a husband who isn't much help when the baby is having full-throttle colic. And a baby who cries nonstop can wear out both Mom and Dad before much time has passed.

The sound of someone else's baby crying is not nearly as nerve-wracking as it is for the mother or father of the child. You may also be able to model some perspective, a reminder of the preciousness of this new life, by cooing and fussing over a baby who may not seem very lovable to her parents at this particular moment.

Take the initiative in asking a new parent how life with the new arrival is going, and in particular if there are any problems with fussing and crying. If you have time, energy, and child rearing skills, offer to look after the baby for a while. You might suggest a specific time ("How about if I come over tomorrow or Wednesday night around six, so you can get out for a couple of hours?") rather than something vague ("Let me know if I can help you"), which may be more difficult to accept without sounding utterly desperate. Your offer to provide a time-out for a frazzled parent may be far more valuable than any baby-shower gift.

spending more time in calm and active alertness, during which you will see several wonderful developments in a variety of areas:

Vision. During the first few weeks, a baby focuses best on objects eight to fifteen inches from her face. You may find her staring intently at the fist at the end of her outstretched arm, which happens to be in her focusing range. She will prefer to study plain, high-contrast, black-and-white images such as stripes, checks, or spirals, or a simple drawing of a face. She may gaze intently into a small, unbreakable mirror attached to the inside of her crib. But her favorite subject to scrutinize will be the face of another person, about a foot away from hers. She will not respond directly to a smile for a few weeks, but a lot of smiles are what she should see.

Your baby will be able to follow an object with her eyes only momentarily at first. You can give her some practice at this ability by moving your face or a brightly colored object slowly from side to side across her field of vision. Around two months of age she will be able to coordinate her eye movements to stay locked on an interesting visual target that passes through a semicircle in front of her. She will also be interested in more complex shapes and patterns and will be able to hold her head steady enough to fixate on simple, high-contrast objects hung from a mobile over her crib. By three months of age her distant vision will be increased to the point that she will recognize you halfway across a room.

Responses to color also develop over the first several weeks. At first she will pay attention to objects with bright, strongly contrasting colors. Ironically, the soft colors that are so often used in decorating a baby's room won't be particularly interesting to her at first. It will take a few months before her color vision has matured enough to distinguish a full palette and varieties of shades.

From time to time all babies will briefly cross their eyes as they develop their tracking skills. But if she frequently appears to have crossed eyes as she approaches the age of six months, she should be checked by her physician and an ophthalmologist.[1]

Hearing. Newborns will vary in their sensitivity to sounds. Some infants seem capable of sleeping through a violent thunderstorm, while others appear to startle when a cat crosses the street a block away. If a young infant is placed in a very noisy environment, he may appear to "shut down," markedly reducing his activity level. This is a protective mechanism, an internal withdrawal from a situation that is overloading him. While you don't need to maintain a hushed silence around your newborn, you should try to keep the noise level around him at a comfortable level—no more than, for example, the intensity of pleasant conversation between two or three people. If you want to go to a ball game or a concert where the crowds and sounds are pumped up, leave the baby at home.

Within a few weeks, he will appear to pay attention to certain sounds, especially the voices of those who regularly care for him. By two months of age, he may begin to shift his eyes and head toward your voice. He may also show some movements and expressions indicating that he recognizes this familiar and comforting sound. As he continues toward three months of age, you will notice him starting to turn toward other interesting sounds, such as a tinkling bell. If the sound is repeated over and over, however, he will tune it out and stop responding to it.

Smell. A very young baby is capable of responding to a variety of smells and can distinguish the smell of his mother's breast from those of other nursing mothers by the end of the first week of life.

Touch. All of us are strongly affected by touch, but babies are particularly sensitive. They will startle in response to scratchy surfaces, rough handling, or sudden temperature changes—especially when their skin makes contact with something cold. Cuddling, caressing, and stroking may help calm a crying episode, but these shouldn't be used merely to stop tears. Touch is an important expression of love and will nourish her emotions before she can understand any words. It should be as routine a part of her day as her feedings.

These developments set the stage for your baby's first true **socializing,** which will probably begin just as you are starting to wonder whether all the nursing and diapers and nonstop caregiving are worth it. You may first notice a brief flicker of a grin after a feeding. Was that a smile or a gas pain? Maybe it was both or maybe neither, but it felt like a puff of fresh air on a hot day. Suddenly—at about the age of four to six weeks—it will be unmistakable: You will lock eyes with your baby, and a big grin will flash across her face. It will be an unforgettable moment, and the next time she smiles will be equally rewarding because you'll know that this milestone was for real.

Over the next month, you will catch smiles in response to your own grinning, cooing, talking, or singing to your baby. You may notice special enthusiastic body movements in response to familiar voices and the turning of eyes and head to seek them out. Even more pleasant are your first "conversations." At about two months your baby will begin to coo, often in response to your speaking to her in soft, soothing tones. At this age, she will not understand the words you speak, but the tone of your voice will communicate volumes.

Even at this young age, your baby may show some selectivity in her responses. Not everyone will necessarily receive the big grin and happy sounds. More often than not, it will go to the most familiar faces and voices. Your baby is already starting to sort out who is important in her life, and so whoever wants to be included in that category will need to log some time with her. This is particularly important for fathers, who may find it harder to interact with a squirmy two-month-old than an older child who likes to "wrestle" on the carpet or play catch. Mothers who are weighing decisions about work outside the home also need to ponder how much time the baby should spend with other caregivers.

Growth and movement. Babies lose and then regain several ounces (about a tenth of their birth weight) during the first ten days of life. From then on, you can anticipate a weight gain of about two-thirds to one ounce per day, or one to two pounds per month. Your baby will add between one and one and a half inches in height each month as well. These amounts will vary, of course, depending on your baby's feeding patterns and on genetics, which will affect whether this growing body will ultimately resemble a ballerina or a fullback. During each medical checkup, your baby's height, weight, and head circumference will be measured and then plotted on a growth chart. Tracking your baby's growth will be an important tool for her health-care provider to confirm how well she is doing.

During the first three months, you will see dramatic changes in your baby's movement patterns. At birth her arms and legs flail and jerk, her chin may twitch, and her hands may tremble. Many of her movements are reflexes, such as rooting, sucking, and grasping. In addition, you may see her do a "fencing" maneuver known as the **tonic neck reflex:** If her head is turned in one direction, you may see the arm on that side straighten and the other arm flex, as if she were about to enter a sword fight. In addition, if you gently hold her body upright, supporting her head, and then lower her gently until her feet touch a firm surface, she will begin stepping motions. This has nothing to do with how soon she will begin walking, and this so-called **stepping reflex** will be gone by the age of two months. However, she will kick her legs quite vigorously when awake and active while lying on her back or stomach.

Hand and arm movements will gradually become less jerky and almost appear purposeful. Between two and three months, she will begin to spend more time with her hands open rather than clenched and will bring them toward her mouth or in front of her face, where she may appear to study them. She still won't have the coordination to reach directly for something that interests her, although she will tightly grasp a small object placed in her hand. In fact, you may have to help her let it go.

At two months she will have developed enough control of her neck muscles to hold her head in one position while lying on her back. When lying on her stomach, she will be able to raise her head briefly, just long enough to turn it from one side to another. But her head control overall will not be secure until three to four months of age, so you must support her head whenever you hold or carry her.

Other people in your baby's life

Just as it is important for you to handle your newborn carefully and appropriately, any older brothers or sisters in the family will need to be supervised during their interactions with the baby. They should have been given plenty of advance warning, in language they can understand, about the new brother or sister who is on the way, and perhaps will have had a chance to say hello to him while Mom was still in the hospital. For very young children, fascination with the wiggly little person will be mixed with an overriding concern about whether there is enough love to go around.

With everyone oohing and aahing over the new baby, your toddler or preschooler may conclude that the best way to get attention is to act like the baby. You may notice him trying to climb into the baby's crib or suddenly forgetting all his potty-training skills. Rather than spending a lot of energy rebuking this behavior, take time to affirm his capabilities and point out some of the advantages of being older. ("You're such a big boy now—you can go to the park and ride on the swings! The baby is too little to do that.") He needs reassurance that he is special and unique, and he needs one-on-one time with Mom and Dad. If Mom is worn out or recovering from surgery, Dad or a grandparent should be prepared to take on this assignment.

Equally (if not more) important is the need to ensure the new baby's safety around children who are not likely to be well versed in the details of newborn care. Toddlers and preschoolers who want to touch and caress the new baby must be shown how to do so gently, avoiding the baby's eyes, nose, and mouth and clearly told that they can only touch the baby while Mom or Dad is there watching them. They should not be allowed to carry a new baby, play any of their physical games with the baby, or touch the baby with anything but their hands that have just been washed. If they have runny noses or a cough, they'll need to wait until the illness is gone before getting near the baby.

If you see an older sibling talking or acting aggressively toward a new baby, immediately separate the two, find out what's going on, and make certain the issue (usually jealousy) is settled before allowing any further contact. Small chil-

dren, especially if they are upset (for whatever reason), are quite capable of in-
juring babies, whether or not they fully realize what they are doing. Toddlers and
two-year-olds are particularly incapable of processing the moral and physical
reasons they should not act aggressively toward a baby, although it is appropriate to define limits for them in this as in other arenas (see chapters 4 and 5, pages
113, 147). Parents and other caregivers will thus need to remain constantly on
guard to protect a young infant from the older sibling—who was himself a baby
not long ago.

The same rules about colds and acute illnesses apply to relatives and friends
who may want to handle your baby. Because her immune system is not as competent as it will be in a few months, you should be careful to expose her to as little risk of infection as possible. This means that, at the risk of upsetting a
well-meaning friend or relative, you may need to be firm about keeping your new
baby away from anyone with an acute infection, especially one involving sneezing and coughing (which can easily spread contaminated droplets). Adults and
older children will have a much easier time getting over their temporary disap-
pointment than your newborn will have recovering from an acute infection. Your
protective stance for the first two to three months of your baby's life should also
include keeping her out of crowds in general and group nurseries in particular,
unless it is absolutely necessary to do otherwise.

Don't hesitate to ask well-wishers to come back at a later date if you are feeling overwhelmed by all your new responsibilities. If the baby is fussy and you're
running on empty with too little sleep, keep visitors to a minimum, place a po-
lite sign on the door asking not to be disturbed, and let the answering machine
take care of incoming calls so you can get some extra rest. You'll have plenty of
time to socialize and show off your pride and joy in the coming months.

NOTES
1. If the position of her eyes is constantly presenting two images instead of one to her brain, she will shut down
the information arriving from one eye or the other, resulting in **amblyopia,** or "lazy eye."

Three to Six Months: Expanding Horizons

Don't forget that compared to a grown-up person every baby is a genius. Think of the capacity to learn! The freshness, the temperament, the will of a baby a few months old!
MAY SARTON

Three to Six Months: Expanding Horizons

As your baby grows and slowly graduates from the newborn stage, you will find yourself entering a phase of increased enjoyment and satisfaction in parenting. During these months your baby will progress from being a pure "taker" of your love and energy to a "giver" as well, someone who can flash a smile and carry on irresistible interactions with nearly anyone who will give him the time of day. For a baby these months are full of intense exploration. No longer restricted to crying as his only method of gaining attention, your baby is now finding all sorts of new ways to investigate and affect what goes on around him. While he isn't exactly capable of propelling himself out the front door while your back is turned, his wondrous new skills will create some safety challenges.

PHYSICAL DEVELOPMENTS: ARMS, LEGS, AND BODIES IN MOTION

During his first three months, one of your baby's major accomplishments was simply learning to keep his head still enough to focus on an object and track a moving object with his eyes. Now he is starting to use larger muscle groups that will eventually allow him to sit up on his own. This begins with more decisive head control, which you will notice when he is lying on his stomach while awake. He will make a more deliberate effort to keep his head elevated so he can see what's going on in front of him. You can encourage the exercise of these upper back and neck muscles by placing a small toy or brightly colored object—or your smiling face—in front of him while he is in this position.

He will then progress to lifting his entire upper chest, with or without help from his arms. When he combines this with vigorous kicking, you will see surprisingly active rocking, and by five or six months, the right combination of movements will send him rolling over front to back. Rolling back to front will not be far behind. (A few babies roll back to front first.) Invariably, he will accomplish this skill for the first time when you least expect it, so never leave him alone on any elevated surface such as a bed or changing table, or he may add free-falling to his new movement experiences.

At this stage he will enjoy being propped on pillows in a sitting position, although he must be watched because he can easily topple forward. He will soon figure out how to "sit" in a hunched position with one or both hands on the floor, precariously maintaining his balance. He can still topple easily, so make sure his landing will be on a soft surface. At six months of age at the earliest, he will be able to maintain a sitting position without using his hands, although he is still a few months away from maneuvering himself into a sitting position.

Another adventure for him at this age is being held by the upper body and "standing" in someone's lap. Most babies love to flex their legs and bounce up and down, as if ready to bear their weight in a standing position. They are, of course, nowhere near achieving this milestone, and the playful bouncing won't bring it along any sooner. But it also won't cause any harm to growing muscles and bones. However, you should not suspend or lift a baby's full weight by holding his hands or arms.

Your baby's ability to use his hands will develop dramatically during these three months. As a newborn he spent most of his time with his little fists clenched and could only respond with a tight reflex grip to objects placed in his hands. Now he will spend more time with open palms, and more important, he will begin to reach deliberately toward interesting things that catch his eye. He will grasp as if his hand were in a mitten, thumb against the other fingers, or rake an item into his hand. (Independent use of the fingers and the ability to pick up an object between the thumb and index finger will not develop until about nine months of age.) You will not be able to tell whether he is right- or left-handed at this point, since this characteristic is not clearly manifested until about the age of three years.

But even without fine tuning, your baby will become a first-class grabber by the age of six months. Not only will he reach for toys in his immediate vicinity (or his own feet), but when someone holds him, he will expertly seize hair, earrings, or the pen in Dad's shirt pocket. Furthermore, all of these items will be inspected carefully and fearlessly, not only with eyes and fingers but invariably with his mouth. You will now need to enter a state of perpetual vigilance for small objects that you would rather not see entering his mouth, either because they are incredibly gross or because they might be accidentally swallowed and/or block his airway.

As his reaching and grasping skills become more developed, he will also discover the joy of "letting go." During these three months you will see him transfer an object from one hand to the other, which requires that one hand release what the other hand takes. At some point he will also discover gravity, as he begins to drop things and observe what happens as a result. In later months this may become a serious pastime as toys, food, and other unidentified nonflying objects are released from various heights (such as crib or high chair) in order to watch them careen or bounce or even shatter. All of this activity is exploratory and not a sign of a destructive streak or a future career in sports. But he will eventually need to be taught what items can be tossed and where.

Vision and hearing

During these three months your baby will continue to gain in the ability to see and hear what's going on around her. By six months she will be able to focus on people or objects several feet away and follow movement in all directions. She will show interest in more complex patterns and subtle shades of color, so this is a great time to hang a mobile over her crib. She will also find stroller rides stimulating times to take in a passing parade of new colors and shapes.

She will become more skillful at localizing the source of sounds and turning her head in the direction of your voice or an interesting noise in her vicinity. In addition, you will begin hearing a wider range of sounds—babbles, belly laughs, bubbling noises, and even a screech or two for good measure. Sometimes she will even alter her "speech" patterns, raising and lowering her voice as if giving an oration in a language only she understands. Rather than parroting back her assorted sounds, which is often irresistible, you can begin to transform some of her favorite syllables into simple words such as *baby, doggie, Mommy,* and feed them back to her. By seven months of age, she should begin imitating sounds you make.

SOCIAL DEVELOPMENTS: THE JOYS OF INTERACTING

For many parents, this stage of a baby's life is one of the most pleasant they will experience, a time when a true personality emerges from the seemingly endless cycles of feeding, sleeping, and crying during the first three months. All of her new skills in movement, vision, hearing, and noisemaking seem to converge and

Spiritual training should begin before children comprehend what it is all about. They should grow up seeing their parents on their knees before God, talking to Him. They . . . will never forget what they've seen and heard.

PARENTING ISN'T
FOR COWARDS

complement each other as she shows off for family, friends, and complete strangers. When her face lights up for Aunt Mary, she'll likely get a big grin and a lot of sweet talk in return. When she babbles and gurgles for Grandpa, she'll probably hear a few new funny noises in response. Even older brothers and sisters will enjoy making the new baby smile.

In all of these encounters, your baby is finding out what kind of world she lives in. What sights and sounds envelop her and what happens when she tries to make an impact, in her own way, on her surroundings? Does she see smiles and bright colors, hear laughter and pleasant voices, and feel hugs, kisses, and cuddling? Is she in a place that is safe physically and emotionally? Even during her first stirrings of independence, she is still completely helpless, depending on the adults around her for her physical needs and her most basic sense of security. She may not be able to understand your words, but she'll get a strong message about her importance to you and your family.

Everyone who cares for your baby plays a role in this process. It is particularly important for Dad to interact with her at this point. Playing with a baby this age isn't all that difficult. With rare exception, your baby can now be entertained simply by laying her across your lap and playing with her hands and feet, making faces, and giving her interesting objects to handle. She will love to wave rattles and toys that make sounds or musical tones. She will enjoy looking at books or magazines with bright pictures. She will like touching and squeezing soft toys, especially if they have an interesting texture.

There will probably be grandparents and favorite uncles and doting aunts around who will also enjoy these simple pleasures. Sometimes a relative who hasn't had all the day-to-day responsibilities and interrupted sleep for the past few months can give you a fresh perspective on your baby, a reminder that tending her is not only worthwhile but a source of enjoyment. This is especially important if you are a single parent, because you will need the break from being on call twenty-four hours a day and the reassurance that raising your child is worth the effort.

FEEDING: NEW ADVENTURES

If your baby is nursing, he will typically need to fill his tank about five times a day and soon should be skipping the late-night feeding(s) if he isn't already. By six months, if he is waking up two or three times during the night, it is far more likely to be for reasons other than hunger (see page 86).

Some mothers who are breast-feeding quite successfully will, for a variety of reasons, begin to think about shifting from breast to bottle before their baby reaches six months of age. If at all possible, however, continue nursing during these months, for all of the reasons outlined in chapter 1 (page 10). If you need to start or resume employment outside the home and cannot nurse your baby during work hours, you do not necessarily need to switch your baby entirely to formula. Depending upon your schedule and your baby's feeding patterns, you may be able to nurse before and after work and even express milk (which can be used at a later feeding) during the time you are away from home. (If you intend to shift from breast to bottle feeding, see sidebar, page 120.)

A formula-fed baby will similarly be consuming five bottles every day, each containing five to eight ounces of formula, depending on his weight. You can discuss the amount with your physician at the four- and six-month checkups, but a ballpark amount for a given feeding is an ounce of formula for every two pounds of weight. By the way, it's too early to begin drinking from a cup at this age. That adventure can begin after your baby reaches the six-month mark.

Parents of babies in this age-group often wonder if this is a good time to introduce solid foods. Thirty years ago, physicians routinely advised parents to begin feeding their babies rice cereal at two months and then speedily progress to other types of foods. Your baby's grandmother may have started you on cereal practically from day one, and perhaps one of your friends has announced with some satisfaction that her baby is already taking all sorts of fruits and vegetables at two months of age. But consuming solids is *not* a sign of advanced intelligence or motor skills. In fact, there are reasons you don't need to be in any hurry to introduce solids before your baby is six months old:

Breast milk or formula can supply all of the calories and nutrients your baby needs for his first six months of life, and it is more easily digested than other foods. The efficiency of the intestinal tract in absorbing other foods increases significantly between the fourth and sixth months.

Babies who are fed solids early may develop food allergies. If there is a strong history of allergies in either parent or other family members, you would be wise to wait. After six months infants are better equipped to process a variety of foods without this risk.

Solid foods are best managed by a baby who has some basic developmental skills in place. (See sidebar, page 82.)

First experiences with solid foods

While you don't need to be in a rush to start solids, most babies are given their first taste of foods other than breast milk or formula between four and six months of age. Like many other everyday concerns in child rearing, directions for introducing solids to babies were not included in the Ten Commandments. Families have made this transition for thousands of years in thousands of ways. What follows are basic guidelines to help you navigate this passage smoothly, along with a few cautions about certain foods and feeding practices that would best be avoided.

Before you decide to let your baby try something other than milk, think about your timing. First, she should be ready developmentally (see sidebar).

The other timing question to consider is the specific setting of your baby's first experience with solids. Pick a time when you aren't going to be rushed or hassled, and take the phone off the hook for good measure. Your baby shouldn't be tired, cranky, ravenously hungry, or completely full. Give her part of a feeding of breast milk or formula before you try the new stuff. *Remember that when you begin solids, they will only supplement milk feedings, not substitute for them,* so the normal feeding should be finished after whatever solid food she has eaten.

What should you start with? The general consensus is that rice cereal specifically formulated for babies is best. It is well absorbed, contains iron, and rarely causes allergic reactions. Whether premixed in a jar or prepared by you with water or formula, it can be adjusted to whatever thickness your baby prefers. You should feed her from a small spoon and not a bottle with an enlarged hole in the nipple. If she sucks solids out of a bottle, she may get too much volume and become obese if this is done repeatedly. And she will delay learning how to swallow solids without sucking.

DEVELOPMENTAL SIGNS THAT YOUR BABY IS (OR ISN'T) READY FOR SOLID FOOD

- While sucking at the breast or bottle, the newborn first protrudes her tongue, pushing it against the nipple as she sucks and swallows. This tongue-thrusting reflex, which gradually subsides over the first six months, interferes with the process of taking food from a spoon and moving it to the throat, where it can be swallowed. A baby who repeatedly pushes her tongue against your spoon probably isn't ready for solids.

- Accepting food from a spoon is much easier for a baby who can control her head position, a skill which will be far better developed after six months than at three or four. A young baby whose head flops everywhere if not supported should be given more time with just breast or bottle.

- By six months of age your baby will be happily grabbing everything in sight and putting whatever she finds into her mouth, an indication that she will find a spoon worth exploring as well.

- If a couple of teeth erupt before six months of age (the usual time of the first appearance of teeth), this in itself is not a sign that your baby is ready for pizza. Your baby won't use her teeth to chew food yet for some months. In fact, even if she still doesn't have teeth at the six-month mark, she will be quite able to swallow the mushy solids you'll be feeding her.

Offer her about half of a small baby spoonful (or use a small coffee spoon if you wish), which should total about a quarter teaspoon. She may not know what to do with your offering and may even appear to reject it with a grimace. Talk to her in soothing tones through the entire process. When she gets the hang of swallowing this amount, she will begin opening her mouth in anticipation of more. Aim for a total of about one tablespoon once a day, gradually increasing to two or three tablespoons per feeding once or twice per day. If she simply refuses or repeatedly tongue-thrusts, don't force her. This is not a moral issue or a contest of wills. Simply wait and try again in another week or two.

When two or three tablespoons are going down smoothly at one feeding, you can try other cereals. Oats and barley are good for the next round, but check with your baby's doctor before trying corn or wheat cereals, which may provoke digestive problems in some infants. After cereals have been successfully consumed for a few weeks, you can think about adding other foods to the mix. Either vegetables or fruits may be the next category you try, but vegetables may hold an advantage because they will not condition your baby to sweet tastes. Fruits can be added later, and meats should be introduced last. By the time your baby is eating from three or four food groups, she will probably be eating three times per day. You may choose to raise a vegetarian and not introduce meats to your baby at all, but if you do, be sure that you are adequately informed so your baby won't be deprived of any necessary nutrients.

Let your baby try each new food (one to three tablespoons' worth) for a few days before introducing another. Observe for any signs of a reaction: diarrhea, irritability, runny nose, coughing or wheezing, or a rash, especially around the face. If there is any possibility that a reaction has occurred, withdraw the food, wait for the problem to calm down, and try again. If you see the same response, put that food aside for several weeks and then run the story by your baby's doctor before serving it to her again. Of course, if any feeding is followed by a more severe reaction, such as an immediate rash or difficulty breathing, contact the doctor immediately. Fortunately, sudden and intense reactions to foods are very uncommon at this age.

You can obtain many foods for your baby in prepackaged forms at the store, or you can prepare them yourself. Commercial baby foods have the advantage of convenience, especially if you are traveling or are short on time for food preparation. Unlike their predecessors of a few decades ago, most are free of sugar, salt, and artificial flavorings—they contain just the straight food in a mushy consistency, ready to feed. When opening a baby-food jar, make sure the safety button in the middle of the lid pops up. If it doesn't, return the jar or throw it away.

Don't feed your baby directly out of the jar because the enzymes and bacteria from her saliva may degrade or contaminate the food she doesn't finish. Instead, spoon a small amount on a plate and refrigerate what remains in the jar; it will be good for a day (or a month if left in the freezer). Whatever she doesn't finish from her plate should be thrown away.

Foods do not need to be hot; room temperature or slightly warm is just fine for most babies. If you need to warm something from the refrigerator, use the microwave with extreme caution—if at all—because of the possibility of uneven temperatures and hot spots within the food that could burn the baby's mouth. Food that is microwaved should be thoroughly stirred so the heat is distributed evenly throughout. If heating food in a baby-food jar, you can place the jar in a pan of warm water for a few minutes.

Don't become a clean-plate fanatic with your baby. When first sampling solids she will take only small amounts—one or two tablespoons at a time—and then gradually increase her intake over time. Watch for signs that she is no longer hungry—turning her head, getting fussy, or general disinterest in what you are offering from the spoon. Trying to force her to eat a prescribed amount is not only an exercise in futility but may also set up a bad habit of eating when she has no appetite.

THE DEBUT OF TEETH

During these months you may notice that your baby is doing a fair amount of drooling. This does not necessarily mean that the appearance of her first teeth is imminent. The ongoing flow of saliva serves partly to protect the mouth from being traumatized by the various objects, including her feet, that your baby will stick in her mouth. Antibodies in saliva may also help prevent bacteria and viruses on those objects from gaining a foothold in her throat or intestinal tract.

Somewhere in the neighborhood of six months, the first two lower front teeth, called the central incisors, will poke through the gums. (However, don't worry if you don't see any teeth for the first year. After that, if none have appeared, check with your baby's doctor.) The central incisors will be followed sometime later by the four upper incisors and then by two more lower incisors. Your baby may ease through this or display a lot of fussiness. She may drool somewhat more than usual and may also try to gum the nearest firm object. Contrary to popular belief, teething does not generate a temperature over 100.4°F taken rectally. If your baby has a fever something else is wrong.

Rubbing your finger against the gum through which the tooth is erupting may help the pain, or she may prefer a teething ring—which should not come from the freezer because it will be too hard. Acetaminophen (Tylenol and others) can help, but topical preparations that are supposed to numb the gums don't usually provide impressive relief because they can't remain in place for long.

A few additional cautions about foods and feeding

Do not feed honey to your baby. Infants younger than twelve months of age who eat honey may develop **infant botulism,** a form of food poisoning that can cause serious damage to the nervous system or very rarely can be fatal. Infant botulism has also been linked to corn syrup.

Keep your baby on breast milk or infant formula (fortified with iron) rather than milk from the dairy case. Infants who drink cow's milk before their first birthday are more likely to develop an allergy to the protein it contains. Cow's milk may also interfere with the absorption of iron contained in other foods.

Steer clear of fruit juices, punch, or other sweetened drinks. Some babies can become so enamored with sweet liquids that they will favor them over more nutritious sources of calories. They may also become hard to separate from their beloved juice bottle, which unfortunately will keep their new teeth continuously bathed in cavity-provoking sweet liquids. A good time for your baby to begin enjoying juices is when she can drink them from a cup.

Don't feed your baby foods with added salt or sugar or with spicy flavors. She needs to become accustomed to the basic, unadulterated taste of high-quality foods.

Don't let your baby become a "grazer." Some parents respond with food (breast, bottle, or snacks) whenever their baby utters any sound remotely suggesting displeasure. The result is nonstop eating by a baby who is never actually hungry or completely satisfied, and who may gain excessive weight.

Remember not to put your baby to bed with a bottle of milk. If she falls asleep with anything other than water in her mouth, bacteria can damage her incoming teeth. A baby who drinks from a bottle while lying flat will also be at greater risk for developing middle-ear infections. If your baby truly seems to sleep better after a bedtime snack, be sure all of it is swallowed.

SLEEP: IS IT TIME TO ESTABLISH A ROUTINE?

Between the fourth and sixth months, your baby will probably have settled into a sleeping routine that is more predictable and easier on everyone during the wee hours. Two naps during the day, one in the morning and one in the afternoon, are a good habit to encourage and maintain. These may last from one to three hours, and at this age you need not awaken your baby from a long nap unless it seems to be interfering with his sleep at night. (Some infants continue to catnap during this period.) Between two and four months or shortly thereafter, your baby should be skipping a night feeding. By sixth months, he should well be able to handle an eight-hour stretch without being fed unless he was premature or is exceptionally small. But whether this translates into uninterrupted sleep will depend on both your baby and your sleeping arrangements.

If he's down for the night by 8 P.M., he may be genuinely hungry at 4 A.M. But at that hour, unless he's sounding off with a sustained howl, you may want to wait a few minutes to see if he might go back to sleep. Delaying his bedtime may help extend his and your uninterrupted sleep in the morning, but a decision to allow him to stay up later must be weighed against other family needs. Ideally, before he is put to bed, there should be some time to wind down with quiet activities—a feeding, some cuddling, some singing, and perhaps a bath. With repetition of a routine, he will begin to associate these particular activities with bedtime and a surrender to sleep. If at all possible, have different people walk through this process with him so he won't come to expect that Mom or Dad is the only person in the world who can bring the day to a close.

Now is a good time to let him learn to fall asleep on his own if he hasn't been doing so already. When he is drowsy but not yet asleep, lay him down, pat him gently, and leave the room. Make sure there's a night-light on so he can see familiar surroundings. If he fusses for more than a few minutes, you can come back for a brief reassurance (perhaps offering some gentle patting on the back) but not a full-blown recap of the nighttime routine. If he persists, let a little more time go by before you return. If there's no end in sight to the crying and you can't stand to let it continue, do whatever works to bring on sleep, and then try again at a later date, perhaps on a weekend night when you have some flexibility in your evening and morning schedules.

If he isn't able to fall asleep by himself by six months of age, the window of opportunity for learning this skill may not be open again for several months. After six months, he is likely to begin a normal phase known as **separation anxiety,** in which a mighty howl may erupt when you or his closest caregivers are out of his sight, especially at bedtime. As a result, if after six months he's still used to being nursed, held, and rocked through several rounds of "Hey Diddle Diddle" until he's sound asleep, you can plan on repeating this ritual for months on end unless you are prepared to endure a vigorous and prolonged protest.

Remember that your baby's nighttime activity may include one or more awakenings that do not necessarily need your attention. If you rush into your baby's room to feed, cuddle, and rock him with every sound he produces, he will become quite accustomed to this first-class room service, and you may find that he is rather reluctant to give it up. Obviously, if he sounds truly miserable and is keeping everyone awake, do whatever is necessary to comfort him and calm things down. At this age it is still better to err on the side of too much attention than too little. After a few more months pass, however, you can become more hard-nosed if he seems intent on having a social hour several times a night.

CRYING: MORE THAN JUST HUNGER OR A WET DIAPER

Your baby's growing list of skills for interacting with her surroundings also includes new expressions of displeasure, and you will notice that a "language" of sorts is developing in her cries. The sounds she makes when she is hungry will be different from those she makes when she is undressed on the doctor's examining table and very different from her reaction to an immunization. Unlike the newborn's intense, almost primitive, crying in response to any and all forms of discomfort, after four months a baby may also cry in order to get attention or other action from the adults in her life. Watch and listen carefully, and you will learn to distinguish a cry that says, "I need to be fed" from one that says, "I'm bored" or "I want that toy I just threw on the floor."

Learning to discern the various intensities and inflections of her cries will also help you decide whether you need to tend to her immediately, or whether she can wait a little while you finish what you are doing. Indeed, as she progresses in her social skills through the first year, she will also need to discover that she is not the center of the known universe. If you know that she is fed, dry, and comfortable, you may want to delay a bit your response to the cry that seems to say, "I want some attention *right this minute.*"

HEALTH AND SAFETY ISSUES: SOME REMINDERS

As your baby begins to show his first signs of mobility and starts inserting everything he can grab into his mouth, you are but a few short months away from the exciting project of keeping him and your possessions safe when he wants to check out *everything in sight.* There will be much more on this topic in the next chapter, but a few basic ground rules are worth stating and repeating.

Don't leave your baby alone on any surface such as a changing table, kitchen counter, or sofa. He will invariably pick that moment to demonstrate his ability to roll over.

Don't leave your baby unattended even for a few seconds while he is in water, whether bathing in the sink, infant tub, or adult bathtub. He can drown in an inch or two of water.

Everyone in your house, including young children, should know how to dial 911 in case of an emergency. All adults and children over twelve should be trained in infant CPR. Local hospitals normally conduct CPR classes on a regular basis.

Be extremely cautious about leaving one of your older children in charge of your baby, even for a few minutes. This assignment should be considered only for a responsible sibling more than twelve years of age who has been observed handling the baby appropriately for a number of weeks. He or she must have explicit information about your whereabouts, instructions about what to do if the baby cries or has any other type of problem, and names and phone numbers of people to call for help if needed.

Always buckle your baby securely into his car seat, no matter how short the ride. Through the sixth month he will still be sitting backward, unless he is well ahead of schedule in size (more than twenty pounds) and in control of his head. The center of the backseat is the safest location for him; thus you should avoid putting him in the forward passenger seat. This means that, should he start to fuss, you will have to resist the temptation to turn around and tend to him while your vehicle is in motion. *If your car has a passenger-side air bag, you should never place your baby in the forward passenger seat.* If the air bag inflates during an accident, it can cause serious or even fatal injuries to a baby.

Never carry your baby while you are also holding a cup of hot liquid. One strong wiggle could result in a scalding injury to one or both of you.

Keep a watchful eye for small objects scattered around your living space. These would include older children's Legos, marbles, action figures, and other toys that might come within your baby's reach and therefore go into the mouth. If your baby is going to spend time on the floor, put your face on his level and scan the horizon. Look for stray coins, paper clips, pieces of dry pet food, plastic wrappers, electrical cords, or unstable objects that might fall on your baby if given a gentle shove.

Beware of parking your baby in an infant swing or doorway jumper and then turning your attention elsewhere. After four months, a baby with enough wiggle power may be able to squirm out of a swing or even bring the whole thing down.

Keep your baby out of walkers, which are responsible for thousands of accidents every year. These devices will not teach him how to walk or speed up his motor development. Instead, they give your active baby the opportunity to propel himself to the edge of the stairs, investigate whatever is sitting on your coffee table, or flip the walker over when he bumps into an obstruction.

Extremely vigorous play (such as tossing a baby a few inches into the air and catching him) is not a good idea at this age. Rapid accelerations and changes in direction, however playful, can have the same effect as shaking a baby, risking injury to his neck and brain.

A baby's skin may become sunburned after as little as fifteen minutes of direct exposure to the sun. Don't allow your baby to have prolonged exposure to direct sunlight (even on a hazy or overcast day), especially between the hours of 10 A.M. and 3 P.M. This is particularly important at higher altitudes or around lakes and seashores where the sun's ultraviolet light (which provokes the burn) can reflect off sand and water. Furthermore, sunscreens containing PABA (the most commonly utilized ultraviolet-absorbing ingredient) shouldn't be used on your baby's skin before he is six months old. If you take your baby outdoors for any length of time, keep him in the shade or use an umbrella and make sure his skin is covered with appropriate clothing (including a hat or bonnet) even if he is in the shade.

Medical checkups and immunizations

If all goes well, your baby will have just two encounters with her doctor during this time period: a well-baby check at four months and another at six months. During these visits, you should be asked questions about your baby's feeding and sleeping patterns, developmental milestones, and indications that she is seeing and hearing well. Some of the practitioner's assessment of your baby's progress will hinge more on observations you have made rather than the actual examination in the office. It will help a great deal if you can offer information about your baby's head control, her use of her hands, rolling over, tracking objects with her eyes, responses to sounds, and her other activities.

Concerns you might have about whether she is "ahead" or "behind" schedule in these areas must be put in perspective because there can be a wide variation in the time when babies accomplish various tasks. In most cases, what matters more is whether your baby is making steady progress overall. If you have questions and concerns about development—or any problems you have encountered—be sure to ask about them during these checkups. It will help if you write them down. If your list contains more than two or three items, let the doctor or nurse know at the beginning of the visit.

Your baby's height, weight, and head circumference will be measured and plotted on a growth chart. At the six-month check, it is likely that she will have doubled her birth weight. During each visit the examiner will look "stem to stern," noting how your baby moves and responds during the entire process. Unless there are specific reasons to do otherwise, your baby should receive DTaP (diphtheria/tetanus/pertussis) and hemophilus B immunizations at both four- and six-month checkups, and the OPV (oral polio vaccine) or IPV (inactivated polio vaccine) at the four-month exam. Your baby's doctor may recommend a third dose of polio vaccine at the six-month check or a later date. If she received her first hepatitis B vaccination at birth and her second at one month, she may receive her third and final dose at the six-month check-up. (Some physicians may delay the third dose until the age of twelve to eighteen months.) If she is on a different timetable, of course, you will have to confirm the date of the follow-up hepatitis injection. Be sure to let the doctor or nurse-practitioner know if your baby had an unusual response to any prior immunizations.

When your baby is ill: common medical problems

You now have a more sturdy, immunologically competent baby than you had three months ago. Infections are not as likely to get out of control and turn into a major medical event or a catastrophe. Unlike the first three months of life, a fever over 100.4°F rectally is no longer a cause for an immediate trip or call to the doctor's office or emergency room. But all of her exploring with hands and mouth is certain to introduce some new viruses and bacteria into her body, and some of these will gain enough of a foothold to cause trouble.

Invaders in the air passages. By far the most common illness you will see will be an **upper respiratory infection** (URI in medical shorthand or colds to everyone else), involving the nose, ears, throat, and upper airway. The most obvious symptoms will be a runny nose and cough, with irritability and disturbed sleep likely as well. Remember, your baby can respond to a sore throat or headache only by fussing and crying. It will be many months before you have the luxury of your child being capable of telling you what hurts. Fever may or may not be present, and you should get in the habit of checking your baby's temperature if she appears ill. Don't rely on your sense of touch to decide whether the temperature is normal, but take the extra time to use a thermometer. If you need to discuss the illness with your baby's doctor or nurse-practitioner, he or she will want to know whether a fever is part of the problem (see sidebar, page 36).

If the cause of this infection is a virus—and there are at least a hundred different varieties of the **rhinovirus,** which is the usual culprit—your baby's immune system will normally deal with it within a week and return things to normal. During these few days, your baby will want and need more cuddling and comforting. Her appetite may be less enthusiastic than usual, or she may want to nurse more often. You do not need to withhold feedings unless there is a significant airway problem, which is rare. Remember to wash your hands regularly, since you can't avoid contact with drool and drainage, and these infections are spread more commonly by contaminated hands than through airborne droplets. Your fingers, which could be hosting some unfriendly organism, make more trips every day to your eyes, nose, and mouth than you think.

Acetaminophen may be helpful for relieving aches and pains for a few hours at a time. It can also help reduce but not eliminate a fever, a capability that is useful only because it can make your baby more comfortable. Although it is an important symptom during an illness, fever rarely causes problems in and of itself, and you do not need to embark on a crusade to drive it away. If you use acetaminophen at this age, your baby will take a dose of 40 mg (0.4 ml of the infant drops that contain 80 mg per 0.8 ml) if she weighs less than twelve pounds and 80 mg (0.8 ml of the infant drops) if she weighs more than twelve pounds.

Review with her doctor or nurse-practitioner about whether to give your baby a cold remedy or cough syrup to relieve symptoms. There are scores of different brands, combinations of ingredients, and dosage schedules on the market, but not many are geared for babies, and some may cause more problems than they solve. Depending on your baby's sensitivity, the ingredients in these medications (decongestants, antihistamines, cough suppressants, and even alcohol) may cause sedation, which could be confusing and worrisome. Is she getting worse, or is it the medication? Or these medications may cause her to be more irritable and wakeful.

The antihistamines in many cold preparations may also thicken the secretions in the nose or airway, making them harder to clear. (In addition, controlled studies of these medications have suggested that they are not likely to be effective in children.) But if coughing and drainage are making your baby miserable and *if your baby's doctor recommends it,* one of these products, whether a single-ingredient decongestant or a combination cold-and-cough reliever, may be tried.

Be careful, and watch yourselves closely so that you do not forget the things your eyes have seen or let them slip from your heart as long as you live. Teach them to your children and to their children after them.

DEUTERONOMY 4:9

If it seems to help for a few hours and doesn't cause any problems, you can continue to use it as needed. Since most colds are caused by viruses, and viruses are not affected by antibiotics, don't be surprised if your baby's doctor doesn't prescribe one of these medications. (Do not pressure the doctor to use them if they're not really needed.)

Remember that you can use a rubber-bulb syringe to suck excessive secretions from your baby's congested nose. Saline nose drops may be helpful in cleansing nasal passages. Three or four drops of nasal saline solution may be instilled in each nostril (one at a time) and then suctioned out. This simple procedure may relieve congestion that is interfering with feeding. A cool-mist vaporizer may also help soothe the nose. However, a vaporizer must be cleaned and rinsed daily to prevent mold and bacteria from growing in it and then being sprayed all over the room the next time it is used. In addition, if everything in the room, including the baby, is perpetually damp from the vaporizer, you're probably using it too much.

Unfortunately, not all colds go away peacefully in a few days. Some allow bacteria to gain a foothold, producing a variety of illnesses for which your baby will need medical attention. One sign that bacteria have invaded is that the nasal drainage not only refuses to disappear after a week or two but turns and stays thick and discolored (gray, yellow, or green). If a cold persists more than two weeks or thick discolored discharge continues more than a few days, give your doctor a call—especially if there is a fever. (This isn't a sinus infection, by the way, because at this age the sinuses are not fully formed.) Antibiotics may be necessary to help your baby deal with these invaders.

The anatomy of a baby's nose and ears may allow bacteria to travel into the middle ear by way of the eustachian tubes. The resulting infection of the middle ear—that is, the air-filled space behind the eardrum—is known as **acute otitis media**. Usually an ear infection will cause pressure to build up behind the eardrum or irritate the drum directly, producing a great deal of discomfort and often fever. Therefore, a baby with a cold who becomes increasingly irritable should definitely be checked, especially if fever is present. Untreated, a middle-ear infection could cause local damage or spread to surrounding structures. Otitis media normally responds to an antibiotic, but *once started, the medication should be continued for its full course.* If your baby reacts to the antibiotic in some way—for example, with a rash or diarrhea—contact the doctor's office for further instructions.

Any virus or bacteria that infects the nose or throat can find its way into the linings of one or both eyes (known as the **conjunctivae**). These eye infections, known as **conjunctivitis** (or pinkeye), produce a reddish discoloration along with a discolored drainage. When this material dries overnight, the eyelids may be stuck together with a crusty debris you will need to remove gently with a warm, wet washcloth. Your doctor will normally prescribe antibiotic drops or ointment, which can be a little challenging to instill in the eyes of your wiggly, unhappy patient for a few days. Careful hand washing is a must for anyone handling a baby with conjunctivitis because the organisms involved have a knack for spreading to others by hitching a ride on unsuspecting fingers.

Coughing will not be hard to miss, but the ultimate source may not be quite as obvious. Mucus draining into the throat from the nose (postnasal drip) can provoke coughing, as will any infection involving the larynx (vocal cords), trachea (airway), bronchial tubes, or lungs. If the very upper portions of the airway are involved, you will notice a barking sound with the cough, in addition to hoarseness and noisy respirations. This syndrome, known as **croup,** is uncommon before the age of six months.

Bronchiolitis is an inflammation of the very small tubes that lead to tiny air sacs called **alveoli** where oxygen is transported into the bloodstream. It may be caused by any of several types of viruses but is most commonly attributed to the Respiratory Syncytial Virus (RSV). Bronchiolitis is usually restricted to infants and young children under the age of three and may become serious enough to require hospitalization. Coughing may actually be less obvious than wheezing and difficulty breathing. **Pneumonia** is an infection of the air sacs themselves and may be caused by bacteria or viruses or, rarely, by aspiration of some foreign material such as water or food. The baby with widespread pneumonia will usually appear quite ill, with fever, rapid respirations, and signs that breathing has become hard work: grunting, flaring of the nostrils, and retracting (sucking inward) of the muscles between the ribs. Sometimes, however, the pneumonia will be so localized to a certain section of lung that coughing and shortness of breath will not be evident. Fever and irritability may be the only symptoms.

If you have any concerns about your baby's well-being during a cold or other respiratory illness, don't hesitate to call your physician for advice or an assessment. A number of situations definitely deserve a call, although the timing and urgency of your contact will depend on the condition of your baby.

If your three- to six-month-old baby is active and feeding well, you can wait to call during office or daytime hours for

- coughing that persists more than a week or is persistent enough to interrupt sleep;
- fever under 103°F accompanying a cold or cough;
- thick, discolored drainage, redness, and/or crusting from the eyes;

- watery discharge from the nose that lasts more than seven to ten days, or thick discolored drainage for more than a few days;
- discolored drainage from one or both ears; this indicates that your baby not only has had an ear infection but has had a spontaneous rupture of the eardrum. This event is not a disaster. In fact, it relieves pressure and pain in the ear, but antibiotics are usually prescribed.[1]

You should call, regardless of the hour, for

- any signs of difficulty breathing other than nasal congestion; rapid respirations (more than forty per minute) or evidence of labored breathing (grunting, flaring of the nostrils, or retracting of the spaces between the ribs) should be evaluated by a physician. If your baby seems to literally gasp for breath, take her immediately to the nearest emergency room, or, if you are unable to do so, call 911;
- relentless crying or listlessness, especially with a fever;
- poor color—pale, bluish, dusky, or mottled skin;
- rectal fever of 103°F or more, especially if your baby is very irritable or lethargic.

You should be aware that many viruses can generate a high fever that a baby over four months of age can tolerate surprisingly well. If your baby is active, feeding well, and in reasonably good spirits despite the fever, your doctor may advise a check during office hours rather than the middle of the night.

Digestive-tract disturbances. As in previous months, you will want to keep a close watch on your baby if he begins to throw up or if his stools increase in frequency and volume. Some babies at this age may still routinely spit up some breast milk or formula after any given feeding and may even seem worse than a few weeks ago. That's because the muscles at the lower end of the esophagus may be looser than they were before. If height, weight, and developmental milestones are still on track, however, the primary focus can remain on minimizing the amount of spitting up. Eventually the problem should correct itself. Helpful measures in the meantime include

- more frequent, smaller feedings;
- more frequent burping during the feeding;
- enlisting gravity's assistance by keeping your baby in an upright position for a half hour after a feeding.

But if your baby's vomiting is forceful, you'll need to watch him carefully. If he is lethargic, running a fever, and/or pouring out loose stools, call the doctor's office for advice and probably a weigh-in and exam, since babies in this age-group can become dehydrated very quickly, especially if they are losing fluids from both ends.

If he throws up once but seems otherwise normal and in good spirits, you can see what happens over the next hour or two. If all is well, you can nurse him for a couple of minutes, watch him again for ten or fifteen minutes, and repeat this process for an hour. If there are no further signs of trouble, resume your normal feeding routine. The same can be done with a bottle-fed baby, except that rehydrating solutions such as Pedialyte or Ricelyte should be tried instead of formula.

A similar approach holds for diarrhea. One or two loose stools in an otherwise happy and active baby need not generate a lot of concern. It happens from time to time, and you won't necessarily know why. If your baby is formula-fed, check to see if his most recent batches of formula have been correctly measured and mixed. If stools are frequent and watery but not accompanied by vomiting or signs of dehydration (see page 96), breast-fed babies can continue nursing as usual because Mom's milk is easy on the intestinal tract. Formula-fed babies, however, should be given a rehydrating solution until the stools begin to slow down and firm up. Plain water will *not* be absorbed nearly as well, and carbonated soft drinks (with or without the fizz) or juices will not contain the ideal blend of electrolytes such as sodium and potassium to replace what has been lost in the stool. Babies who are already taking solids can try some foods that are mildly constipating such as rice cereal, applesauce, or banana.

After your baby has experienced an intense bout of diarrhea, your physician may suggest using a lactose-free formula, since the illness may temporarily cause lactose intolerance. *Medications used to control diarrhea in adults, such as diphenoxylate (Lomotil) or loperamide (Imodium), should generally not be given to young infants.* They don't actually treat the cause of the loose stools, and they may cause the extra stool to accumulate in the bowel rather than pass into the diaper. This could lead to a false sense of security because it *looks* as if your baby has stopped the diarrhea.

If diarrhea lasts more than one or two days, especially if a fever is present, call your baby's doctor—even if the baby seems to be doing well. He should be evaluated if he is listless, passing blood with the stool, or having vomiting episodes along with the diarrhea.

Whether brought on by mild or moderate vomiting, diarrhea, or both, you should be aware of signs that **dehydration** (loss of body water) is becoming significant. A decrease in activity level, fewer wet diapers than usual, and fewer tears with crying suggest mild to moderate dehydration. If these occur, call your health-care provider for advice, which may include a doctor's evaluation.

Signs of more severe dehydration—indicating a much more urgent need for a trip to the doctor's office or emergency room—include the following:

- Dry mouth and no tears
- No urine for five to six hours, indicating that your baby is working hard to conserve his fluids
- Sunken eyes
- A sunken fontanelle (the soft spot in the skull)
- Skin texture that is no longer elastic, but more like bread dough
- Persistent fussing, especially if it is more of a moan or whine than a vigorous cry
- Cool and/or mottled skin
- Marked listlessness, with lack of interest in play or feeding. A baby this age who lies still while awake, shows little interest in people or things

WHAT CAUSES VOMITING AND DIARRHEA IN INFANTS?

Vomiting can be provoked either by an intestinal infection or by illness somewhere else in the body. When vomiting and diarrhea begin suddenly at the same time, the problem is usually **gastroenteritis** (or stomach flu), most often caused by a virus. Occasionally bacteria or even parasites are at fault.

Vomiting may also signal a problem elsewhere: an ear infection, pneumonia, urinary tract infection, or even meningitis. Because of the number and variety of possible causes of persistent vomiting, a medical examination will nearly always be needed, especially in a baby less than a year of age.

Diarrhea, with few exceptions, indicates a problem focused in the bowel. Usually this is an infection—most commonly viral, especially in the winter when an unsa-vory character known as rotavirus makes its rounds—but bacteria and parasites may have to be ruled out by taking samples of stool to a local laboratory for culturing and other tests. Contaminated food can be a cause of infectious diarrhea in older babies and children.

Antibiotics are a notorious cause of diarrhea in infants and children because they directly irritate the bowel or wipe out the normal bacteria in the intestine and allow less friendly organisms to multiply.

Food allergy, lactose intolerance, or a problem with formula may also provoke loose stools, though without other signs of illness such as fever or lethargy. Some detective work with your health-care provider may be needed if your baby has persistent loose or watery stools but is otherwise doing well.

around him, and has markedly reduced movements of arms and legs may be in serious trouble and should be evaluated immediately.

ARE WE HAVING FUN YET?

As you progress toward the halfway mark of your baby's first year, you will probably find yourself increasingly "settled in" with this new person in your life. Feeding and sleeping should become generally more ordered and predictable, so you can spend less time in maintenance mode and more in playful and pleasant interactions with him. You don't yet have the challenge of keeping track of a crawler/cruiser/toddler who is fervently seeking to explore every nook and cranny of your home. This child has yet to look you in the eye and communicate in his own unique way, "I know what you want, and I'm not giving it to you—what are you gonna do about it?"

Obviously not every infant approaching six months of age is a complete joy, and some will still be spending a lot more time fussing than cooing. But, if at all possible, this would be a good time for you to take a deep, slow breath and marvel at the wondrous gift God has entrusted to you. This project called parenting should include times when you momentarily lay aside your quest to catch up with the bills, laundry, projects brought home from work, dishes in the sink, and general clutter. At least once every week take the phone off the hook, sit back in a comfortable chair, place your baby on your lap, and take a good long look at him. Watch his eyes; see how he is beginning to use his hands; catch the details of his toes. If you can elicit a few sounds from him, carry on a little "conversation." Jot down in a notebook some thoughts about what you now behold. In a few short years, long after you have forgotten whatever cares and annoyances were floating through this particular day, these memories will linger in your mind like a sweet song.

NOTES
1. Before the development of antibiotics, as a therapeutic measure physicians deliberately made small incisions in the drums of infected ears to relieve pressure and allow drainage.

CHAPTER 4

Six to Twelve Months: Explorers

A child more than all other gifts
That earth can offer to
declining man
Brings hope with it, and
forward-looking thoughts.
WILLIAM WORDSWORTH

Six to Twelve Months: Explorers

During the six months prior to her first birthday, your baby will begin a momentous transition. As Sir Isaac Newton might have put it, she will change from a "body at rest" to a "body in motion." Her blossoming ability to control arms and legs will enable her to propel herself from point A to point B, usually by way of points C, D, and E. This exciting development will also set in motion a series of conflicts that you and your child will reenact in thousands of ways over the next two decades.

She will want to investigate everything she can get her hands on but will be completely clueless about risks and consequences. And, though fervently desiring to explore whatever she can see, she will also be afraid of separation from familiar faces, voices, and hugs. Your challenge will be to protect her—and her environment—while allowing her to stretch her wobbly legs and find out how the world works.

Before the end of the first year, she will also need to discover that, contrary to her own belief, she is not the center of the universe. She will need to learn about limits, that she cannot have or do whatever she wants, whenever she wants. She will need to discover that someone is in charge, and it isn't her. Your job will be to introduce her to these realities in a way that is loving, firm, consistent, and respectful.

Welcome to a whole new chapter of parenting!

DEVELOPMENTAL MILESTONES: FROM SITTING TO "CRUISING" AND CLIMBING . . .

Between six and nine months, your baby will be figuring out how to sit up and remain steady. First she will need support from pillows or the nearest adult. Then she will begin to prop herself up using her outstretched hands in a "tripod" posture. Eventually she will sit up for minutes at a time without toppling. By nine months, half of all babies are able to maneuver themselves into a sitting position from any other posture. This will give her considerable satisfaction, because her hands will be free to examine interesting objects while she remains upright.

Once your baby discovers the wonders of her world that are visible from a few inches off the floor, she will develop a keen interest in moving herself closer to whatever she spies across the room. Whether she eventually tries to roll, slither, scoot, or crawl toward them and when she first makes the attempt will be impossible to predict. If she takes to crawling, her skill will peak between seven and ten months, at which point you will be amazed at the speed with which she can cross the floor. She may use the traditional hands-and-knees approach, scuttle sideways like a crab, or inch forward military-style.

Some babies rarely or never crawl, and crawling doesn't actually appear on standard charts as a developmental milestone. Babies don't need to learn to crawl before they walk, and there is no correlation between this skill and future athletic or intellectual ability. Learning to crawl is not necessary for visual development, hand-eye coordination, or learning to read later in life. If other skills are moving ahead and your baby's doctor confirms that all else is going well, don't panic if she decides to skip crawling and move on to bigger and better things.

At around nine months of age, she will make another discovery: Standing upright is really, really fun. Usually someone in the family will pull her to a standing position next to the sofa or a soft chair, and she will gleefully remain there, using her hands to hold her position. Eventually she will figure out how to pull herself to her feet, using any available object that appears tall enough. Next comes the ultimate prewalking thrill of "cruising" from one place to another while holding on to whatever will keep her upright.

There will be three potential problem areas during this phase of exploration. First, expect a minor commotion if she pulls herself to a stand but can't figure out how to let herself down. You can teach her to bend her knees and lower herself to the ground without a fall, a skill that will save her a few bruises and spare you several trips to wherever she has become hung up, including her crib.

Second, your baby will have no ability to judge the stability of whatever she sees around her. If she decides to pull herself up using a wastebasket, a petite end table, a houseplant, or a floor lamp, both she and her unsteady support may end up on the floor. The results can be unpleasant if she pulls down a loose tablecloth on which sits your favorite china, or dangerous and disastrous if she applies her weight to an object that is both unstable and heavy such as a wobbly bookcase.

The third problem arises from a variation on cruising—climbing. Some babies find the lure of heights irresistible and will startle you with their ability to scale low-level furniture, stairs, or even combinations of pillows and stuffed animals to explore the upper atmosphere of the room. A few climbers will carry out remarkable acts of problem solving in their efforts to gain increased elevation. Unfortunately, their interest in heights will not be matched by an appreciation of the discomforts caused by a fall.

If your budding cruiser is going to be turned loose in a room, take a quick visual survey or a brief tour at her level to make certain that she won't find out about the force of gravity the hard way. Particularly important is keeping her off the stairs, which she will find irresistible once she discovers them. After her first birthday, she can begin to learn, with your direct supervision, how to get herself downstairs backwards. But until she is clearly "stair safe" many months from now, you will need to consider getting one or more barricades if her activity areas include potential access to a flight of stairs. These barricades should be the sturdy, horizontal gates with narrow slats (two and three-eighths inches or less apart), not the old-fashioned accordion-style, wood-slat barriers, which are less stable and are potential traps for inquisitive heads.

Letting her suffer some bruising consequences to "teach her a lesson" is a bad idea at this age. Not only will this risk unnecessary injury, but she is in fact not yet capable of understanding and judging the risks involved in her explorations. (She won't start on this learning curve until she is about fifteen months of age.)

Standing and walking

As your baby continues his relentless efforts to stay upright, he will at some point let go of his favorite support and stand on his own for a few seconds. At the same time or shortly thereafter, he will take a few shaky steps, perhaps with one or both parents cheering him on. Within a week he likely will be purposefully walking from one end of the room to the other, with or without a few unscheduled drops to the floor along the way. His legs will be bent and toes pointed outward, giving a thoroughly precarious appearance to his efforts. But all the lurching and plopping, which you may find nerve-wracking to watch, won't slow him down at all. (Don't forget to grab the camera so you—and he—can enjoy seeing it later.)

When will all this ambulating begin? Depending upon his size, center of gravity, genetic code, and temperament, anywhere between eight and fourteen months of age. If he is on the hefty side, he may have more difficulty hoisting his weight and maintaining his balance. The timing of his first steps has nothing to do with his future batting average or his chances of getting into college, but if he arrives at his first birthday and cannot stand even while being supported, your health-care provider—who will be doing a routine checkup at this age anyway—should be consulted.

What about shoes? Shoes serve little purpose prior to the onset of walking other than to decorate the feet for a family portrait. Once your baby starts to walk routinely, however, you may want to get shoes to protect his feet if he will be walking somewhere—such as the backyard or a park—where terrain is more likely to contain objects that are unfriendly to little soles.

Shoes should be big enough to allow a half inch of space between his toes and the tip of the shoe, and since his feet will be growing rather rapidly, there is no sense in blowing the family budget on designer footwear. A simple pair of tennis shoes with a sole that grips will suffice. Unless prescribed by a qualified health-care professional to remedy a specific problem, he shouldn't need wedges, heel lifts, or other hardware in his shoes. He won't need arch supports because his arch is covered by a fat pad that will gradually recede over two to three years.

Furthermore, you may notice that while his toes point outward when he walks (because of looseness of the hip ligaments), his feet will tend to point inward (pigeon toes) when he lies down. Both of these situations should straighten out by the time he is about eighteen months old. If any positioning of feet or legs seems extreme or not symmetrical, have your baby's doctor (or, if necessary, an orthopedist who deals with young children) take a look. If you see your baby limp, whether now or in the future, a medical evaluation should be carried out as soon as possible. *Limping is never normal,* and it may indicate that any number of significant medical problems is occurring.

Eyes and hands

By seven or eight months of age, your baby's visual capabilities will have matured to the point that she can focus on people and objects across the room, though not quite with the clarity with which she sees things directly in front of her. She may find a mirror entertaining, as she watches the interesting little person who responds exactly to her own movements. She will be more attentive to a variety of colors and shapes and will be rapidly absorbing visual information about the world around her. You will at times notice her staring intently at something across the room. More often she will become fixated on, and apparently fascinated by, some tiny object directly in front of her—a wad of lint, a stray Cheerio, or a little bug.

Her increased visual skills will be matched by new abilities with hands and fingers. By nine months she will have progressed from the mitten or rakelike grasp (using four fingers as a unit against the thumb) to the more precise "pincer" grasp between thumb and one finger. She will also begin cooperative efforts between her two hands such as picking up toys, passing an object from hand to hand, or smacking two items together to enjoy the sound they produce.

Over the next three months, these investigations with hands will become more sophisticated. She will discover the joy of releasing something from her hands, or actually throwing it, and watching what happens. She will turn it around and look at it from a variety of angles, rub it, and shake it. If it has a hole, she'll poke a finger into it. If it has parts she can move, she'll push, pull, twist, or spin them. Toward the end of the first year she will enjoy dumping small objects out of a container and then putting them back in, one at a time. She will knock something over and then set it upright, over and over. And, of course, she will bring *everything* directly to her mouth for examination by lips, gums, and tongue.

Sounds, syllables, and speech

One of the most pleasant developments between six and twelve months is watching your baby begin to make all sorts of new sounds. After six months he will begin imitating various syllables, primarily with vowels at first. By nine months, gurgling and babbling will be replaced by sounds with consonants such as "baba" or "dada," either in short bursts or repeated at length. He will probably not assign these sounds to a particular person (for example, "mama" for his mother) until twelve months or after.

As he progresses toward his first birthday, his "speech" will sound more sophisticated, though without much obvious meaning. Your one-year-old is likely to utilize a vocabulary of a few words, along with some wonderfully modulated babbling that rises and falls with the inflections of real speech. You can almost imagine that he is a visitor speaking a foreign language. He will also begin to communicate with gestures, such as pointing to something he finds interesting, waving bye-bye, or shaking his head to signify no. You may also hear exclamations such as "Uh-oh!"

While his speaking vocabulary may not be lengthy at his first birthday, he can understand quite a bit more (in fact, far more than you probably realize) well

Two distinct messages must be conveyed to every child during his first forty-eight months: (1) "I love you more than you can possibly understand" and (2) "Because I love you I must teach you to obey me."

DR. DOBSON
ANSWERS YOUR
QUESTIONS ABOUT
RAISING CHILDREN

before that date. After nine months he will begin responding to his own name and may show recognition of familiar people, pets, or objects. He will likely (we hope) respond to the word *no* before he starts using it himself. He may turn his head toward a person or toy you name, and before long he will surprise you by following a simple command.

You can make a major contribution to your child's language development during these months, even if you're not yet having much conversation. All day long you can name objects that you both see, talk in simple terms about what you are doing, and even look through simple picture books together. Try to keep your vocabulary straightforward and consistent, and don't expose him to hours of convoluted baby talk. Instead, coo and fuss and caress with your voice to your heart's content—using real words. His little computer will be processing all of this input, associating objects and pictures with words that you provide, and he might as well get it right the first time.

As cute as you will find his babbling, resist the temptation to repeat back his garbled versions of new words. If he points to a truck and says, "Guck!" be sure to say, "That's right, truck!" rather than leading him to believe that he has truly seen a guck. (One exception: Grandparents almost always proudly assume the names given to them by the first grandchild, such as "Nana and Papa," "Gomba and Bumpa," etc.)

Now is a good time to think about the kinds of sounds your baby will be imitating. Does everyone in the family speak in calm, pleasant tones, or do conversations sound loud and confrontational? Are compliments or complaints exchanged across the kitchen table? Is your baby likely to learn "Shut up!" before he says "I love you"? Is he hearing more words from the adults in his life or from the TV set droning in the corner? If you don't like what your baby is hearing, hold a family meeting and prayer time to help launch some new conversation patterns (and perhaps lower noise levels) at home.

Gestures and games

In addition to imitating your words and speech patterns, your six- to twelve-month-old will also begin to mimic gestures and movements. You will be pleasantly surprised one day to see him holding his toy telephone to his ear rather than banging it on the floor, or stroking his toy brush across his hair rather than gumming it. By one year of age, he will also enjoy a number of gesture games, such as peekaboo, pat-a-cake, and "so big." ("How big is Tyler?" Tyler's hands will imitate yours reaching for the sky, as you say, "So-o-o-o big!")

You can have fun with your baby and watch some developmental milestones being reached as he develops his sense of **object permanence.** At four or five months of age, if something is out of sight, it's also out of mind. If he pushes his rattle off the edge of the sofa, he won't pursue it with his eyes. But at about nine months of age, he can keep an image of something fixed in memory long enough to look for it after it disappears.

Take one of his toys, show it to him, and then hide it under a small cloth. Voila! He will pull the cloth away to reveal the toy, much to everyone's delight. As he practices this skill, you can try putting two or more obstacles between him and the toy. With increasing maturity of his sense of object permanence, he will be more persistent in finding it. To make the game even more exciting, you can "hide" yourself behind a chair or around a corner and then let him "find" you. (You may need to leave a foot in view or peek around the corner the first time until he gets the idea.)

Other games you can play (which for your baby are actually explorations of the world around him) include rolling a ball back and forth, building a small tower out of plastic blocks and letting him knock it over, and plopping all sorts of smaller objects into a large container and then dumping them out. There are, indeed, very few fancy gadgets that babies this age will appreciate any more than simple, inexpensive toys (or, for that matter, household items): all sizes and types of plastic containers, lightweight unbreakable bowls and cups, balls of all sizes (as long as they are too big to fit into his mouth), building blocks, toy telephones, and plastic cars, trucks, and planes (whose edges aren't sharp and whose parts won't come loose).

SAFETY MEASURES: CURIOSITY, CHAOS, AND CAUTIONS

All of these activities with eyes and hands are not random or meaningless. On the contrary, they are vital to your baby's development. Her brain and nervous system are assimilating information at a rapid pace, and all of the staring, touching, and gumming are providing important input about how things are and the way they work. By nine months of age, your baby's curiosity will be insatiable. She will not be content to merely inspect every item within her reach. She will also be itching to get her hands on all those interesting shapes that she's been seeing for weeks on end from across the room. Her intense curiosity will thus become a driving force in advancing her motor skills.

This normal—and necessary—development will generate extra work and worry for everyone in your baby's life. Her explorations should be encouraged, but they will inevitably require some adjustment of your living arrangements. You'll need to balance your baby's healthy curiosity against her need for a safe environment and your need for some semblance of order.

Avoiding extremes is important. Confinement for hours on end in a playpen, which might be convenient for the grown-ups, will impair the flow of information to baby's developing brain. But giving her unlimited access to all parts of the home without some thoughtful preparation is an invitation to harm or disaster. *Furthermore, attempting to train a baby at this age by subjecting her to a nonstop*

SPECIAL TOYS, AND TOYS TO AVOID

Short attention spans and nonstop investigation of one item after another mean that you don't have to spend a lot of money on a special toy, since your young explorer probably won't spend any more time with it than with the box containing it. However, if Uncle John really wants to unload some cash on a toy for his nephew, you could steer him toward the following:

- Push toys, especially if they have a low center of gravity that allows your baby to cruise or "walk" behind them.
- Busy boxes with all sorts of switches and levers to push and noises to make.
- Bath toys that can be emptied and filled (a few plastic cups may suffice for this) or toys that float, squeak, and squirt.
- Sturdy picture books with thick cardboard "pages"; your baby will probably get less of a charge out of the pictures than he will from moving the pages back and forth, since they function as a colorful hinge, and many babies at this age are hinge fanatics.

Toys to think twice about or avoid altogether at this age include:

- Stuffed animals. That's right, stuffed animals, especially for the baby younger than nine months who has no idea who Barney or Mickey Mouse is or has any interest in finding out. These toys can collect

dust, aggravate allergic noses, shed hair and stuffing, and lose plastic eyes and noses that might end up in someone's airway or even in an older toddler's nose. If the stuffed toys accidentally get in the line of fire when your baby spits up, they'll reek for weeks. As your baby passes the nine-month mark and separation anxiety becomes more evident, a soft something may be enlisted for duty as a transitional object to help keep him calm when you are out of the room or out for the evening. Whatever is used must be sturdy enough to survive lots of handling and washing and must not be adorned with little decorative items that might come loose.

- Anything with sharp edges, little parts, or big parts that might easily become little parts.
- Balloons. Aside from scaring the daylights out of your baby when they pop, those little rubber fragments are very easy to choke on.
- Toys that are supposed to "educate" your baby about abstract concepts such as letters and numbers. It will be some time before your baby will comprehend this type of symbolism, and efforts to introduce him to the ABCs and 1-2-3s are unnecessary at this point in his life. Right now your baby's education is going on during every waking hour as he handles, gums, bangs, and drops everything in sight and as he listens to older people talk to him.

torrent of No's! and hand-slapping while she is merely trying to find out what's what in her world will make everyone miserable and exhausted.

Some reasonable baby-proofing and commonsense precautions will spare everyone a lot of toil and grief.

Take a child's-eye tour of whatever living space will be available to your crawler/ cruiser/walker. Are there any top-heavy items—chairs, tables, floor lamps, bookshelves—that might fall if pulled by your baby? Any electrical cords or outlets within reach? (Install plastic plugs to block unused outlets from inquisitive fingers.) Do you see any wires with frayed insulation? These are a hazard to everyone, not just the baby. What about cords dangling down from a curling or steam iron resting on a counter or ironing board? A yank on one of these could cause not only a hazardous bonk on her head or body but also a very painful burn.

Are there any small objects lying around that, upon entering her mouth, might end up in her airway? Your vigilance regarding small objects will be a daily concern if you have older children at home, because their toys and games tend to have lots of tiny parts and pieces that have a way of dispersing throughout your home. How about cords attached to draperies and blinds? These should be looped or tied on a hook well out of reach to prevent the baby's getting tangled in them.

Don't leave your prized china or other valuable breakables within reach of a newly mobile baby and then demand that she not touch them. She will have no concept of the difference between a cup made by Wedgwood and one brought home from Wendy's, except, perhaps, the sound they make when they hit the floor. Your expensive collectibles should be displayed (or stored) out of reach during this season of your child's life.

While some recommend that your kitchen be kept off-limits to little explorers, this will probably not be a realistic option. Most parents and older children traverse the kitchen many times each day, and dealing with a barricade every time is a major nuisance. Lots of family interactions take place in kitchens, and your baby will not want to be left out.

This will mean, however, relocating cleaning compounds and other chemicals to higher ground. Bleach, furniture polish, and drain cleaners are particularly hazardous, and automatic-dishwasher powder can be extremely irritating if it gets into the mouth. Sharp objects, which of course are abundant in kitchens, must also be kept out of reach at all times. If you have an automatic dishwasher, be sure to keep the door latched when you are not loading or unloading it. A wide-open dishwasher door is not only an irresistible climbing spot but also a gateway to all sorts of glassware and sharp utensils.

Many families set aside a low cupboard for "baby's kitchen stuff"—a collection of old plastic bowls, cups, spoons, lids, and other safe unbreakables that she can examine and manipulate to her heart's content. (By the way, she will probably spend a fair amount of time moving the cupboard door back and forth on its hinge.) You may want to steer her toward this particular cupboard and away from the others (this will take lots of repetition) or make the arrangement more formal by installing plastic safety latches in the cupboards and drawers that are off-limits.

While kitchens are difficult to barricade, bathrooms are another story. Like kitchens, they are full of potential hazards: medications, cleaners, and, most important, bodies of water. Any medications (prescription or over-the-counter, including vitamins and iron) and cleaning substances must be stored well out of reach and returned to their secure spot *immediately* after each use (see sidebar).

Never leave a baby unattended in the bath, even at this age, and be certain to empty the tub as soon as you're done with it. Open toilets are an irresistible destination for a cruiser. The possible consequences of a baby's investigation of an unflushed toilet are both unsafe and stomach turning. More important is the possibility that a top-heavy toddler might lean over far enough to fall in.

Never leave hair dryers, curlers, or other electrical devices plugged in after you use them. For that matter, no one should be using any of these items when the baby (or anyone else) is in the bathtub, unless you have a very large bathroom with a lengthy distance between appliance and water. If your baby or an older child tries to take the hair dryer for a swim, *even if it's turned off but plugged in,* the resulting shock could be lethal.

TIME TO BUY IPECAC

If you haven't done so by now, buy a small bottle of syrup of ipecac, a drug that may be used to induce vomiting if your baby eats or drinks something that might harm her. *However, you should give a dose of ipecac only if you are told to do so by the doctor, the emergency room, or a poison-control center.* Ipecac should *not* be used with many substances, especially caustic materials (such as drain cleaner) or petroleum products (such as gasoline or furniture polish) because they can do as much or more damage on the way up as they have done on the way down. For medications and some other items, however, you may be instructed to use ipecac to empty the stomach. One tablespoon (15 cc) followed by two glasses of water will induce vomiting, normally within fifteen to twenty minutes.

Unlike most kitchens, bathrooms have doors that can be shut to prevent unsupervised entry. If an enterprising explorer learns to turn door handles, an additional high latch may need to be installed.

Survey your home for "what's hot and what's not." Radiators, heaters, floor furnace grills, and fireplace screens can all become surprisingly hot, and a protective barrier between these surfaces and little fingers will be needed, at least at some times of the year.

Never leave pots cooking with their handles extending over the edge of the stove, since one healthy pull could result in a severely scalded child. Some stoves also have exposed knobs that babies and toddlers might love to twist and turn. If these are easily detachable, you may want to remove them between meals.

A similar reminder applies to hot liquids such as soups and gravies near the edge of your dining table, especially if they sit on a tablecloth that could be pulled from below. Avoid carrying your wiggly explorer and a cup of hot coffee or tea at the same time. One sudden twist on her part could fling hot liquid over both of you.

Set your hot water heater temperature below 120°F to minimize the risk of an accidental scald from the tap.

How about those houseplants? Infants and toddlers can be quite adept at doing some impressive pruning on your prized houseplants if they are within reach. A more worrisome possibility is that these young children might choose to sample the leaves and stems, which may be irritating to the lining of the mouth or even overtly toxic. Now is the time to move the plants out of reach, unless you know for certain that they are nontoxic and you don't care if they get mangled sometime during the next few months. In order to prevent your explorer from having a close encounter with the dirt around any plants that remain at floor level, you can cover the soil with screen mesh.

Finally, think about your baby's introduction to the great outdoors. When the weather's nice and the family gathers in the backyard, what interesting but hazardous items might cross her path? Once again, make a baby's-eye survey of any area that she might reach (if she's a skilled crawler, keep in mind how fast she can move while your attention is diverted).

If you have a swimming pool, make sure that a childproof fence surrounds it. (Some states by law require this safety barrier.) If your yard contains a spa, it should be securely covered when not in use. Pool and hot-tub drain covers should be checked periodically to make sure they are properly in place. If not, a child's hand or even hair could be pulled into the outlet by the suction created by the pump, and she might be unable to break free. Children have drowned in such circumstances. As a backup precaution, make sure that the pump's on-off switch is readily accessible.

Check the lawn for mushrooms, and if you are not absolutely certain they are nontoxic, get rid of them, because anything your baby finds at this age is likely to go straight into her mouth. Are there any garden tools, insecticides, fertilizers, or other unfriendly items lying around? The more potential dangers you can eliminate from her immediate access, the more you can enjoy your time outdoors with her.

One other outdoor hazard you must not ignore is the sun. A baby's skin is very sensitive to the ultraviolet (UV) light generated by the sun, and at peak times of the day (between 10 A.M. and 3 P.M.) as little as fifteen minutes of direct exposure can provoke an unpleasant burn. This is a particular problem at higher altitudes, where UV light is more intense, and around lakes and oceans, where UV can reflect from water and sand. Sunburns can also occur on hazy or overcast days because UV light penetrates both haze and cloud cover.

If your baby is going to be experiencing the great outdoors for any length of time, try to avoid the 10 A.M. to 3 P.M. time of peak intensity, keep her in the shade as much as possible, and utilize appropriate clothing (as well as a hat or bonnet) for protection. An explorer who is going to be in and out of sunlight will benefit from a sunscreen with a sun protection factor (SPF) rating of at least fifteen, applied an hour before she ventures forth. If you are going to take her with you into the pool, use a waterproof version and reapply it after you are done. Occasionally a baby will react to the common UV-protecting ingredient known as PABA, which is used in many sunscreens. If your baby has very sensitive skin, you might take your sunscreen for a "test drive" by applying some to a small area of her skin (an inch or so wide) for several hours to see if any reaction develops.

Parental vigilance . . .

Many of these guidelines represent passive restraints—fixed barriers between child and hazard. But you cannot anticipate every possible risk or create enough safeguards for a 100 percent-safe environment, unless you want to turn your home into a padded cell. You will need to take more active measures as well, involving both your own surveillance and some basic training for your baby.

From your standpoint, perpetual vigilance is the price of child rearing, at least for now. You must develop an ongoing sense of your child's whereabouts, a third eye and ear that are tuned in to him, even when he is in a confined and seemingly safe space such as his crib. You will need to monitor his activities constantly to see what new perils might cross his path in the immediate future.

The riskiest times will be those when you are distracted, frazzled, or just plain weary. You may be in the middle of a project involving hazardous tools or materials—a long overdue deep cleaning, for example. Suddenly the phone rings, or someone is at the door, or another child cries out in another room. Before you drop everything to attend to the new situation, look at what might be open, exposed, or available to your baby. Could he get to any of it? You may have to delay your response for a few moments while you ensure there is no way your baby in motion can get his hands on something dangerous.

Beware of those times in the day—especially the late afternoon—when your energy may be low, your mind preoccupied, and your patience short. One or more other children may be irritable at this time, competing for your attention. But don't lose track of your youngest crawler/cruiser/toddler, who may have just discovered something interesting that was dropped under the kitchen table.

Sometime in your parenting career, you may reach a point of such sheer exhaustion that you just have to lie down for a little while. Do you let an older child watch the baby or let him roam around your bedroom while you close your eyes for a few precious minutes? Think hard before you stretch your safety boundaries. Some cautions about using older children as baby-watchers were brought up in the previous chapter, but you must be even more wary when you have a new explorer. An older child is more likely to become distracted by a friend or toy, and a major problem could develop during a few moments of inattention. If you are really that tired, see if a trusted adult such as a friend, neighbor, or relative might relieve you for one or more hour's respite.

. . . and baby's boundaries

The other side of the safety coin involves your child. As her first birthday nears, she must learn that there are some boundaries in her world, even if she has been given access to a substantial amount of your living space. Of course, she will have no way of knowing what is okay to touch and what is off-limits until she is given that information. And give it you must, remembering that—for now—her driving force is nearly always her intense curiosity rather than a specific desire to put you and your limits to the test. At this stage of development, in fact, you can take advantage of her curiosity, along with her short attention span, to help shift her interest away from the things you want her to avoid.

Keep in mind that your limit setting will require a lot of legwork because you can't use much verbal "remote control" until she's a few months older. If she is

He who spares the rod hates his son, but he who loves him is careful to discipline him.

PROVERBS 13:24

examining something that is unsafe or inappropriate, it is extremely unlikely that she will understand the command ("Emily, don't eat that bug!") you issue from across the room. The tone of your voice may get her attention and perhaps stop the deed momentarily. But you will also have to separate the offending item from her fingers (or mouth) while making a simple and concrete statement about it. ("No, no—not for Emily" or "Don't touch the stove—ouch!")

Will she understand what you are saying? Probably not at first, although she will pick up your reaction about what she has been doing. More important, her amazing little computer is continually processing information about "What happens when I _____?" and you definitely want to provide a lot of the input. In particular, when setting boundaries, your tone of voice should communicate that you mean business. (You can't project much of a warning or a sense of authority if you sound like the Lullaby Lady.) On the other hand, yelling, haranguing, or (worse) sounding off without taking any action will definitely work against you. Sometimes a verbal and physical response at the same time can turn your statement into an object lesson: "Don't touch the curtains" will make more of an impact while you are physically removing her from them.

Her short attention span will usually allow you to distract her focus elsewhere after you have made your point. Most likely she will forget about whatever she found interesting if you offer her something else that is equally intriguing. But she may also forget whatever you were originally trying to tell her. If she is really intent on pursuing her investigation, she may promptly head back to the shiny knobs on the stereo or the ill-tempered cat's flopping tail, even when you have just taken her away from it—for the seventh time.

When your mobile baby seems determined to override your intentions and repeatedly bears down on the forbidden target, *don't back away from the limits you have set*. Take action *every time*, making your statement by using an increasingly firm tone of voice (which won't be difficult). One approach to consider when she crosses your line over and over again is to remove her completely from the temptation zone. A time-out in a crib or playpen, where her roaming privileges are temporarily curtailed for a few minutes, may be appropriate at this point.

At some point, however, you may need to take more direct and immediate action, especially if she is repeatedly reaching for something that is dangerous. A quick thump on the hand (not hard, but enough to get her attention) may need to accompany your verbal warning, but this should be done only if

- you are certain that she understands what you want (which is not likely before nine months of age);

- her safety is on the line; and
- you have no other way to separate her from the hazard.

The point of your response is not to lash out in anger and frustration but to change behavior for her benefit and protection. If she is bent on playing with the handle on the oven, for example, the brief sting of your rebuke will be far less painful than a burn on her fingers. When she cries as a result, take a moment to comfort her and talk things over. While she won't understand a lecture on burn prevention, some simple input such as "Mommy said not to touch this" will usually be understood by a baby approaching the first birthday.

Indeed, at this age your objective is not to teach great moral principles or the whys and why nots of home safety. Later when her language and reasoning skills are more sophisticated, you will carry out that assignment on an ongoing basis. In the meantime, she must assimilate some reasonable house rules into her ever increasing fund of knowledge about how her world works. Your consistent enforcement of boundaries, even at this preverbal stage, will establish that you are in charge and position you to handle the more overt challenges to come.

If it hasn't become apparent by now, you will soon become acutely aware that you cannot guarantee the absolute safety of your child. In addition to loving, comforting, teaching your child, and taking appropriate safety precautions where you live, now is the time to renew your commitment to pray for her as well. Remember that she is on loan, entrusted to your care for a season, and her Creator ultimately knows and loves her far better than anyone can imagine. Acknowledging that fact and seeking His wisdom on a daily basis—even for the everyday routines of parenting—will help keep your concerns in perspective and tap into strength and insight that extend far deeper than your own.

FEEDING: SOLID FOODS—BEYOND THE BASICS

During these six months your baby will make another important transition as he becomes nourished primarily by solid foods. Chapter 3 described the process of introducing your baby to solids in some detail (page 80), and if you are just now beginning to offer your baby any food other than milk, you should review that information.

Chapter 3 also mentioned some reasons not to begin solids too early (before four months of age), but you don't want to wait too long either. As your baby passes the sixth month, breast or formula feeding alone will fall short of providing the calories and nutrients he needs. Between six and nine months he may be more willing to try a variety of foods than after the one-year mark. Your goal at six months will thus be to begin solids if you haven't by now and then to expand his food horizons gradually and steadily.

By the end of the first year, the general outline of his eating patterns should resemble your own, except for amounts and textures. This raises the question of where you will take your baby nutritionally. If your family's eating habits are chaotic and your diet loaded with fat, salt, and sugar, do you want your baby to reach the same endpoint? This may be a good time to reevaluate and reconfigure your own food choices.

By nine months you will see some side-to-side chewing movements that signal readiness for foods with a thicker texture. This is a good time to begin trying some mashed or chopped food from the family meal and some finger foods that your baby can feed himself. The latter include items such as small pieces of soft fruit (peaches or pears, for example), little squares of bread or toast, unsalted crackers, pieces of pancake or soft waffle, and cooked soft pasta.

Don't become a clean-plate fanatic with your baby. When first sampling

INTRODUCING YOUR BABY TO SOLID FOODS

1. After three tablespoons of rice cereal are going down smoothly at one feeding, you may want to try other cereals such as oats and barley. Check with your baby's doctor before trying corn or wheat cereals, which provoke digestive problems in some infants.

2. After cereals have been established on the menu for a few weeks, you can introduce either fruits or vegetables. Vegetables may hold an advantage because they will not condition your baby to sweet tastes. Fruits can be added later, and meats introduced last. You may choose to raise a vegetarian and not introduce meats to your baby at all, but if you do so, be sure that you are adequately informed so your baby won't be deprived of any necessary nutrients.

3. Remember to let your baby try each new food (one to three tablespoons' worth) for a few days before introducing another. Observe for any signs of a reaction: diarrhea, irritability, runny nose, coughing or wheezing, or a rash, especially around the face.

If there is any possibility that a reaction has occurred, withdraw the food, wait for the problem to calm down, and try again—unless the reaction is severe; then consult your baby's doctor. If you see the same response again, put that food aside for several weeks, and tell your baby's doctor before serving it to her again. If there's a more severe reaction, such as an immediate rash or difficulty breathing, contact the doctor immediately. Fortunately, sudden intense reactions to foods are very uncommon at this age.

4. Once your baby is taking food from different groups (for example, cereal and vegetables), you can feed her solids twice daily and expand to three times daily when three or more types of food are part of her daily routine. In addition, her daily intake should include about sixteen to thirty-two ounces of breast milk or formula. (A rule of thumb is that one nursing session at this age delivers six to eight ounces of milk.)

solids he will take only small amounts—one or two tablespoons at a time—and then gradually increase his intake over time. Watch for signs that he is no longer hungry—turning his head, getting fussy, or general disinterest in what you are offering from the spoon. Trying to force him to eat a prescribed amount is not only an exercise in futility, but may also set up a bad habit of eating when he has no appetite.

Chapter 3 listed a number of cautions about foods and feeding. Because of their potential impact on your baby's health, these caveats will be repeated here along with some additional notes for the more experienced solid-food consumer.

- *Do not feed honey to babies under the age of twelve months* because of the risk of infant botulism, a form of food poisoning that can cause serious damage to the nervous system, or very rarely can be fatal. Corn syrup has also been found to cause infant botulism.
- Keep your baby on breast milk or infant formula (fortified with iron) until he reaches the age of twelve months. Infants who drink cow's milk

(continued)

Once she has become well acquainted with solids, for most feedings you'll probably want to offer breast milk or formula *after* your baby has had other foods. (Milk can also be given between meals and at bedtime.) Solids won't hold much interest if her tank is already full of six or eight ounces of milk.

A FEW REMINDERS ABOUT FOOD PREPARATION: If you are using commercially prepared baby food from a jar, make sure that the safety button in the middle of the lid pops up when you open it. If it doesn't, return the jar or throw it away. Don't feed your baby directly out of the jar because the enzymes and bacteria from her saliva may degrade or contaminate the food she doesn't finish. Instead, spoon a small amount on a plate, and put what remains in the jar into the refrigerator, where it will be good for a day (or a month frozen). Whatever is left on her plate should be thrown away.

You may prefer to prepare your own foods rather than (or in addition to) using commercial baby-food products. At first, keep them simple: adequately cooked and

then pureed in a blender or baby-food grinder or mashed with a fork. Fruits other than bananas should be cooked rather than served raw.

Avoid salty, sugary, and spicy concoctions as well as foods that might provoke allergic reactions. When your baby has had her fill of a particular item, you can store any extra in the refrigerator. However, before serving rewarmed food to your baby at a later meal, inspect and smell for any signs of spoilage. If in doubt, toss it out.

Solid foods do not need to be hot; room temperature or slightly warm is just fine for most babies. If you need to warm something from the refrigerator, use the microwave with extreme caution—if at all—because of the possibility of uneven temperatures and hot spots within the food that could burn the mouth. Microwaved food should be thoroughly stirred so the heat is distributed evenly throughout. If heating baby food in a jar, you can place the jar in a pan of warm water for a few minutes.

before their first birthday are more likely to develop an allergy to the protein it contains. This may lead to the loss of small amounts of blood from the intestine. Cow's milk may also interfere with the absorption of iron contained in other foods. Both of these could lead to a shortage of red blood cells (anemia). After twelve months, when you do begin to offer cow's milk, use whole milk, not low-fat or nonfat, because your baby will need the extra fat to construct his growing central nervous system.

◆ Keep your baby away from chocolate, peanut butter, shellfish, egg whites, citrus fruits, strawberries, and tomatoes before his first birthday; these can induce future allergies. Some physicians also add wheat and corn to this off-limits list for the same reason.

◆ Even more risky to your baby are foods that might cause a choking accident. Avoid any foods that are small and hard such as seeds, nuts, small candies, uncooked peas, and popcorn. Also keep your baby away from foods that are sticky, chewy, stringy, or small and round. Peanut butter and hot dogs are thus off-limits, along with grapes, uncooked vegetables, raw apples, and dried fruit. In a nutshell, foods that can't be smushed by gums or easily dissolved in saliva or that might fit snugly into a small airway don't belong in your baby's mouth.

◆ Don't feed your baby foods with added salt or sugar, or with spicy flavors. He needs to become accustomed to the basic, unadulterated taste of high-quality foods. Offer fruit for dessert rather than calorie-drenched sweets such as custards and puddings. Don't let your baby develop a taste for soda, punch, or other sweetened drinks.

◆ Keep up the variety. If your baby seems to ignore everything but one or two foods—crackers and bananas, for example—don't be frightened or blackmailed into allowing him to establish a major food rut. Hold these items and offer him a variety of alternatives from the other food groups instead. If he refuses, don't panic. When he's hungry, he'll eat what you've offered, especially if he hasn't filled his tank with milk before mealtime.

◆ Don't let your baby become a "grazer." Some parents respond with food (breast, bottle, or snacks) whenever their baby utters any sound remotely suggesting displeasure. The result is nonstop eating by a baby who is never actually hungry or completely satisfied and who might acquire a long-term habit of turning to food for comfort. You would be wise to avoid feeding patterns such as this that might result in overeating, especially if obesity is a problem on either side of your family.

Between six and nine months, you can establish mealtime routines: breakfast, lunch, and dinner, with midmorning and midafternoon snacks if you and your baby desire. But when meals are over, let them be over.

- Don't put your baby to bed with a bottle of milk or juice. If he falls asleep with anything other than water in his mouth, bacteria can damage his incoming teeth. A baby who drinks from a bottle while lying flat will also be at greater risk for developing middle-ear infections. If your baby truly seems to sleep better after a bedtime snack, be sure all of it is swallowed and then carry out a gentle toothbrushing with water (if he has any teeth) before going to bed.

- Don't let your baby become a "juiceaholic." Some become so enamored with the sweet taste of juices that they will favor them over more nutritious sources of calories, including milk. Furthermore, juices sucked from bottles may stay in contact longer with the teeth and lead to early decay. Juice bottles have a way of becoming an entrenched habit.

  Hold off on juices until he can drink them from a cup. Once he has started drinking them on a regular basis, set a four-ounce daily limit, or dilute four ounces with an equal amount of water if you want to offer them more often. Since citrus fruits may provoke allergic responses during the first year, you may want to hold the orange juice until after the first birthday. (Check with your baby's doctor.)

Avoiding high-chair hazards

As your baby begins to spend more time with solids each day, you may find it easier to feed her in a high chair. As with all baby equipment, a few simple precautions will help prevent unpleasant or even serious accidents.

- As with bathtubs and car seats, rule number one with high chairs is *never leave your baby unattended while she is sitting in it.*

- Make certain that the chair has a broad base so it cannot be easily tipped over. Grandma's high chair might be a venerated family heirloom, but if it doesn't sit rock solid on the floor, use a newer one. If you use a chair that folds, make sure it is locked into place before your baby gets in.

- Take the few extra seconds to secure your baby with the chair's safety straps. This will prevent her from wiggling and sliding out of position or standing up to survey the horizon, both of which could result in a serious injury.

- Before your baby is seated, make sure the chair is at a safe distance from the nearest wall or counter. Otherwise, a healthy shove from your young diner might topple her and the chair to the floor.
- Don't let other children play under or climb on the high chair.
- Clean food debris off the chair and tray after each meal. Your baby may have no reservations about sampling any leftovers—in various states of decay—that are within finger range.

If you use a portable baby seat that clamps onto a table when you travel or eat out, observe a few additional precautions:

- Make sure the table is steady enough to support both chair and baby and that the chair is securely clamped to the table before your baby gets in. Card tables, glass tops, tables supported only by a center post, and extension leaves are not strong or stable enough for this job.
- Position the chair so your baby can't push against one of the table legs and literally "shove off" for a voyage to the floor.

MAKING THE TRANSITION FROM BREAST TO BOTTLE?

If breast milk has been your baby's primary nutrition source through the first six months of life, you will need to introduce her to solids during the coming months (if you haven't started already) as has just been described.

But should you switch to formula feeding as well? The answer depends entirely on you and your baby. On one hand, if the two of you are a smoothly functioning nursing team and everyone is quite happy with this arrangement, there's absolutely no need to change. If a well-meaning relative thinks you're "getting a little carried away with this breast-feeding thing" because you're still nursing a baby who is nearly a year old and perhaps starting to walk, you can let her know, without any embarrassment, that this arrangement is working very nicely for you. In other words, at this point in your baby's life, "if it ain't broke, you don't need to fix it."

On the other hand, baby or mother (or both) may be ready to make a change during the months approaching the first birthday. As babies become more mobile and

fascinated with the world around them, they may also become squirmy and distracted during nursing sessions—especially during the day when they are wide-awake and their hunger is being satisfied by other foods. They may suck a few times and then display body language that says, "Sorry to eat and run, Mom, but I got things to do!" To add injury to insult, some babies may absentmindedly chomp into a nipple with their newly erupted teeth.

Many moms have their own reasons to wean a baby from nursing to formula between six and twelve months of age. Perhaps they feel the need to devote more of their time and attention to other people and activities within the home, to educational pursuits, to outside employment, or to a combination of these interests. Some begin to long for "having my body back," especially if nursing is starting to feel more like alligator wrestling. There may be a budding (or even full-grown) desire to pursue weight reduction and physical conditioning without worrying about affecting a baby's nutritional well-being.

- The chair should attach to the bare surface of the table, not a tablecloth or place mat that can slide off.
- Don't let older children play under the table and/or seat, since they might accidentally bump and dislodge it.

Dining area or "mess" hall?

Some babies are quite content to let you feed them one spoonful of food after another, while others can't wait to take matters literally into their own hands as soon as possible. When your ten-month-old reaches for the feeding spoon, she is primarily interested in it as an object to investigate and manipulate—just like everything else she touches. It is quite unlikely that she will use it to transfer food into her mouth with any consistency until she has passed the fifteen-month mark. Instead, she will probably bang her spoon against the nearest hard object, fling it to the floor, or perhaps dip it into her food—before she bangs and flings it.

(continued)

Even more fundamental and important for many mothers is the realization that an inevitable passage is arriving: The totally helpless and dependent newborn, who derived all of her sustenance from her mother who carried and nursed her, is now taking the very first steps toward independence. She now needs more nourishment than she can obtain from milk. She is starting to move in all directions under her own power. She most certainly needs to be loved and cherished and must have plenty of Mom's attention if she is going to thrive, but her direct physical attachment to her is coming to a close. Whether it occurs now or sometime after the first birthday, allowing this brief season of intimate dependence to end is but one of hundreds of ways in which she will need to be released, step by tiny step, over the next eighteen to twenty years.

Whatever your reasons might be, if you are ready to move from breast feeding to a bottle or cup:

- Substitute the bottle or cup for a feeding in which your baby tends to be distracted or not interested in a long nursing session. (Usually this is one in the middle of the day.) Each week add a bottle substitution to a different feeding. Usually bedtime nursing is the last to go.
- Eliminate nursing for reasons other than nourishment. If you need to comfort your baby, caress and rock her rather than using the breast as a pacifier.
- Cut down the duration of nursing sessions. If your baby wants a "hit and run" session, don't try to keep her at the breast longer than she seems interested.
- If your breasts are becoming engorged and uncomfortable as your baby nurses less often, express just enough milk to stay comfortable. If you empty them fully, they will produce larger quantities of milk.

A final note: If you have second thoughts during this transition and decide to maintain your nursing relationship for a few more months, you can reverse the process by having your baby nurse longer and more often. Your milk supply will increase accordingly.

Many babies could care less about the spoon, no matter who is holding it, and simply want to turn every solid into a finger food—or an unidentified flying object. Either scenario will serve as an impressive illustration of the word *mess*. After a prolonged mealtime with a self-feeder in this age-group, food may be everywhere—from head to toe on the baby, scattered over a radius of several feet around her high chair, and perhaps decorating a few walls, people, and pets as well.

One theoretical advantage of giving your baby free rein in feeding herself before her first birthday is that her prowess with the spoon might develop more quickly. However, it is questionable whether early spoon practice really matters in the long run. A more realistic benefit of self-feeding is that she'll tend to regulate her own food intake. She'll get down to business (eating and making a mess in the process) when she's truly hungry, then shift into other activities (making a mess full-time) when her appetite is satisfied. The end result is a baby who stops eating when she's no longer hungry, an eating habit that will serve her well the rest of her life, making it less likely that she will turn to food for needs other than hunger or unwittingly overeat on a regular basis. In contrast, a baby who happily accepts any and all food offered to her, even after she is no longer hungry, is at risk of becoming overweight.

The major disadvantage of a do-it-yourself feeding at this age, of course, is the extra cleaning effort needed to round up the wayward food. To protect floors and carpets, some parents buy special "splash mats" at stores that sell baby paraphernalia or even set up an empty plastic wading pool around the high chair. Unfortunately you can't haul all this gear to a restaurant or a friend's house, and you may grow tired of hosing off the high chair after every meal. Furthermore, just as imposing some limits on your baby's explorations is necessary for safety and sanity, imposing some semblance of order at mealtimes is a reasonable and worthwhile goal.

Some parents go to the opposite extreme, trying to control and orchestrate every bite taken by the baby. If this is your intention, keep an eye on your blood pressure, because you'll be repeatedly going to the mat with your child over the fine points of what she will or won't eat. *Whatever else you do, don't attempt to force a baby to eat when she's not hungry and don't let your concern over her lack of interest in a particular food escalate into trench warfare.* If she doesn't like bananas, for example, find some other fruit she does enjoy.

A balanced approach is for you to manage the spoon with the gooey stuff—the cereal and strained foods—for the first several months, until she is able to handle this assignment herself with a minimum of mess making. You can let her handle a spoon all she wants, of course, without getting food involved. As she passes her first birthday, see if she will imitate you as you show how it's used. At the same time, let her have some of the self-contained finger foods described above, either before or after spoon feeding. Pay attention, however, to the signs that she isn't hungry: turning her head, not accepting the spoon, getting restless in the chair, or tossing the finger foods overboard. If she doesn't want to eat, don't try to feed her, but don't let her play with the food.

Cup control

Another skill to work on in the high chair is drinking from a cup. Since this project involves hand control, new swallowing skills, and liquid that might go anywhere and everywhere, take your time. The cup you choose for your baby may be easier to handle if it has two handles or, depending on his preference, no handles. A weighted bottom will help keep it oriented topside up, and sturdy construction is a must. The pretty china cup illustrated with Beatrix Potter characters might be nice to look at, but for everyday use unbreakable plastic is the only way to go. You may wish to get a transitional cup that has a lid with a small spout, but when it's time to use the real thing, he may not know whether to sip or suck. The spouted version might best be used for the baby who resists the cup in favor of his beloved bottle.

After he's gotten the hang of taking food from a spoon, you can try putting a little water in his cup. When you first put it to his lips, he will probably not know quite what to do. After you let a few drops enter his mouth, he may swallow, or let it run down his chin, or some of each. Be patient. Only one in four babies will master this skill by the age of nine months, and it may be an additional six months before most of the liquid goes where it belongs.

Overall, it's better to start cup training earlier rather than later. A one-year-old who is a confirmed bottle user or who has been exclusively breast-fed may take a dim view of this plastic contraption you are handing him. Some babies, left to their own devices, become attached to their bottles as an ongoing source of comfort and security. You will definitely want to avoid having a toddler (or a preschooler!) who wanders around all day with a bottle in his mouth.

HEALTH ISSUES: MEDICAL CHECKUPS

During this six-month period your baby will not need as many routine checkups as he did during the first six months of life. Normally, visits are carried out at six months, nine months, and one year. Your baby's doctor will, as before, measure progress in height, weight, and head circumference. A review of developmental milestones and a check from head to toe will also be on the agenda. You should feel free to ask questions about feeding or behavior problems that might concern you, and check for any specific guidelines about the introduction of solid foods. You can expect some input about safety at home as well, including directions about appropriate action to take in case your baby accidentally swallows a toxic substance or an overdose of medication.

As noted in the previous chapter, the third DTaP (diphtheria/tetanus/pertussis) and hemophilus B immunizations will be given at the six-month check. The third hepatitis B vaccination may be given now if the series was started at birth, although some physicians may delay the third dose until the age of twelve to eighteen months. If for any reason your baby has fallen behind on his basic immunization schedule, talk to the doctor about a timetable for catching up. Now that he has reached the six-month mark you may be tempted to slack off on vaccinations, especially if your budget is tight. But you should press on and complete this process because the illnesses that you may prevent can be devastating (see chapter 1, page 31). If you are short on funds, check with your local health department about the availability of low-cost immunizations. Many communities have vaccination programs that are carried out on a regular basis throughout the year.

Between a baby's ninth and twelfth months, some health-care providers administer a skin test to detect any possible exposure to tuberculosis. At the one-year checkup your baby may have blood drawn to check for **anemia** (a shortage of red blood cells) or exposure to lead. If anemia is present at this age, it usually indicates a need for more iron in the baby's diet. Your doctor will give you specific recommendations if this is the case.

Common illnesses in infancy, including upper respiratory infections (colds), ear infections, intestinal upsets, and other disturbances were discussed in chapter 3 in the section entitled "When Your Baby Is Ill: Common Medical Problems." These will not be repeated here, but if you need a quick review, turn to page 90.

SOCIAL DEVELOPMENTS

While no two babies interact with the rest of humanity in exactly the same way, there are distinct trends you will likely notice during this very eventful six-month period.

At six months of age and for the next two or three months thereafter, babies tend to socialize easily with the world at large. As you walk by a seven- or eight-month-old who is peering over someone's shoulder in the church foyer, flash a grin and you'll probably get one in return. This sunny responsiveness—to just about anyone—is pleasant and certainly endearing, but it won't last forever. It also does not mean that a baby is equally attached to every grown-up on the planet. All the attention and care that have been given at home have been making a profound impact, and the bonds of attachments for the immediate family will continue to strengthen during these important months.

Strangers and separation

As early as six months of age, but usually between eight to twelve months, a new phase will develop. Your baby, who may have seemed so comfortable around everyone, will begin showing anxiety among unfamiliar people. The approach of someone new or someone she hasn't seen for a while will provoke a wide-eyed stare, usually followed by wailing and clinging to you for protection. This is called **stranger anxiety.**

This behavior may bother Aunt Mary, who hasn't seen your baby yet and was expecting a warm embrace from her newest niece. Since fear of strangers is virtually universal as the first birthday approaches and continues well into the second year, both you and Aunt Mary should relax about it. In fact, a simple strategy can help her and your baby get acquainted.

First, Aunt Mary shouldn't try to touch, kiss, or hold the baby right away. In fact, even a direct return of your baby's stare may set off a healthy cry. Instead, you should chat with Aunt Mary as if nothing else is going on. Let your baby see that this is someone you are comfortable with, and let her get used to the sight of this new person in your home. After a while, some simple exchanges of looks, touches, and eventually play will likely begin as Aunt Mary becomes one of the gang.

The flip side of stranger anxiety is **separation anxiety,** an increased unwillingness to be separated from the main caregiver—usually (but not always) Mom. Your baby may begin to cry when you simply step into another room for a moment or put her into her crib for a nap. If and when she's about to be left with a relative or a sitter, the crying may escalate into a wailing and clinging session of spectacular proportions.

Separation issues can turn into an emotional upheaval for parents and baby alike. On one hand, it's nice to know that your child thinks so highly of you, so to speak. But having your baby/toddler cling to you like superglue, or hearing a prolonged chorus of protest every night at bedtime, or wondering whether you can't have a night (or weekend) away without massive guilt can begin to feel like a ball and chain.

Your approach to this development should be, first of all, to avoid extremes. Some parents, especially with the first baby, feel that their supreme calling in life is to prevent their child from having one minute of unhappiness. Whatever it takes to prevent crying they will do, and whatever the baby seems to want they will provide, immediately and without question. But this is an exercise in futility, and a setup for creating an overindulged, selfish, and miserable child. Conversely, parents who take a very controlling approach to child rearing may not be very concerned about separation anxiety. But they also run the risk of being inattentive and neglectful of a young child's emotions in general. Both approaches stake out a path of least resistance that may seem to work for now but may also exact a terrible price in the future.

Since you are no doubt sensitive to your child's emotions but probably don't want to feel entirely controlled by her cries and moods, you'll be relieved to know that separation anxiety is a normal phase of development. It's virtually inevitable, but you can buffer its impact. For example, if a sitter is coming to your home, take an approach similar to the one just described for Aunt Mary. Have your sitter arrive a half hour early so she can get acquainted with your baby in an unhurried manner. If you are dropping the baby off at a place that is new to her, try to stick around for a while to allow your baby time to explore and get accustomed to the new environment. When it's time for you to depart, don't stoke the emotional fires with a hand-wringing send-off. Let your baby get involved in an activity with the caregiver, say a short and sweet good-bye, and then leave. (If your baby or toddler is going to spend time with a favorite set of grandparents or an aunt and uncle whom she knows well, you may find that your departure barely provokes any response at all.)

The separation process will be much more unpleasant if your baby is tired or hungry. If you can schedule your departure after a nap or a meal, it may go more smoothly. There is no harm in finding a so-called transitional object to serve as a comforting reminder of things that are familiar to her. (It can also help at bedtime—see next page). This can be a soft toy or small blanket, much like the world-famous security blanket belonging to Linus in the "Peanuts" comic strip. Once this object has been picked out by your child, you may want to buy a duplicate (or in the case of a blanket, tear it in half) to have on hand if the original is lost or in the washer. Tattered, stained, and probably a little smelly, this item may become a treasured souvenir of your child's early years.

Separation and sleeping

For some babies separation becomes a major issue at bedtime. As was mentioned in the previous chapter, if your baby isn't used to falling asleep on her own by eight or nine months of age, you may be in for some stormy nights ahead if you try to revise her routine. If she wakes up during the night, not only will she sound off, but she may also pull herself to a stand in her crib and rattle it vigorously until you tend to her. (Make sure you have adjusted the mattress and side rails of the crib so she can't tumble out.) Even a baby who originally was doing very well at bedtime may start resisting the process, crying and clinging to you when it's time to go to sleep.

You can still work toward bringing her into a state of drowsiness (but not quite asleep) using a little nursing or formula, rocking and singing, augmented perhaps by her favorite soft object. Then lay her down, pat her gently, reassure her, say good night, and leave. The same approach should be used if she begins awakening during the night. If this is a new behavior for her, check to be sure she isn't ill, grossly wet or soiled, or tangled in her blanket. Tend to these concerns if needed, but keep your visit quick, quiet, and businesslike and then say good night. She shouldn't need any middle-of-the-night feedings at this point; if you continue offering them well after the six-month mark, you'll only be providing room service and bleary-eyed companionship, not meeting any nutritional needs.

If you have an infant older than nine months who is still routinely rousing everyone from sleep two or three times a night, even after you have been providing a boring response for weeks, you may want to consider more deliberate measures to bring this behavior to a close. This would involve picking a time—usually on a weekend—when you can say good night and then resolve not to return until the next morning—if you can handle it—no matter how often and how long the crying goes on. *Keep in mind that returning to your baby after a prolonged bout of crying may convince her that endurance pays off.* Obviously, you would not want to try this "commando" approach with a child who is sick, or on a hot summer night when the windows are open, or when you need to be wide-awake the next day, or (most important) if *both* parents are not wholeheartedly ready for it.

You should greet your baby in the morning with smiles, hugs, and reassurance. Yes, indeed, you love her as much as the day is long, but nighttime is for sleeping. Normally after three, or at most, four nights, she will get the picture and sleep through the night thereafter (unless, of course, something else is wrong). Obviously, if interrupted sleep doesn't bother anyone, you may choose to leave things alone.

Eventually your child will sleep through the night on her own—but with some children it may take many more months before this occurs spontaneously.

Relationships and security

This six-month period of your baby's life begins an extremely important phase in development, not only for his motor skills but for his intellectual and social abilities as well. The intense curiosity and exploration described earlier isn't limited to the world of objects. It also includes a huge amount of information gathering about the people around him. He will make the transition from having limited forms of communication—crying when he's uncomfortable or hungry and random babbling when he feels good—to owning a wide array of sounds, gestures, and body movements.

As he exercises these abilities, he will be learning how his parents, siblings, and others around him respond. If he is uncomfortable and cries as a result, does anyone come to make him feel better? Does this happen when he makes different kinds of sounds? Does crying evoke a response more often than other behaviors? If he can't get to something he wants and cries (or makes other sounds), will someone get it for him? What happens when he touches or plays with various objects he finds? If he seems unhappy when he is taken away from a particular object, is your response consistent? Who makes him feel warm and comfortable? Who smiles and makes pleasant sounds—and who doesn't?

Your baby won't be formulating these questions (he hasn't the words for them yet), but he will be paying close attention to your reactions and responses, and he will be taught by them.

He will need to know that he is deeply and consistently loved. He will flourish when someone responds to his sounds of frustration or pleasure and comes to assist him or to share in the joy of a particular discovery. Paradoxically, he will also develop some security when he learns that those who love him don't necessarily come "right this instant" every time he calls out. A little delay in getting what he needs—and not always getting what he wants—will not harm him when it occurs in a setting where there is an abundance of smiles, caresses, and sweet conversation. On the contrary, it will teach him that he is secure in your love, even when you are not immediately present or even when your love for him causes you to overrule his immediate desires.

CHAPTER 5

Twelve to Twenty-Four Months

Oh, that our home on earth might be to them the pathway, the gate to the Father's home in heaven! Blessed Father, let us and our children be Thine wholly and forever. Amen.
ANDREW MURRAY

Twelve to Twenty-Four Months: Declarations of Independence

During the first twelve months of life, your baby will have undergone an incredible transformation—from a totally helpless newborn to a mobile explorer who is interacting vigorously with everything and everyone around him. During the next year of life, the physical changes you see in your child from month to month will not appear nearly as dramatic. You will, however, start the year with a "baby on wheels" and end it with a small child whose mind and body have, in fact, undergone some very significant developments.

Because of his mobility, your one-year-old will keep you hopping during nearly all of his waking hours. Track shoes, a sense of humor, and a little tolerance for disorder are a must from here on. Striving to ensure that he (and everything in his path) stays in one piece will be a full-time project, and you would be wise to review carefully the cautions regarding safety and sanity set forth in the first half of chapter 4 (page 101).

But as much attention as this assignment rightfully requires, a common mistake made by parents of toddlers is to enter a maintenance (or, in some cases, raw survival) mode and never move beyond it. As much as they need food, safety, endless cleanups, and diaper changes, toddlers also need the important grown-ups in their life to be *fascinated* with them. "Lord, give me the strength to get through this day" may be the repeated cry of the parent's heart (usually about 5 P.M.). But with it should come a postscript: "Lord, help me understand, appreciate, and marvel at this incredible creation You have loaned to me." Your toddler is no less "fearfully and wonderfully made" now that he is tearing all over the house than he was while he was being knit together in his mother's womb.

Your need for both of these prayers may become more intense, at least at times, as your child begins to demonstrate a reality that is painfully obvious to parents and often ignored by the most learned philosophers: Little children aren't inherently virtuous. They are not born brimming with selfless instincts and kind gestures. They have no concept of other people's viewpoints or needs. In fact, they are not even morally neutral "blank slates" who will readily follow whatever direction you give to them. They come hardwired with a will, boundless energy to express their interests, and powerful emotions to display if they aren't satisfied at any given moment. They don't need to be taught to grab, fight, howl in anger, or bluntly defy you (or anyone else caring for them). If you have any doubt that humankind is a fallen race (as painfully set forth in Genesis 3 and demonstrated in every generation thereafter), you have yet to spend any length of time in close quarters with a toddler.

Your response to this reality should be, as much as possible, measured, loving, calm (at least most of the time), and, like everything else, governed by an avoidance of extremes. If you don't believe that your sweet, innocent baby could ever challenge you ("Not *my* boy, whom I love so dearly . . ."), you're in for a rude shock this year. And if you aren't prepared and willing to meet him confidently when he does, you may find yourself living with a miserable, demanding two- or three-year-old, or even a full-fledged miniature tyrant.

However, if you are bound and determined to meet every departure from perfect decorum with harsh words and an iron fist, your opportunities to shape his will, impart moral standards, and serve as a role model will be squandered. Whatever good behavior you see will be based on raw fear and, once soured with a few years of resentment, will be spectacularly discarded at the first available opportunity.

During these next several months—which will pass more quickly than you might imagine—you will enter into some crucial interactions with your child. By the end of this year he needs to know and understand that you love him fervently and unconditionally and, at the same time, that you are in charge and he isn't. *If either or both of these messages are not clearly established by the second birthday (or within the few months that follow), your child rearing tasks during the following years are likely to be far more difficult.* His patterns of relating to you and any other people close to him, whether generally pleasant or continually combative, are likely to become more firmly entrenched by the third birthday and may continue for years thereafter.

You don't need to do everything perfectly this year to bring up a healthy, delightful child, however. An isolated mistake or even getting on the wrong track for a number of weeks isn't going to ruin his life. God has granted parents a good deal of time on the learning curve and children a great deal of resiliency. So take a deep breath, fasten your seat belt, stay on your knees (not just when you're picking up toys), and amid all the challenges, don't forget to step back once in a while to marvel at this little person you are nurturing.

PHYSICAL DEVELOPMENTS

Height, weight, and other physical progress

If you haven't already done so during one of your child's well-baby checkups, take a look at the growth curve that should be in her medical chart. Better yet, ask the doctor or office staff for a copy you can continue updating on your own. You'll notice that the average rate of growth during the second year is slower than it was during the first twelve months. A normal one-year-old will have tripled his or her birth weight but then will gain only three to five more pounds by age two. Similarly, regardless of gender, your child will add roughly four inches of height between the first and second birthdays, less than half the height gained during the first year. Interestingly, while your child's head will increase in circumference only about an inch over the next twelve months, by age two it will have reached 90 percent of its adult size.

The percentile curves shown on the growth charts begin to diverge more noticeably after the first twelve months. In other words, the differences in height and weight between a child who is at the 90th percentile (that is, larger than 90 percent of the children his age) and one of the same age who is at the 10th percentile will become more dramatic after the first birthday. For most children, position on the growth chart depends largely on genetics, with a height and weight trajectory that will be fairly predictable after the first eighteen to twenty-four months of life have been tracked, barring an unusual problem or chronic illness. If your child is "falling off" a curve—that is, she has been at a certain percentile of weight and height for a number of months and then appears to shift to a significantly lower level during subsequent checkups—a medical or nutritional problem may be present, and your health-care provider may recommend further evaluation.

Even though she will not be making drastic changes in height and weight, the baby look will begin to fade away between her first and second birthdays. With more muscle motion, her arms and legs will look longer and leaner and the abdomen less prominent. Her face will gradually shift from the round, nonspecific but universally appealing look of a baby to more well-defined features that will give you a preview of her future appearance. As you watch her enthusiastically attempting to blow out two birthday candles, don't be surprised if you find yourself wondering, "Where did my baby go?"

As described in the previous chapter, the debut of walking may already have occurred two or three months before the first birthday, or it may be a few months away. By eighteen months, your child should have this skill down pat. While early starters won't have any long-term advantage over the late bloomers who are otherwise normal, they will be somewhat ahead of the game in maturity of their gait. It takes a few months to progress from the broad-based, lurching, hands-up, toes-out, frequent-faller "toddling" walk to a smoother, more narrow-based gait with fewer falls, improved maneuvering, and—a big thrill for many kids—the ability to use hands to carry things while on the move.

Parents watching a toddler career around the room may wonder about the alignment of the legs: Are they turned outward too far? Does one foot point in a different direction from the other? During the first several weeks of walking, this may be impossible to answer. If you see an obvious, consistent difference in the orientation of the legs, however, you should have your toddler's health-care provider watch her move up and down the office corridor. He or she may want an opinion from an orthopedist to determine whether specific intervention is in order.

The treatment for the vast majority of toddler gait concerns is "tincture of time"—they resolve as weeks pass and coordination improves. However, an obvious limp or a toddler's sudden unwillingness to walk after she clearly knows how is always abnormal and should be evaluated medically as soon as possible.

Vision, hearing, and language

The average one-year-old can see well enough to spy small objects across the room or planes flying overhead. By the age of two he will probably approach normal vision, although it is difficult to measure accurately at this age. If he seems to be squinting a lot or bringing objects right up to his face before he interacts with them or doesn't seem to be tracking objects with his eyes, an exam by an ophthalmologist (a physician who specializes in eye problems) would be a good idea.[1] This should also be done if you see obvious crossing of his eyes (even temporarily) or if they don't seem to be moving in the same direction.

While major visual problems are uncommon in one-year-olds, hearing can become impaired if ear infections and colds—which are not at all unusual in this age-group—leave persistent thick fluid behind one or both eardrums. If the problem persists untreated for weeks or months, your child's ability to understand and generate language can be delayed.

If you have any concerns about hearing loss (see sidebar), by all means have his ears and hearing checked—the sooner the better. While your health-care provider can usually determine whether there is fluid behind the eardrum or identify other physical problems, a detailed assessment of hearing in this age-group requires special training and equipment. A relatively new and painless test with the intimidating name "brain stem evoked response audiometry" can test hearing without your child's cooperation, but you may have to travel some distance to have it done. If your toddler's physician recommends this test or a consultation with an ear, nose, and throat (ENT) specialist, don't hesitate to do so.

Assuming that hearing is intact, your child will probably have a speaking vocabulary of a few words at his first birthday and about ten times that many at his second, some of which he may combine into two- or three-word sentences. What he can *understand*, however, will become much more impressive as the year progresses. As he moves past the eighteen-month mark, he will point to all sorts of things—people, objects, body parts—when asked about them ("Where is your nose?" "Where's Auntie Linda?"). By the second birthday, the unintelligible strings of sounds that sounded like a foreign language at the beginning of the year will be honed down to simple statements or even questions. Even more amazing is seeing your walking baby, who not long ago lay helpless in a crib, following a simple command such as "Go get the ball."

Over the next several months, you will have the unique and important opportunity to help expand your child's language skills. You won't need a teaching credential, a master's degree, or special training in child development to do this. Instead, you will simply need to "be there" when you are with him. Keep your antennae up and be ready to give him dozens of little doses of your attention and conversation throughout the day.

WHEN MIGHT YOU SUSPECT YOUR ONE-YEAR-OLD HAS A HEARING PROBLEM?

- He doesn't turn in response to sounds or ignores you when you call him. Many parents have had the humbling experience of repeatedly disciplining a toddler for failing to respond to them, only to find out later that he really couldn't hear them.
- He isn't using any single words (such as *mama*) by the age of twelve to fifteen months, or his speech is unintelligible by the age of two. Babies and toddlers normally love to experiment with all sorts of sounds, and one who seems to be specializing in making noises he can feel (such as gargling or growling) may not be able to hear his own vocalizations.
- His responses to sounds seem to be selective. While you might suspect that he is choosing to pay attention to some and not others, he may be hearing low-pitched sounds better than high-pitched ones, or one ear may be affected but not the other.

Take advantage of his curiosity. When he approaches you with an object or points to something and makes a sound (which may rise at the end like a question—"Car?"), you've got his attention. Name the object and say something simple about it ("Yes, that's Daddy's car"). He doesn't need a lecture about auto mechanics, of course, but don't be afraid to aim your comment a little beyond what you think he might understand.

Talk to him while you're doing everyday chores. Folding clothes may be boring to you, but if he's watching, it doesn't take any extra time to name the items or say what you're doing with them. Remember, his little computer is on all the time.

Read to him. Reading simple stories to your child, especially at bedtime, is an extremely worthwhile activity to begin this year, if you haven't already. (Be sure to let him see what you are reading and to identify for him anything he finds interesting in the pictures.) His interest and understanding will increase dramatically over the course of the year. By age two, in fact, he may be able to fill in the blanks in a story he knows well, anticipating and saying one or more words at favorite spots along the way.

A few cautions about language:

Remember to speak to your child using clear, meaningful words. Use a pleasant tone of voice, but avoid baby talk, and don't repeat his unique mispronunciations of words, even if they *are* cute (see page 105).

Don't make reading to him an issue if he's not interested at the particular story time you have in mind. Usually you won't meet much resistance at bedtime when children are attentive to just about anything that delays lights-out, but they may not be as interested during daylight hours.

Don't expect Big Bird, Bert and Ernie, and the rest of the gang on *Sesame Street* to take care of your child's language development or other learning experiences. Even if he pays attention (which at this age he probably won't do for any length of time), live humans who are paying attention to *him* do a much better job.

Hands, minds, and safety

This year your toddler will continue the process of exploring whatever she finds around her. Her ability to pick up and manipulate objects both large and small will become much more refined and coordinated during the coming months. By her second birthday, she will enjoy scribbling with crayons (preferably not on the walls), stacking four or five items and then knocking them over, playing with clay, and sticking pegs of various shapes into similarly shaped holes. Many toddlers also become fascinated with things that go around. Wheels that spin on toy cars, pedals on bicycles, a lazy Susan you don't need anymore, or a saucepan lid turned upside down on the kitchen floor may become objects of your child's greatest affection.

Between eighteen and twenty-four months of age, most toddlers also become enamored with balls; holding, rolling, tossing, watching them bounce around, and then chasing them hold endless interest and delight. Beware, however, of small round objects (such as marbles) that might be put in the mouth and then accidentally inhaled. Best bet: Buy your toddler her own inexpensive inflatable twelve- to eighteen-inch beach ball. It's quiet, it can't do much damage, she can carry it around when she doesn't want to throw it, and it's easy to replace.

By her second birthday, you may get a preview of your child's preference for using the right or left hand. But she may also use the spoon with her right, scribble with her left, and throw a ball with either. Don't try to push the use of one hand over the other and don't worry about speeding up the process. She'll sort out her handedness in due time.

This year your child will significantly increase her grasp of the way things work. Her sense of object permanence—the idea that something is still present even if she can't see it—will become more sophisticated. Not only will she learn to search for a toy she saw you place under two or three blankets or pillows, but she will also become a whiz at little hide-and-seek activities. If she sees you stick a toy in your pocket, she won't forget where it went.[2]

Brief episodes of playacting and imitation will become more sophisticated over the course of the year. Watch her hold the toy phone to her ear (or yours), try to brush her hair, rock her "baby," or turn the steering wheel on a toy car. As the months pass, she will try to engage you in some of these scenarios. If you can stop for a few moments to pretend to drink out of the toy cup she offers you or talk on her phone, you'll make her day. Finding the right balance between responding to these overtures often enough to satisfy your child but without endless interruption to whatever you're trying to get done is an art in parenting (see Social and Emotional Development: The "First Adolescence" later in this chapter).

Because of your child's maturing motor and problem-solving skills, your vigilance for her ongoing safety must not only continue but become more sophisticated. Her developing fine-motor coordination will also include new abilities that can lead to new hazards: turning doorknobs, manipulating latches, flipping switches, and pushing buttons. Turn your back for a moment and she may be locked in the bathroom or out the door and down the street, peering over

Children cannot raise themselves properly. There is no substitute for loving parental leadership in the early development of children.

DR. JAMES DOBSON
ANSWERS YOUR
QUESTIONS ABOUT
MARRIAGE AND
SEXUALITY

the edge of Grandma's swimming pool. Her interest in climbing to precarious new heights may increase, along with her ability to find new and clever ways to get to them.

Her tendency to "gum" everything as a means of gathering information will wane, but she may not hesitate to place small objects in her mouth. Remember to stay vigilant for any such items that might cause choking if accidentally inhaled. She may very well take a swig or a bite of *anything* that looks interesting. Medicines, plants, cleaning products, dog food—you name it—nothing is off-limits for an oral sampling. You cannot assume that a bad taste will keep her from guzzling the furniture polish or anything else. This year and the next are the most risky for your child's having an accidental ingestion of a dangerous substance.

If you haven't done so by now, buy a small bottle of **syrup of ipecac,** a drug that may be used to induce vomiting if your baby eats or drinks something that might harm her. *You should give a dose of ipecac only if you are told to do so by the doctor, the emergency department, or a poison-control center.* Ipecac should *not* be used with many substances, especially caustic materials (such as drain cleaner) or petroleum products (such as gasoline or furniture polish) because they can do as much or more damage on the way up as they have done on the way down. For medications and other items, however, you may be instructed to use ipecac to empty the stomach. In a child over one year of age, one tablespoon (15 cc) followed by two glasses of water will induce vomiting, normally within fifteen to twenty minutes (see "Time to Buy Ipecac," page 110).

FEEDING: ESTABLISHING PATTERNS FOR EATING

By her first birthday, your toddler should have a working knowledge of a variety of foods from the well-known groups in addition to her milk. Remember that while cow's milk may be introduced after the first birthday if your child doesn't demonstrate any allergy to it, *whole* milk—not low-fat or nonfat—should be on the menu. Cholesterol is not an issue at this age, and the fat in whole milk is useful in building a number of tissues, including the central nervous system. Beware, however, of allowing a budding milkaholic to push her milk consumption past sixteen to twenty-four ounces (one to one and one-half pints) per day. Not only will this curb her interest in other types of food, but large amounts of milk may also interfere with the absorption of iron from other foods, which in turn can lead to anemia (a deficiency in red blood cells).

During this year you will want to establish a routine with meals and snacks if you haven't already. Three meals and two small snacks at generally consistent times are far preferable to nonstop grazing, which trains a child to eat for all kinds of reasons other than hunger, scatters food everywhere, and may lead to a choking accident if a toddler stumbles with food in her mouth. This is a good time to establish a routine of sitting down at the table before eating, which actually is beneficial for adults and older children as well.

A fair amount of the food she eats at a meal can consist of small portions of whatever the rest of the family is having, as long as it

- isn't too hot in temperature;
- isn't too hot in seasoning, or overly salty, sweet, or swimming in butter or grease—which isn't so great for the rest of the family either;
- is either mushy or cut into small, easily chewed pieces. Continue to avoid foods that could easily lodge in the airway: hot dogs (that aren't cut into bite-size pieces), nuts, seeds, hard candy, grapes, popcorn, peanut butter, raw vegetables, dried fruit, etc., as described in chapter 4 (see page 115).

One development on the food front that catches many parents off guard is the erratic appetite of the toddler. She may eat voraciously one day and show little interest in food the next, or consume a sizable breakfast and then quit after only a few bites of the day's other meals. With her nonstop activity during waking hours, this apparent inconsistency in fueling patterns may not make sense, but it is not uncommon. In fact, at this age her intense curiosity and compelling desire to explore the world around her will tend to limit her interest in food to two primary activities: eating it if she's hungry and examining it if she isn't. If either of these isn't happening at the kitchen table, she'll probably want to move on to more interesting pursuits. Also remember that growth is not as rapid now as it was during the first year, and that the average toddler needs only about one thousand calories a day—not a huge amount of food—to meet her nutritional needs.

Your goal should be to offer her a variety of foods in modest amounts each day. If she turns you down, don't turn your mealtime into a battle zone. Attempting to force a toddler to eat anything is an exercise in futility, and insisting that she can't leave the table or have another meal until she has finished every last speck of her vegetables (which might get a few days old while you wait) will lead to miserable, exhausting times around the dinner table.

Don't panic and then offer your toddler something she really likes out of fear that she won't get enough to eat. This may turn into a subtle form of dietary extortion and is a surefire way to create long-term food habits that may be nutritionally inadequate. If she doesn't want much now, put the plate back in the fridge and warm it up for the next meal. When she's hungry, she'll eat. If you are worried about her food intake, write down what she has eaten over a week's time and run it by her doctor. If she is active, showing developmental progress, and gaining on the growth chart, she's getting enough. Remember: No normal child will voluntarily starve herself.

You should discuss with your health-care provider whether or not your toddler should be on vitamin supplements. Some use these routinely, while others feel that well-balanced food intake essentially eliminates the need for vitamins. Fluoride supplements may be recommended, however, based on the content of your local water supply. Your child's doctor or local pediatric dentist should have this information, or you can obtain it from the agency that supplies your water.

Weaning

As the year progresses, you will see improving skill in your toddler's use of the cup and spoon, which will enable you to turn more of the feeding assignment over to her. With increasing cup proficiency (see chapter 4, page 123), you can begin phasing out bottles. This process may meet with some resistance but should be started by the first birthday and accomplished by the fifteen-month mark. Plan on substituting cup for bottle one meal at a time (or all three at once, if you're adventurous), and then do likewise for her snacks. Usually a bottle before bedtime is the last to go, since it has a way of becoming part of the night-time routine. Remember: No milk or juice should ever be given to your baby while she is lying down and falling asleep, because this practice (which is all too easy to start as a last resort during a restless night) can lead to dental cavities and ear infections. A little snack just before bed and before brushing teeth is fine, but food should not be part of any middle-of-the-night activity at this point (see page 127).

Once you've decided to bid the last bottle feeding farewell, your best bet is to pack all of them away when your toddler is asleep. If she begins to ask (or cry) for her "baba," be matter-of-fact and upbeat: "Your bottles are gone! And you're so big, you don't need them anymore!"

If your baby is still nursing at this point and has never used a bottle, she can graduate directly from breast to cup and avoid bottles altogether. As mentioned in the previous chapter, you should still introduce your baby to drinking from a cup even if most of her fluids are coming directly from Mom. If you wait too long, you may face resistance when it's time to stop nursing.

With solids, you will need to decide how much mess you can tolerate. Some postmeal cleanup will be necessary while your child learns the fine points of hand-spoon-mouth coordination, but you shouldn't confuse the pitching of food and fluids in all directions with her self-feeding learning curve (see chapter 4, page 121). One way to minimize the mess is to keep the serving sizes small. A typical balanced menu for a one-year-old equals measured quantities of half a cup of a fruit or vegetable, two to three ounces of meat, or a slice of bread made into a half-sandwich. (Remember, of course, that your toddler on any given day may eat less or more than these amounts.)

Depending upon everyone's schedule, make an effort to include your toddler at the family table for at least one meal per day. Traditions and timetables will vary, of course, but for many families, a shared meal (usually dinner) may be the one occasion when everyone at home can share conversation as well as food. (Shutting off the TV and perhaps taking the phone off the hook will enhance this experience.) While not exactly participating at the same level as everyone around the table, your one-year-old will be watching

---

MENU FOR TODDLERS

◆ breads and cereals	*4 servings per day*
◆ milk	*2–3 cups per day*
◆ vegetables and fruit	*4 servings per day*
◆ meat/poultry/fish, eggs, beans	*2 servings per day*

A child's serving is generally one-fourth the size of an adult serving.

Keep in mind:
- Children will often consume a lot in the bread and grains group. As long as they are eating from other food groups as well, this is usually not a problem.
- Too much milk will add fat to a child's diet and replace valuable nutrients from other food groups.
- Too much fruit or fruit juice will add sugar to a child's diet and lessen the appetite for other necessary foods.

---

and listening and will become accustomed to being included in these gatherings. Let her see the family pause for a blessing. Indeed, it would be well for her to hear brief words of thanks before her other meals too, a practice that will prepare her for that time in the near future when she begins to understand the meaning of prayer.

SLEEPING: ESTABLISHING A ROUTINE

By his first birthday, your child should have been sleeping through the night for some time. If not, remember that by now his nocturnal awakenings aren't the result of any nutritional needs. Instead, he has become accustomed to the fact that having company or a snack feels good during the night. Why go back to sleep after awakening momentarily in the wee hours when there are other pleasantries to enjoy?

If you really don't mind working the nursery night shift, you may choose to put off dealing with the inevitable protest that will break forth when you cancel room service. But if he is otherwise well, you can usually establish uninterrupted sleep for everyone within one or two days, typically over a weekend, once you decide to take the plunge (see chapter 4, page 127, for details).

Even a seasoned all-night sleeper, however, may depart from his pattern during an illness, while on a trip, after a move, or perhaps because of a bad dream. Under these circumstances, you'll need to provide care and comfort (though not snacks, unless you have been specifically directed by the doctor to push fluids when he is sick) until things settle down, then nudge him back toward his old habits.

WHEN SHOULD I WEAN MY TODDLER FROM BREAST FEEDING?

Some authorities discourage nursing as a frequent daily activity after a toddler reaches 12 to 15 months of age. Others (especially members of nursing advocacy groups) encourage a completely open-ended approach, noting that in some cultures mothers may nurse a newborn on one breast and a child as old as five on the other. If you are pondering this question, remember that there are both nutritional and behavioral aspects to consider.

Unlike the first months of your baby's life, nursing does not serve a life-sustaining function after solids have been introduced. In fact, at this age if frequent trips to the breast are substituting for solid foods, your toddler may become anemic or even gradually undernourished. The role of nursing thus becomes increasingly social and emotional as the months (or years) pass, especially after eighteen months of age. This can be a source of ongoing nurturing, closeness, and even relaxation between

mother and child. If all else is going well, there may be no compelling reason to bring it to a close in the immediate future.

On the other hand, nursing for an extended period of time could cause or prolong problems such as:

- A toddler who is overly dependent on or demanding of Mom. If she is clinging to you and your breast day and night and not spending much time exploring the world around her, she needs to expand her horizons. If she wants to nurse whenever she's unhappy or bored, she needs to learn how to find comfort in other ways (such as cuddling without the oral intake). If she refuses to take liquids from any other source but Mom, parental activities are going to be stifled. If you are still nursing because your toddler throws a tantrum whenever she can't have access to

For many toddlers the Good Ship Slumber may be rocked in other ways. At some point, you're likely to run into bedtime resistance, manifested either by winsome appeals (requests for another kiss, one last drink, and in subsequent months, answers to riddles of the universe) or by outright rebellion against getting or staying in bed. Some of this may arise from separation anxiety, from negativism, or simply from the fact that other people are up doing interesting things, and lying in a crib or bed seems awfully boring by comparison. You may be tempted to take the path of least resistance and let him decide when he's ready to sleep—in other words, when he eventually collapses from sheer exhaustion. This is a bad idea for a number of reasons:

- You need to spend time with older children (if you have any) without an increasingly tired and irritable toddler wandering around.
- You need to spend time with your mate or by yourself without *any* children wandering around.
- Your toddler needs the sleep—a good ten or eleven hours at night, which probably won't happen if he's staying up until your bedtime.

If not already in place, establishing a fixed bedtime routine and a fixed bedtime will be an important task this year. Even if his vocabulary is limited, you can

---

(continued)

your breast, you are under siege. In this case, you may need to curtail nursing simply to gain control of your (and her) life.

- A mom who is overly dependent on the toddler. As was mentioned in the last chapter (see sidebar, page 120), the intimacy of nurturing a dependent young infant occurs for a special but brief season. Acknowledging that it is over is a necessary step for both mother and child. If you feel that your meaning and purpose in life are going to evaporate if you are not nursing, you may need to explore some more basic issues relating to your identity and importance as an individual. This may be worked out informally in conversations with other mothers, but more formal counseling may be appropriate as well.
- Friction in the marriage. If your husband is beginning to feel that personal and physical intimacy with you

is hampered by the ongoing presence of one or more children at your breast, the duration of nursing should be open for discussion.

- Modesty problems. A small child burrowing under Mom's blouse can be an awkward event at the mall or in the neighbors' living room, and appropriate limits must be set for the location of nursing an older toddler. A preschooler who is still accessing Mom's breast may well be crossing modesty boundaries, even in the privacy of the home.

If one or more of these problems have developed, it may be time to get the weaning process under way. There is rarely, if ever, a need to do a "cold turkey" approach, however, and a gradual phaseout is likely to provoke less turmoil. The principles for shifting from nursing to bottle or cup described in the previous chapter (see sidebar, page 120) apply at this age also.

talk him through the steps you choose: bath, jammies, story, song, prayer, for example, carried out in a manner that winds him down. A raucous wrestling match or chasing the dog right before bedtime probably won't help set the stage for turning in. Keep in mind that whatever bedtime routine you establish (including one that takes one or two hours to complete) may become entrenched and expected every night for years to come.

As with a blessing before meals, your child will learn the routine of a short bedtime prayer before he understands the words or the theology. Over the coming months and years, however, this brief but important moment should take on new meanings and should not become a singsong patter repeated every night for no apparent reason other than long-standing habit.

As happened (hopefully) when he was an infant, your toddler should be placed in his crib or bed sleepy but not asleep. If he becomes accustomed to falling asleep on the sofa, floor, or your bed, he is more likely to resist signing off on his own pillow—both at bedtime *and* during the night.

Parents who have maintained a "family bed" through the first year should take the baby's first birthday as an occasion to review the current sleeping arrangements. Does your child need a parental body next to him to fall or stay asleep? (If one or both parents were to go away on a retreat for a night or two, would there be a problem?) More important, how is the presence of a much larger and more mobile baby affecting your sleep and your intimacy? Mother and Father should be in complete agreement about this situation or seek to resolve any difference of opinion if they are not—even if counseling is needed. Serious and damaging rifts in a marital relationship can develop if one spouse feels displaced physically and emotionally by a child who is taking over an ever increasing area of bed space. In general, if either Mom or Dad feels that it's time for the baby to sleep elsewhere, the other parent should oblige—not only out of respect for the other's feelings but in recognition that the marital relationship needs to be nurtured and preserved.

At the first birthday, most children are still logging three to four hours of daytime sleep, usually in two naps. The amount of daytime sleep will decline to two or three hours over the next year, and as a result, the morning nap will eventually phase out. When your toddler shifts to a one-nap-per-day routine, don't start too late in the afternoon or you may increase his bedtime resistance. (Who wants to go to bed after just getting up?) And, though he may seem intent on playing through the entire afternoon, don't be conned into eliminating nap time altogether, even if he resists it. Without daytime sleep, afternoons will probably be more notable for combat than for companionship.

SOCIAL AND EMOTIONAL DEVELOPMENT:
THE "FIRST ADOLESCENCE"

During the second twelve months of life, your child will display a gamut of behaviors and emotions that, depending on your frame of mind, you may find confusing, amusing, or downright exasperating. A little preparation and some insight into the emerging worldview of the one-year-old can help you sort out and manage this important developmental passage.

First and foremost, keep in mind that above all else your baby/toddler needs to know that she is loved, accepted, and "at home" with you and that you are on her side without reservations—even when you won't give her everything she wants. She needs kind and loving words and actions all day long, and she will come to you frequently for them.

Expect overtures of all sorts, often with arms outstretched, many times during the day as your toddler seeks

- cuddling and hugs;
- comforting after a bump or bruise;
- reassurance after being frightened;
- help with a problem, such as getting something out of reach or fixing a misbehaving toy;
- your enthusiastic reaction to something she has brought to you;
- a response to a simple question (or sounds that resemble a question);
- relief from being hungry, thirsty, or having a wet or dirty diaper;
- an invitation to role-play (at her direction)—pretending to talk on her toy phone, for example;
- confirmation that you are still "there" when she has not seen you for a few minutes.

These approaches for comfort, input, and help will not last forever, and to the best of your ability they shouldn't be ignored. For a toddler they provide some critical fact-finding about how things work, how to get help, and who cares about her. They probably will also have a major impact on the way she interacts with the world at large in subsequent years. In a very real sense, you are her "launching pad," and after determining that her base of operations is safe and secure, she will be able to explore an expanding world around her.

You may find it difficult or impossible to stop whatever you're doing and respond immediately every time your toddler comes or calls to you. In fact, a little wait at times won't hurt: She needs to learn that she is important, but not Queen of the Domain. If you're on the phone or up to your elbows in dishwater, it's quite all right to acknowledge one of her overtures with "I hear you, and I'll help you in a few minutes."

As with everything else in parenting, extremes are best avoided. If your toddler is clinging to you every minute of the day or whining and crying if you pay attention to anything or anyone else, she may be too attached to you and not spending enough of her day exploring and learning about other parts of the known universe. In this case, you may need to be more assertive about delaying your response to her when you need to tend to other business. On the other hand, if you find yourself issuing a steady stream of brush-offs, uh-huhs, or irritated sighs ("What is it now?!"), take a few minutes to review your own state of mind or think about some ways to recharge your batteries (see sidebar).

AVOIDING TODDLER-CARE BURNOUT

There is no getting around it: Bringing up a toddler requires a seemingly limitless supply of time and energy. If you have other children at home, especially if one or more of them are under five, the demands on your attention may seem even more overwhelming. Simply maintaining some semblance of order can be a daunting task, and worrying about such niceties as a child's language development may sound like a fantasy if you feel immersed in total chaos.

There may be other pressures too. The parent who elects to stay at home (usually the mother but not always) may feel that her brain is rapidly turning to mush and that the stimulating worlds of education and career are passing her by. ("I've got a degree in history, and all I'm doing is changing diapers and listening to babbling.") If both parents work or if a single parent is rearing a toddler, much of the work may need to be done at home after a full day working elsewhere.

Because so much is going on in your toddler's life, he needs meaningful attention and input from the most important people in his life. If you feel that you're just marking time, becoming demented, or enduring in a state of slave labor, consider the following antiburnout ideas:

- There should be some time during your day when things become quiet. This usually can occur only after little people are in bed. You cannot collect your thoughts or anything else if kids are up until all hours of the night. Early bedtime for small children is not only good for them but necessary for you.
- Some of this quiet time should be real quiet time, designated for reflecting, reading, praying, and journaling. A daily devotional will provide not only refreshment but perspective on how your parenting tasks fit into the big picture of who Jesus is and what He's doing.
- Don't feel as if you are wasting your time and education to focus your primary attention on your children at this age. Believe it or not, the world isn't passing you by, and there will be plenty of time to make your mark in it later on. This doesn't mean that you have to put your brain in neutral, however, or that all outside activities must come to a screeching halt.
- Try to remember that this particular period of your child's life is not only extremely important but, in fact, highly interesting. Many people take sophisticated classes and earn advanced degrees to understand what is unfolding in front of you every day.

Exploring: pushing the boundaries and the advent of negativism

At some point during the second year of life, usually between fourteen and six-teen months, your child will begin a phase that may seem exasperating but is quite normal. Up until this point, his explorations of the world will have been fact-finding missions. He has been finding out "what happens when I eat the mashed banana, turn the knobs on the stereo, push my toy car across the floor, flip the light switch, pull the cat's tail, bounce the ball, laugh, cry, yell, babble . . ."

Some of these acts have results that are interesting or feel good, some tweak little fingers, some get attention, some make the big people laugh or get upset, some are still under investigation. If the important people in his life have re-sponded consistently, he will have figured out many of the ground rules of his world or at least have a good sense of the odds that a particular consequence will follow a certain deed.

(continued)

You can, in a very real sense, become a student of child development and the human condition in your own living room by being an observer as well as a caregiver. You may even want to consider doing some additional reading about this phase of your child's life.

- Take time for yourself. If you are a full-time parent at home, you will need regular time-outs—not merely for errands but for personal refreshment. These might include exercise workouts, walking in the park or strolling through the mall by yourself, or meeting a friend for lunch. Yes, you will need someone to watch your offspring while you do this, but it's worth the trouble and expense.

- Don't become starved for adult communication. When you reunite with your mate at the end of the workday, the first order of business should be some unhurried and attentive conversation between the two of you. Your child(ren) should see you do this and should be informed (as often as necessary) that this is "your time" together and "their time" will arrive shortly. Not only will this help maintain your marriage, but children who see their parents regularly connecting and showing affection will feel much more secure about the stability of their world.

- Married couples should also maintain their date night, once a week if possible. Important news for fathers: Never stop courting your wife, especially now. Notes, flowers, and unexpected gifts speak volumes and breathe new life into your relationship.

- Build relationships with other parents who have young (or even older) children. Many parents meet regularly in small groups, whether assembled spontaneously or organized by their church.

Hundreds of local groups affiliated with MOPS—Mothers of Preschoolers—meet on a regular basis across the United States (and in a number of other countries as well), offering support, conversation, and pleasant activities for mothers and their small children. (For the location of a MOPS group in or near your community, call 1-800-929-1287.) Local crisis pregnancy centers often put together single-moms' groups and activities. In the setting of such a get-together, you can share wisdom and woes, find support and encouragement, release laughter and tears, and even receive exhortation, if necessary.

Now, however, he will take his explorations a step further and up the ante. Instead of merely observing cause-and-effect relationships, he will want to find out how much power he wields. What will happen if he pushes the limits? Who's really in charge here? Mom may have said not to do this or touch that, but did she really mean it? Older sister's dolls are supposed to be off-limits, but will anyone do something about it if I carry one away?

During the months that follow, most, if not all, of the limits you have set will be challenged. At times they will receive a spectacular full-frontal assault. To call him "oppositional," a developmental term applied to this period, may be an understatement. By eighteen months, his favorite word may well be *no* followed by three exclamation points. What parents usually find astonishing, and at times humorous, is the extent and irrationality of this negativity:

> "Would you like some water?" you ask innocently, holding his cup.
> "No!"
> You put the cup on the counter.
> "Waaber!" he cries, reaching for it.
> You fill it and give it to him.
> "No!" He pushes it away.
> You put the cup on the counter.
> "WAABER!!" he howls.
> You offer him the cup.
> "NO!!" He swipes at the cup, nearly knocking it out of your hand.

What fuels this temporary insanity is, in fact, a very simple premise: If it wasn't his idea, he won't have anything to do with it.

Another startling variation on this theme is his disobeying a rule you have made abundantly clear—and making sure you're there to see it broken. This is not what was going on at eleven or twelve months, when his insatiable curiosity would override his very short memory, so he might explore an object after you have told him to leave it alone—seven times.

By eighteen months he can understand simple rules very well. Furthermore, the toddler in this phase won't always operate in stealth mode, a routine practice for older rule breakers. Instead, he may trot right over to the curtains you just told him not to touch, wait until you're watching, look you in the eyes (perhaps with a grin to boot), and give them a healthy tug. He is extremely interested in your response, and it is crucial that you give him one with more substance than "Isn't he cute. . . ." Dr. James Dobson has described the appropriate parental response in a memorable adage: "If he's looking for a fight, don't disappoint him."

This doesn't refer to taking part in a literal brawl, of course, but to taking a consistent posture of standing your ground when your authority has been clearly challenged.

The duration and severity of this oppositional stage will vary, but you can count on manifestations of it for at least six months. Some children who are particularly agreeable and compliant won't give you much to write home about. (There aren't too many of these.) Others who are especially strong-willed seem to put on the war paint and push the boundaries on a daily basis.

To some degree, this behavior represents an important developmental milestone for your toddler. He is developing a budding sense of identity, an awareness that it is possible to make things happen, and a compelling need to find out how far his newfound capabilities can take him. At the same time, of course, he is emotionally volatile, lacking in wisdom, and extremely primitive in his handling of relationships. And when there is a conflict, any attempt at reasoning is usually an exercise in futility.

These characteristics are, indeed, strikingly similar to some seen in another age-group—teenagers. You might think of this phase of your child's life as a preview of adolescence, a turbulent but universal passage for which there is, thank goodness, light and sanity at the end of the tunnel. As with adolescence, some parental wisdom can keep the family boat from rocking too hard. Aside from the fact that a teenager is a lot bigger than a toddler, there is one crucial difference in the way you manage these two periods of your child's life. During the teen years, your goal will be to let go, to escort your son or daughter to independent, responsible adulthood. But with a toddler, it is critical that he understand without any doubt that you are in charge.

If this fact is not established with absolute certainty (though always with an abiding sense of love and respect) by twenty-four to thirty months of age, your child may be very unpleasant to live with for months—or even years—thereafter. Indeed, for many children the "terrible twos" are but an extension of the "ornery ones," only with more horsepower. But a child who comes through this developmental stage knowing he is surrounded by unshakable love and consistent limits will generally be happier and more civilized throughout the rest of childhood.

How do you make it clear to your toddler that you are in charge? Some basic approaches and specific techniques of discipline—the word literally refers to teaching and molding, not merely corrective action or punishment—are discussed in detail in Special Concerns, page 177. How to deal

with tantrums, breath holding, head banging, and other spectacles is included in that section.

Relationships with other children

Very often two or more sets of parents who have toddlers of similar ages will have
the bright idea of getting their offspring together for a little fun and group play-
time. After all, isn't this a good time to learn how to get along and make new
friends?

Believe it or not, the answer is "probably not," *especially* if the children are
closer to one than to two years old.

With rare exception, a one-year-old is incapable of playing cooperatively
with children her own age. Her universe is centered around herself, and she cannot comprehend such niceties as understanding the viewpoint or feelings of
someone else. Parents and other adult caregivers are important to her, of course,
but another small child will generate little more interest than another toy—except when each is interested in the same item.

If there's one concept that is foreign to the toddler's outlook, it is sharing.
She cannot grasp the idea that one of her toys can be "borrowed" or used by
someone else and still remain hers, or vice versa. She lives in the here and now,
and "waiting a turn" is a meaningless phrase. Her outlook has been summarized
quite amusingly by child-development expert Dr. Burton L. White:

> THE TODDLER'S CREED
> If I want it, it's mine.
> If I give it to you and change my mind later, it's mine.
> If I can take it away from you, it's mine.
> If I had it a little while ago, it's mine.
> If it's mine, it will never belong to anyone else, no matter what.
> If we are building something together, all the pieces are mine.
> If it looks like mine, it's mine.[3]

Therefore, if you turn more than one toddler loose in the same room, keep
a close watch and plan to serve as referee. Having plenty of toys available will
help, of course, but you will need to be ready to intervene at the first sign of combat. This is important not only as a means of keeping the flow of tears to a minimum but also to prevent physical consequences. All too often if a desired item
can't be pulled easily out of the grip of another child, pushing and hitting will
follow.

Should this occur, separate the opponents with a clear rebuke ("No hitting!"), tend to any wounds, and then administer consequences. In this case, immediate withdrawal of a privilege (such as access to the toy she wanted) or a time of isolation from the others and the toys is an appropriate response.

If the skirmish includes biting, you will need to take decisive action to reduce the risk of a repeat performance, because human bite wounds carry a significant risk of infection. The biter should be removed from the scene and given a firm, eyeball-to-eyeball order: "Do not bite Amanda or anyone else! Biting hurts very much." A long lecture about manners or infections isn't necessary, but you may want to maintain a steady (but not painful) grip on the upper body to prevent any wiggling or movement for a minute or so. A toddler normally becomes quite unhappy after a very short period of this restraint, and continuing it for fifteen to thirty seconds after she begins to complain will reinforce your point. (Say it again before you let go.) Do not shake or slap her and never bite the biter in an effort to show "how bad it feels."

Along with maintaining zero tolerance for your child's biting anyone, consider some preventive measures as well. If you hear a conflict brewing between two toddlers, don't wait for them to negotiate through their disagreement because they can't (and won't) at this age. Distract, separate, take whatever is in dispute out of the picture, or simply call it a day if it looks as if everyone is tired and cranky.

Depending upon the spacing of your children, conflict between a toddler and other siblings is virtually inevitable. If your children are spaced less than two years apart, the older at first will be wary of the attention being showered on the younger and may even regress to babylike behavior in an effort to regain center stage. Once she is assured of her place in your affection, however, she probably will pay little attention to the baby—until he becomes mobile. Once this happens, the insatiable curiosity of the new explorer will inevitably lead to an invasion of big sister's possessions. If your older child isn't yet two and a half, don't expect her to embrace any high-minded ideals about sharing. Try to keep your older child's prized possessions out of harm's way, and in return, make it clear that any hitting or other physical action taken against the younger sibling will have unpleasant consequences.

Even with very basic ground rules, however, some combat is inevitable. Furthermore, when it erupts, you may not always be able to figure out who did what to whom or who was at fault. This problem often gives parents considerable grief, and you will need plenty of wisdom, prayer, and patience to deal with it. In

The rod of correction imparts wisdom, but a child left to himself disgraces his mother.

PROVERBS 29:15

general, your response will have to depend on the age of the children involved. With very young children, separation from one another and whatever they were fighting over will be your most common tactic. Remember that this age-group is not terribly responsive to logic and reason. Later on, more sophisticated ground rules, "rules of evidence" when stories contradict, and consequences that fit the crime will need to be carried out.

If there is a difference of a few years or more between children, the likelihood of conflict with a toddler will be reduced. Not only will the older child have her own circle of friends and interests, but depending on her age, she may serve, at least at times, as a caregiver. She should not, however, be given disciplinary authority or responsibilities that belong to you alone.

HEALTH ISSUES: CHECKUPS AND IMMUNIZATIONS

Your toddler should have a routine exam at age one, at fifteen and eighteen months, and at age two. As before, along with the normal gentle poking and prodding, his measurements will be taken and charted, and his developmental milestones (walking, etc.) should be reviewed. Remember to bring something to entertain your toddler in case you have to wait before the visit.

Don't expect a great deal of cooperation from your toddler during these exams. Typically the same physician who was greeted with coos a few months ago will now elicit howls of terror. Most of the exam will need to be done with your child sitting on your lap, and at times (such as when his ears are being checked) you will need to hold him still, pinning arms and head to your chest in an affectionate hammerlock. Occasionally, a more prolonged look into the ears will be needed, especially when wax needs to be cleared, and you may be asked to help keep your screaming and thrashing patient quite still on the exam table while this is going on. You will be impressed at how strong he is, how upset he sounds, and how guilty you feel. Remember, however, that he is experiencing far more fright than pain.

Everyone will have an easier time at the doctor's office if you can maintain a cheerful and confident demeanor throughout the visit. If your toddler senses that you are apprehensive or ambivalent about what is going on, his fright level may increase tenfold. When he cries or resists, don't plead with him to stop. Keep your voice mellow and reassuring, and your grip tight.

Between twelve and fifteen months of age, your child should receive his MMR immunization, which protects him from measles, mumps, and rubella. He may develop a fever or even a slight rash after seven to ten days, but more serious reactions are extremely unlikely. *If your child has shown a severe allergic reaction to eggs, notify the doctor ahead of time, since the production of the vaccine involves the use of egg products.* If necessary, consultation and testing by an allergist may be needed before the vaccine is given. If you are pregnant, it is safe for your child to receive the vaccine, as there are no reported cases of rubella being transmitted from toddler to mother as a result of the toddler's being immunized.

At fifteen to eighteen months, another diphtheria/tetanus/pertussis (DTaP) immunization will be due. In addition, he will probably receive another immunization against hemophilus influenza B bacteria. (The timing will depend on the particular type of vaccine used.) Between twelve and eighteen months your child's physician may also recommend a vaccine against chicken pox (varicella). Finally, if the third dose of polio or hepatitis B vaccine has not yet been given, it should be given between twelve and eighteen months.

IS IT TIME TO START POTTY TRAINING?

Probably not.

Some children may show signs that they are ready to learn this skill before the second birthday, and you may begin the process of training them if you desire. But most toddlers are still in the throes of discovering their place in the world and dealing with their emotions during this eventful year, and adding any pressure to get rid of diapers and use the toilet may create even more turmoil. Take your time.

NOTES
1. Ideally this would be a pediatric ophthalmologist—a physician who specializes in children's eye problems—although many ophthalmologists deal with all age-groups. Unless specially trained and equipped, your primary-care physician will not be able to determine the visual acuity of a one-year-old.
2. Don't try to fake her out with some sleight of hand, by the way. "Magic tricks" where items appear or disappear unexpectedly will confuse the toddler's budding sense of object permanence. Save the disappearing ball and card tricks for the older kids.
3. Burton L. White, Ph.D., *Raising a Happy, Unspoiled Child* (New York: Simon and Schuster, 1994), 161.

When Your Child Has a Fever

In order to function properly, the human body is intricately designed to maintain its internal (also called **core**) temperature within very narrow limits. The normal human core body temperature is 98.6°F (or 37°C), but temperatures as low as 96.8°F (36°C) or as high as 100.4°F (38°C) are not necessarily abnormal. Normal variations in body functions brought about by a child's biological clock can cause temperatures to be lower in the early morning and higher in the later afternoon and evening. A child who has been in vigorous perpetual motion will have a higher body temperature than one who has been resting quietly.

The control center for regulating temperature is in the **hypothalamus,** a structure at the base of the brain that governs a number of critical bodily functions. The hypothalamus monitors body temperature and balances heat production and heat loss to maintain the temperature within very narrow limits. This **set point** is much like the desired temperature that you set on your thermostat at home. Heat is increased by shivering and by constriction of blood vessels at the body surface, and it is lost through sweating, breathing more rapidly, and dilation of surface blood vessels.

WHAT IS FEVER, AND WHAT CAUSES IT?

A fever is an abnormal elevation of core temperature. Most medical practitioners define a fever as a temperature higher than 100.4°F taken rectally in an infant and in a toddler up to three years of age.

There are several important points to remember about fever:

- *A fever is not a disease in itself* but a sign that the body's regulation of temperature has temporarily changed. Fever in children is most commonly a response to infection, and it is now known to serve a useful purpose by stimulating activity of white blood cells and other functions in the immune system.
- While it is a significant sign of an illness in progress, *fever itself is rarely dangerous for an infant or child.* A persistent temperature of 106°F or higher can be harmful, but this level occurs only in unusual circumstances such as in an extremely hot environment or during a heatstroke. Fever generated by the hypothalamus in response to an infection only occasionally exceeds 105°F, but essentially never rises above 106°F. Even at this level a fever will not cause damage except in very unusual circumstances, although it will usually be accompanied by some general discomfort (especially headache or body aches).
- *The height of the temperature does not always indicate how serious the problem is.* An infant with roseola, for example, will typically be quite active and cheerful even with a temperature climbing past 104°F. Conversely, a baby or child can be gravely ill with a temperature that is much lower.
- Whether or not a fever is specifically treated, it may go up and down several times during the course of an illness. Some parents mistakenly fear that a fever will climb relentlessly if they don't take active measures to lower it.

Body temperature is elevated in three ways:

- *Elevation of the body's internal thermostat.* This is by far the most common mechanism. Chemical factors released by the body in response to invasion by viruses or bacteria can raise the set point of the hypo-thalamus, provoking shivering and other mechanisms that raise body temperature. Rare causes of a rise in set point are certain cancers (for example, leukemia) and illnesses such as arthritis syndromes, which generate inflammation within the body but are not infections.
- *Heat production exceeds heat loss.* This can occur if heat loss mechanisms are thwarted by high environmental temperature or even when a child is wearing too many layers of clothing. Uncommon disorders such as hyperthyroidism or an overdose of certain types of drugs (for example, aspirin) may cause the body to generate excessive heat.

♦ *Malfunction of the body's normal heat-loss mechanisms.* This may result from an overdose of certain drugs or from the syndrome known as **heatstroke**. This is also an uncommon reason for a child's fever.

WAYS TO MEASURE A CHILD'S TEMPERATURE

There will be many occasions during your child's life when you will need to determine her body temperature as accurately as possible. Even though the touch of your hand might suggest that your child is "burning up" or "cold and clammy," this impression based on surface temperature can be very misleading. Most fevers below 102°F cannot be detected this way, and children who feel warm to the touch are as likely to have a normal temperature as an elevated one. Plastic liquid-crystal strips placed on the forehead aren't much better and may miss a fever entirely. To obtain a reliable core temperature measurement, your best bet is to use a thermometer in one of these locations:

♦ *Rectal* temperature most accurately and reliably reflects core temperature, especially in infants and young children. It is typically 0.9°F (or 0.5°C) higher than oral temperature. *Measuring temperature rectally is specifically recommended for infants under three months of age,* for whom significant medical decisions may hinge on the numbers that are obtained.

♦ Taking an *oral* temperature is usually more convenient than a rectal temperature in older children (preschool age and older), assuming they can cooperate. It will be less reliable if the child is breathing through her mouth or has taken hot or cold liquids within ten minutes prior to the reading.

♦ Temperatures taken using a thermometer whose tip is held in a child's *armpit* (also called **axillary readings**) are not as reliable as those properly taken rectally or orally. However, they may be more accurate than a temperature taken improperly in an uncooperative child.

♦ *Ear* temperatures taken with special electronic thermometers are both quick and convenient, but they may be less accurate in infants and toddlers (see next page).

When talking to your physician, tell him the exact temperature and method used. Do not add or subtract a degree because this could make a significant difference in the care of your child, depending on his age.

TYPES OF THERMOMETERS

Glass (mercury) thermometers are inexpensive ($3 or $4), have no batteries that need replacing, and when properly used can provide a very accurate temperature reading. However, they don't work as quickly as digital or ear thermometers, and some people find them difficult to read. They also must be shaken down and cleaned with alcohol after each use.

Rectal glass thermometers, which have a short bulb-shaped tip, are used with infants and small children, while oral glass thermometers (with an elongated tip) are appropriate for children who can cooperate when the tip is placed under their tongue.

Digital thermometers use battery-driven heat sensors and take about thirty seconds to arrive at a reading (usually signaled by a beep), which is displayed on a small screen. They can be used to take temperatures orally, rectally, or under the arm. Typically costing about $10 or less, they come with a package of disposable polyethylene sleeves. A new sleeve should be used each time a temperature is taken, so you will need to maintain a supply of these if a digital thermometer is your preference.

Ear (tympanic membrane) thermometers can give an estimate of core temperature instantly by measuring the energy emitted from tiny blood vessels within the eardrum. Many doctors' offices and clinics utilize them because of their speed (less than two seconds to get a reading) and convenience, since very little cooperation is required from the child. In fact, these thermometers can be used when a child is asleep. However, the readings may be less accurate, especially in infants and toddlers, because of the children's smaller external ear canals; the reliability of the reading can also be affected by the position of the thermometer's tip within the ear. Another disadvantage of these devices is their cost of $60 or more.

TAKING A CHILD'S TEMPERATURE

When taking a rectal temperature, the infant or young child should be placed stomach-down across your lap. Lubricate the metallic tip of the thermometer with petroleum jelly and also put a little around the child's anus. Then gently insert the thermometer into the child's rectum about one inch. *Do not force the thermometer into the rectum.* Leave the thermometer in place for two or three minutes or until the temperature stops climbing in a mercury thermometer; then remove it and read the temperature.

When using an oral thermometer, the tip should be placed under the mid or back portion of either side of the tongue. The child should hold the thermometer steady with her lips and fingers, not with her teeth. Be sure your child is not biting down on the thermometer, which could cause it to break. The mouth should be closed, so she will need to breathe through her nose for two to three minutes until the mercury is no longer rising. (If her nose is extremely congested, she may need to take intermittent mouth breaths, or you might want to consider using a different method of checking her temperature.)

If you use an ear thermometer, be sure to follow the manufacturer's directions for proper use, being especially attentive to the position of the tip in your child's ear. During its first few uses you may want to compare your reading with a simultaneous temperature taken by a glass thermometer, in order to confirm that you are obtaining consistent readings.

If you are taking an armpit temperature, first make sure that this area is dry. (If damp, the reading could be inaccurately low.) Place the thermometer tip in the center of the armpit and hold the child's elbow against her chest until you hear the beep (for a digital thermometer) or for three minutes if using a glass thermometer.

WHAT TO DO IF YOUR CHILD HAS A FEVER

First, stay calm—which may be easier said than done if your child is very young—and then assess the situation. The actual height of the temperature is important, but equally significant are *the age of your child and what else is going on.* Before calling the doctor, determine if there are other symptoms such as coughing, runny nose, sore throat, rash, or (in children who can communicate) pain in some location.

Even more important is *the way your child is acting,* which will help you determine how urgent the problem is. A normal child will usually become somewhat irritable, less active, more clingy, and less hungry when a fever is present. (This shouldn't be surprising if you remember how you felt the last time you had a significant fever.) In a typical acute illness such as a cold, your child may act like her old self again when the fever subsides. With more serious infections, however, changes in behavior tend to be more profound, and if one or more of these are present, call the doctor immediately.

Most acute illnesses that generate a fever in infants and children are caused by viruses and will disappear on their own, while some illnesses may involve bacteria that will respond to specific antibiotic treatment. (Certain viral illnesses, such as influenza, may also improve more rapidly with treatment.) If the fever persists for more than twenty-four hours, a call to your child's physician and possibly an evaluation may help determine the problem. In addition, there are some other general measures that may be helpful.

Dress your infant or child in light clothing and keep her room at a comfortable temperature. Turning up the heat at home or bundling her up in hot clothes will not speed recovery, and doing so may actually keep her temperature elevated. If she is shivering, give her a light blanket for comfort. (Remember, though, that shivering is a process that will raise the body temperature.)

Give your sick child fluids of all kinds, since some body fluids will be lost during sweating. Appetite is typically reduced during an illness in which fever is present. Large or fatty meals should be avoided, since fever tends to slow movement of food through the digestive tract.

Your child does not need to be strictly confined to bed, but activities should be kept on the quiet side, since vigorous exertion might increase her temperature. If the illness is potentially contagious (and most viruses are), she should be kept away from other children or anyone (such as an elderly person) whose health might be jeopardized by an acute infection.

Sponge bathing an infant or child to bring down a fever is *not* necessary, except in unusual situations (such as heatstroke) where temperatures exceed 106°F. However, sponging might help her feel more comfortable, especially if her temperature is higher than 104°F. It is helpful to give a dose of acetaminophen or ibuprofen (see next page) at least thirty minutes before doing so to lower the set point of your child's thermostat. (Otherwise, she will simply shiver back to her original temperature.)

Set the child in an inch or two of lukewarm water (85°F to 90°F, which should feel just slightly warm to the touch). *Do not use cold water,* which will make her shiver (and thus raise her temperature), and *do not use rubbing alcohol,* which can be dangerous when absorbed through the skin or inhaled. Use a sponge or washcloth to keep body surfaces wet for thirty to forty-five minutes, during which time she will lose heat as water evaporates from her skin. You do not have to bring her temperature down to normal—lowering it a couple of degrees will help her feel better.

USING MEDICATIONS
TO LOWER TEMPERATURE

Three medications that are available without prescription can help reduce an infant's or child's fever. Before using them, keep these things in mind:

- The primary reason to give these drugs will normally be to make your child more comfortable. They will not make an infection disappear more quickly. If your child has a fever but is otherwise contented, you don't need to give her anything to make the fever go away.
- *The fever's response to any of these medications is not an indication of the severity of the illness.* One dose may only reduce the fever 2° or 3°F over a couple of hours, or it may merely limit the height of an upward temperature "spike." Don't panic if the thermometer reading doesn't drop right away or if it rises again after a few hours.
- *Do not give medication to lower fever to a baby under three months of age without contacting your physician.* In this age-group, determining the *cause* of the fever is far more important than lowering the temperature itself.

There are several medications on the market that can help lower fever:

- Acetaminophen (Tylenol, Panadol, Liquiprin, Tempra, and other brands) is available in a variety of oral and rectal suppository preparations and may be given every four hours as needed. While this medication has been widely and safely used for a number of years, an accidental overdose can be potentially dangerous.

    Most acetaminophen products list recommended doses based on age, but if possible, it is better to determine the dosage based on weight, especially if your infant or child is above or below average.
- Ibuprofen (Children's Motrin, Children's Advil, and other brands) has the potential advantage of a longer-lasting effect—six to eight hours per dose, as opposed to acetaminophen's four to six.
- Aspirin is effective in lowering temperature and relieving aches and pains *BUT it is not recommended for this purpose in anyone younger than twenty-one years of age* because of its link to an uncommon but serious disorder called **Reye's syndrome**.

Febrile Convulsions

Febrile convulsions—seizures precipitated by fever—occur in 2 to 5 percent of children sometime between four months and five years of age. These seizures often begin early in an acute illness, usually during the rapid upswing of a fever (which doctors refer to as a **spike**). In fact, an infant or child whom you find hot and cranky with a 104°F temperature is *not* likely to have a seizure in the immediate future because with rare exception she has already arrived at the high temperature without incident. (Temperature spikes tend to occur so quickly that it is unlikely that you will be able to take a temperature while one is actually taking place.)

Caregivers: Who Will Care for Your Child While You Are Away?

Even if you are the most dedicated and attentive parent(s) on earth, you cannot (and indeed should not) provide hands-on care for your child twenty-four hours a day, seven days a week, from the delivery room to the college dormitory. Many times during your child rearing career you will need to release her to the temporary care of another person. Whether this involves an occasional time-out to run errands or a routine of several hours every workday, transferring responsibility for your child to someone else raises many questions:

- How do you choose a caregiver?
- Is it better for your child if the caregiver comes to your home, or is it okay to take her elsewhere (such as to another home or day-care center)?
- How long is it appropriate for you to be away from your child?

Without question these are extremely important topics. Like many other concerns of parenting (such as discipline), there is no surefire formula that will apply to every family or even to one family through the development of all its children. What follows therefore are a few basic—but very important—overriding principles.

Child-care issues overall cluster around two major situations:

- Extended periods of child care on a regular basis, usually occurring when both parents (or a single parent) are employed outside the home.
- Short-term or episodic care, commonly referred to as baby-sitting, which is discussed at the end of this section (page 175).

The first of these concerns—and the question of whether the mother of one or more young children should be employed outside of the home—is by far the more complicated, emotional, and controversial of the two.

WORKING IN AND OUT OF THE HOME

Whether you are a young couple enthusiastically welcoming the first baby to your nest, seasoned parents with a home full of children of all ages, a blended family, or a single mom or dad, you must deal with some of the following issues:

- How much income does the family need, and where will it come from?
- How will we divide labor in the home? Will one parent be the main income producer while the other's primary role is caring for children? Or will both parents share more equally in these tasks?
- How will bringing up one or more children mesh with one or both parents' work schedule, not to mention education and career plans?
- Is it wise for both mother and father to work outside the home? If this is done, who is going to take care of the child(ren)?
- How can a single mother or father best cope with the simultaneous demands of earning a living and rearing children?

Every family will have different circumstances that affect the answer to these questions:

- Age, abilities, and temperament of each child
- The state of the marital union or the absence of a marriage partner
- Educational background
- Job/professional skills
- Financial resources
- Relationships with immediate and extended family members
- Involvement with a church community
- Goals, plans, and dreams for the future

For some parents there will be many ways to approach these questions. For others, options are very limited and the answers will be defined by current circumstances. Most single parents, for example, have the daunting dual role of primary income provider and full-time parent. There is no standard solution that will work for every family or even for one family throughout its entire lifetime. But when thinking through these very important and often emotionally charged questions, it is important to keep some broad perspectives and reality checks in mind.

Faulty expectations, identity, and the "end of life" test

Much discontent over the question of balancing child rearing and career(s)—for both mothers and fathers—can arise from several powerful but faulty expectations:

The expectation that rearing one or more children won't require considerable effort or many changes in lifestyle. An infant cannot be fed and changed and then left to her own devices, nor can an older child be expected to grow up on her own. Not only must a child's basic health and safety be assured, but her intellectual and emotional development requires continuous monitoring and frequent interaction with adults who are deeply committed to her.

The expectation that a certain lifestyle is necessary for happiness. With rare exception, whatever standard of living young parents envision for themselves in the immediate or distant future will probably require more income than expected. Remember Murphy's Law of Money: Everything costs more than you expect—both to purchase and to maintain. The belief that a particular home or car, travel, and certain experiences are necessary for contentment in life can push the budgetary limits to the point that a second income becomes a necessity. But this could have the ultimate effect of trading irreplaceable interactions with one's own children for material goods that will eventually be worn out and discarded.

The expectation that mother can be Supermom, effortlessly managing a career, nurturing children, and experiencing extraordinary marital satisfaction—all with great style and finesse. TV commercials and magazine ads have helped create this fantasy, which more often than not leads to frustration, guilt, and, most of all, fatigue. There may be a few true Supermoms around, but the other 99 percent who are more earthbound usually realize that they must accept a number of compromises at home and/or work in order to survive.

An issue more often but not always for women: The expectation that being at home will result in the evaporation of one's intellect and ambition. Women have received this message from numerous voices, including popular media, friends and acquaintances who work outside the home, even insensitive husbands and family members who either don't understand or have forgotten what is involved in running a household and nurturing children. The decision to remain at home is often made at considerable sacrifice, and many women find themselves disadvantaged later when they try to reenter the outside marketplace after a few years' absence from it. However, to assume that staying home with the children will erode a woman's mental or professional powers is to subscribe to an extremely narrow view of life.

The rewards of participating significantly in a child's development cannot be measured. A parent who chooses to stay home is aware that her children will only be home for a season and that her impact on their intellect, development, and values will probably continue for decades. Rearing children is a career that requires a host of skills as well as insight, patience, and wisdom.

The world of work is changing to accommodate parents who have decided to spend more time with their children. An increasing number of options for working part-time or from a home office are making it possible for both moms and dads to be with their children more often and more consistently. Many women for whom an outside career or interest is important have created satisfying professional options for themselves from within the home setting. These are encouraging developments, both for women who want to pursue a career outside the home (whether now or in the future) and for women who are content to make home their career but who want to pursue artistic or community interests.

An issue more often but not always for men: The expectation that the career track defines identity and that all other concerns pale in comparison. Men are notorious for defining themselves in terms of their occupation and position. (How often do you hear a father answer the question "What do you do?" with "I'm Trevor and Amanda's dad"?) But the danger of this orientation is that the demands of a career and the "pursuit of excellence" at work can result in rampant absenteeism from home and mediocrity in parenting. Many fathers and mothers buy into the myth that a few minutes of time spent with one's children every day is just fine, as long as it's "quality time." But will a one-ounce steak be satisfying because it is "quality steak"? Or (perhaps more relevant for men) will sex every six months be adequate because it is "quality sex"?

Both mothers and fathers need to think very carefully about these issues. The truth is, *a true and lasting sense of worth, identity, and satisfaction comes ultimately from being present and accounted for in God's family and going about His business every day.* In the final analysis, these qualities are not derived from the initials after one's name, the title on one's door, the plaques on the walls, or the money in the bank. They do not come from being CEO of Universal Widget or having a home that is the envy of the neighborhood—or having kids who are perfect. Parents must beware of the "If only . . ." syndrome: "If only ____, then I'd be satisfied/content/happy." These are the longings of those who are perpetually restless and discontented, who never fill the gaping hole remaining in their lives, no matter how often they successfully accomplish last month's "If only . . ."

The "end of life" test. Parents who are making decisions about who will rear their children should ask themselves an important question: When you are staring down death's corridor, what in your life will really matter? Will you look back fondly at the hours spent at the office and pine over the fact that you weren't there longer? You may be the world's greatest Monopoly player—on the game table or in the real world—but eventually you will have to fold up the board, put the money back in the box, and put it in the closet. No one will remember for very long who won the game, but those who were at the table with you will long recall whether their time with you was pleasant or miserable.

More specifically, will your children arrive at your bedside and thank you for all the career goals you accomplished? They will probably remember most fondly and thank you for the times you spent with them—rocking them, listening to them, wrestling on the carpet, having lunch at their favorite restaurant, going fishing, walking on the beach, or helping them out of a jam. At that moment, what will matter most will be the people you care about, the lives you have touched, and the prospect of hearing, "Well done, my good and faithful servant."

Best and second best

These considerations are not intended to incite great pangs of guilt nor to say that careers launched from within or outside the home are somehow evil. They are, however, meant to raise serious questions about priorities, about what *really* matters, and to lay the foundation for the following observations.

While children are growing up, they should be cared for primarily by people who are *passionately and sacrificially committed to them.* In the vast majority of cases, the people who best fit this description are their own parents. However, grandparents, other relatives, or close friends may feel this way too.

People who are hired to take care of other people's children can and should be responsible, mature, kind, and attentive—but they will rarely be passionately and sacrificially committed to those children. Most paid caregivers are probably not going to develop a deep emotional bond or a relationship with a child that will last for years.

If at all possible, then, it is most desirable for children to spend the majority of their waking hours with one of their own parents or with someone else who has an equally intense commitment—especially during the first few years of life when children are dealing with basic issues of security and trust.

This will not always be possible for a variety of reasons. If it isn't and your child is going to spend a significant amount of time in the care of others, your energy should be expended not on guilt but on finding the best possible caregiver arrangements, a process that will be reviewed in the next section. As much as possible, continually seek ways to arrange schedules and time commitments that will maximize parental time with each child at home.

SEEKING A CAREGIVER

Assuming that your child is going to be spending time on a regular basis with a caregiver other than one of her parents, what options are available?

In-home care: the caregiver comes to your child

This person might be a relative such as a grandparent, a nanny that you hire for an extended period, or perhaps a college student or *au pair* from another country who provides care in exchange for room and board. There are several advantages of in-home care:

- Your child remains in a completely familiar environment—with access to his own crib or bed, toys, yard, etc.
- Assuming that the same person comes to your home regularly, there will be greater stability and consistency in your child's life.
- The caregiver's attention is focused specifically on your child(ren), rather than on a larger group.
- There is no exposure to contagious diseases from other children. If your child becomes ill, care does not have to be interrupted or rearranged.
- Convenience is maximized—there is no need to transport your child and the items she needs to another home or facility.
- Depending upon the caregiver's availability, there may be more flexibility in this arrangement; your home doesn't have "closing hours."

Disadvantages of in-home care are as follows:

- If you are hiring the caregiver, in-home care is likely to be more costly. In this case, the individual will in effect be your employee, so you will need to be aware of possible tax implications and even liability concerns. (For example, who pays the bills if the caregiver is injured in your home? Your homeowner's insurance may or may not cover such expenses.)

♦ What do you do if the caregiver is ill or can't come for some other reason? You will always need to have Plan B ready in case such a problem arises.

Family child care: your child stays in the caregiver's home

In this arrangement, an individual (or perhaps a couple) provides care in his or her home for a number of children who may be of similar or widely variable ages. (If the caregiver is a devoted relative who is responsible only for your child(ren), this situation may be essentially the equivalent of in-home care.) The advantages of family child care include:

♦ Your child remains in a home rather than a "facility" environment. If the family is someone you and your child already know, there will be some familiarity (and perhaps less separation anxiety).

♦ As with the in-home arrangement, having the same caregiver every day will provide consistency in your child's experiences.

♦ There are likely to be fewer children than in a day-care center, and thus less exposure to contagious diseases.

♦ Costs are sometimes less than for in-home care or a day-care facility.

♦ As with care in your own home, there is often more flexibility with hours.

Disadvantages of family child care include the following:

♦ There may be no licensing requirements for family caregivers in your state. In this case, you will need to rely more heavily on your own assessment of the caregiver and the home environment to determine if all is safe and sound. (Obviously, it is helpful if you know the family beforehand.)

♦ Plans may have to be rearranged (sometimes without warning) if the caregiver becomes ill, has an unexpected family problem, or simply goes on vacation.

♦ If the caregiver is responsible for several children, you will need to determine if she or he can give adequate attention to your child and not become overwhelmed.

Facility child care: your child stays at a day-care center operated by a church, university, or commercial entity

There are several advantages to this type of child care:

♦ These are normally licensed and thus accountable to regulations regarding the facility and the staff. These places may have extremely well-trained employees, age-appropriate learning programs, and physical resources (such as playground equipment) not available in homes.

• Facilities normally have predictable staffing and hours of operation. You will not need to make sudden adjustments because a caregiver is ill or unavailable.

• If care is provided by a church whose beliefs you share, your child might be exposed to songs, stories, and other input that build spiritual and moral values.

The disadvantages of facility child care include:

• Day-care centers sometimes have relatively large child-to-staff ratios so that individual attention for your child is in short supply.

• If the facility does not offer competitive wages, it might not attract well-trained or attentive staff. Staff turnover in some centers can be rapid, leading to unpredictable relationships between the children and their adult caregivers.

• Infections are spread much more easily among groups of children who are interacting at close range and handling the same toys. Both upper-respiratory infections (including middle-ear infection) and diarrhea are more frequent among children in day-care centers.

• While hours of operation are more predictable, they might not be very flexible. What happens if you are stuck in traffic or experience some other delay at the end of the day?

All things being equal, if care is provided on a regular, ongoing basis by someone other than a parent, the order of preference for choosing a caregiver would be as follows:

1. One or more relatives, either in your home or in theirs
2. A nonrelative in your home, such as a nanny or a live-in
3. Nonrelatives in a home setting
4. Large-group day care in a facility

This ranking is based on several key assumptions:

• A relative is more likely to be attached and attentive to your child than a nonrelative would be.

• A stable, predictable situation is more desirable than one in which there is constant change.

- If there are fewer children for each caregiver, your child is likely to receive more individual attention.
- Infections are less common among small numbers of children than in large-group settings and even less frequent in your own home.

As with so many other parenting concerns, there are always exceptions to these guidelines. For example:

- A conscientious nonrelative is preferable to an irresponsible family member.
- A large day-care center that is well maintained and staffed by adults who love children is preferable to a home setting that is unsanitary and poorly supervised.
- A caregiver that you hire to stay in your home may not necessarily devote herself to your child's well-being while you are gone.

If you need, but do not yet have, child care available, ask some trusted friends or coworkers for suggestions or referrals. Your church might have references or a bulletin board listing caregivers in your community. Newspaper and yellow-page listings are also possibilities, although with these you do not have the advantage of a specific recommendation. Ultimately you must survey the options available to you and then consider carefully which might best meet your family's needs. In doing so you will need to keep three factors in balance:

1. Is your child likely to thrive in this situation? How closely will the care duplicate (or at least resemble) the way *you* care for your child at home?
2. How well will the availability and location of the caregiver mesh with your own schedule and daily logistics?
3. Are the child-care arrangements affordable?

There are also specific considerations for infants and toddlers. A baby's physical and intellectual development, as well as emotional security, requires *ongoing* adult attention. Infants need mental, emotional, and physical stimulation; they should not be left lying or sitting for hours in a crib or playpen. They need to be changed when wet, comforted when crying, and played with when awake and comfortable. They should be hand-fed; propping a bottle in an infant's mouth creates a risk of choking and of ear infections. (If you are looking into a center that provides care for infants, check to see if there are a number of comfortable chairs in which adults can hold and feed babies.)

Mobile babies and toddlers need room to explore—safely. They can neither be confined to a small enclosure nor allowed to roam far and wide without supervision. Their attention can shift as rapidly as their mood, and they are not capable of playing cooperatively with other children.

In order to give adequate attention to the needs and development of infants and toddlers, there should be:

- at least one caregiver for every three children younger than two years of age. If at all possible each infant or toddler should have a main caregiver— that is, someone with whom she has an ongoing and consistent relationship.
- at least one caregiver for every four children between two and three years of age.
- at least one caregiver for every eight children between three and six years of age.

With these basic principles clearly in mind, you must also evaluate several aspects of any potential child-care arrangement, including short-term (baby-sitting) care:

The person or people involved (This is the most important.) *You should get to know those who are going to be responsible for your child's welfare.* Don't hesitate to request one or more interviews, and take the time to observe the caregiver's interactions with your own child as well as with other children.

- Does the caregiver appear comfortable, relaxed, and pleasant with children?
- How well does the caregiver interact with *you?*
- What prior experience does the caregiver have?
- Are references available?

If you are dealing with group care in a home or day-care center, ask the following questions about the staff before you make your decision:

- Who is in charge, and what are her or his credentials?
- What is the ratio of children to caregivers?
- If assistants are used, are they at least fourteen years old and properly supervised?
- Is everyone trained in child CPR?

The child-care setting (assuming it is not your own home) Before choosing the best facility for your situation, look at the following:

- Is it clean, cheerful, and attractive to you and your child?
- Do tables, chairs, and other equipment appear to be in good repair?

- Are there any potential safety problems?
- Are electrical outlets covered?
- Are smoke detectors and fire extinguishers present?
- Are heating, air-conditioning, and overall ventilation adequate?
- Are cleaning supplies, medications, and other hazardous products inaccessible to children?
- Are appropriate toys available?
- Is the outdoor play area properly fenced and secured?
- Are enough mats, cots, cribs, or beds available for naps?
- Is there an area specifically designated for diaper changing? Is it cleaned after each use? Is it anywhere near where food is prepared?
- Are pets present? Are they child-friendly? Is your child allergic to animals?

Philosophy, policies, and programs (in day-care centers or group home care)
Consider the following when choosing your facility:

- Are there written policies and procedures you can review?
- Is the basic worldview of the caregiver or facility compatible with yours?
- Will the values you teach at home be honored?
- Is there any spiritual input for older children?
- What is the caregiver's outlook on training and discipline?
- Are the disciplinary policies delineated and followed by all caregivers?
- Does there appear to be an appropriate balance between love and limits in dealing with behavior problems?
- What types of measures are used to maintain order?
- Is disciplinary spanking ever carried out, and if so, under what circumstances?
- Is disruptive or destructive behavior handled appropriately?
- If you observe a child's behavior being corrected, is it done with respect?
- Are children adequately supervised at all times?
- What kind of food is offered to children?
- Are activities planned and available for older children?
- Do these activities enhance learning and overall development?
- Are arts and crafts available?
- Is there excessive reliance on TV or other passive activities?
- Are there opportunities for physical exertion and outdoor play?
- What happens when a child is ill?
- Do children who are sick remain in contact with those who are not?

- Are the caregivers willing and able to give prescribed medications to infants and children?
- Are parents encouraged to drop in at any time to see how things are going? (*This is very important.* Be wary of any place where your access to your child or the facility is discouraged or restricted.)
- Is the caregiving situation appropriately secure?
- Are there clear policies regarding releasing children to adults who are not their parents?
- Can the facility prevent unauthorized individuals from entering?

RED FLAGS

While stable and nurturing child care is desirable, *safe* child care is an absolute necessity. Injuries resulting from adult carelessness, physical or sexual abuse, or assaults on a child's emotions are a parent's nightmare—and all are unacceptable in any setting. Unfortunately, signs of neglect or wrongdoing may not be especially obvious, and even if they are, it can be impossible to prove that the caregiver was at fault. Nevertheless, you will need to keep your eyes and ears wide-open for any of these potential indicators of trouble:

- Does your child become unusually upset or fearful about being left with a particular caregiver?
- Does the caregiver appear impatient, irritable, or stressed?
- Has your child become more withdrawn or shown other signs of not being herself after spending time with a caregiver?
- Have you discovered unexplained bruises, welts, or other marks on your child's body?
- Has your child exhibited inappropriate language or sexual behavior?
- Do you feel uneasy whenever you leave your child with a particular caregiver?
- Are you discouraged from dropping in on the caregiver unannounced?
- If you have made an unexpected visit, have you found things in disarray, children improperly supervised or extremely upset?

If you observe one or more of these red flags, you should strongly consider removing your child from that situation until you can determine with greater certainty what is best in the long run. You may need to speak candidly to the caregiver about what you have observed and see if the response you receive is appropriate, evasive, or overtly hostile. If you believe that your or someone else's child has been abused in a child-care setting, you should contact your nearest child-protection agency and explain your concerns. Even if you are not certain whether abuse has actually taken place, it is their job to investigate more fully and take appropriate action if needed.

BABY-SITTERS

While it is vitally important to be diligent regarding the choice of a long-term caregiver for your child, it is also important to be careful about your choice of baby-sitters, even though the time your child spends in their care may be considerably shorter. During the first six months of your child's life, it is best to leave her in the hands of experienced relatives or other adults. As your child grows older, however, younger baby-sitters can be utilized. Indeed, some of the best baby-sitters you may find will be students in high school or middle school. (Most states require that a baby-sitter be at least twelve years old if he or she is going to be unsupervised. Check your local statutes.) In many communities, hospitals or other organizations offer short courses (including CPR training) for baby-sitters, and those who have completed such a program could be excellent candidates for you to consider.

It is best to build a roster of trustworthy baby-sitters before you actually need one. Ask other mothers of young children whom they recommend and why. Responsibility, experience, and good rapport with young children are important qualities to seek. You might find some excellent sitters and have a chance to see them in action in the church nursery or Sunday school.

Once you have potential candidates, it is helpful to spend time with each one in your home. If possible, have him or her watch your child while you do some other work at home. This will give you a chance to observe how the sitter interacts with your child; it will also allow your child time to become familiar with the baby-sitter, thus reducing separation anxiety (if the child is old enough to manifest it) when you leave.

When you leave your child with a sitter, always leave the address and phone number of the location(s) where you can be reached, along with the number of your doctor, the local hospital, and another relative or friend who will be home in case you can't be reached. You might want to invest in a pager to allow you more geographical flexibility.

Let the baby-sitter know when you expect to be home and what you expect to happen while you're gone—including feeding, bathing, and bedtime routines. If a child needs medication, make sure the baby-sitter knows exactly how much and when to give it. The sitter should also know any other family rules, such as those applying to TV or video watching, as well as any reliable ways to comfort your child when you leave. The baby-sitter should allow no visitors into your home unless you have made prior arrangements. If it helps you feel comfortable, check in with the sitter by phone after you've been gone awhile to find out how things are going.

Make sure that your pay rate is clear from the start. Ask a friend what the going rate is for each age-group and don't hesitate to offer more for the best sitter on your list. If you would like the sitter to clean up dishes or straighten up elsewhere in the home, offer to pay a little extra.

If your child is old enough to understand, tell her that you are leaving and you will be back. Don't sneak out when she isn't looking, and don't be pulled into a long, emotional parting scene. Your child will survive and, with rare exception, will calm down shortly after you leave. Enjoy the night out!

A Final Note: Who Will Provide Care If You Are Gone . . . for Good?

Planning for a disaster is never enjoyable. But an accident during even the most routine errand might unexpectedly leave your child(ren) without one or both parents. If such a tragedy were to take place, who would care for your children, and how would their material needs be met?

All parents must consider this possibility, carefully decide whom they would want to care for their children—along with a number of other financial, practical, and spiritual considerations—and then express their desires in a legally binding document. The specific steps involved in the preparation of a will or a living trust are beyond the scope of this book and should be reviewed with an attorney who is well versed in estate planning.

What matters most is that parents not succumb to the notion that "it can't happen to me/us" but instead take the proper measures to provide for their children should the unthinkable happen.

Principles of
Discipline and Training:
Balancing Love and Limits

Discipline: Training and instruction that is intended to produce a specific pattern of behavior, character development, and moral or mental improvement. (From the Latin *discipulus:* "pupil," derived from *discere:* "to learn.")

Mention the word *discipline* in connection with rearing children, and images of various forms of punishment may come to mind. *But discipline encompasses the entire process of shaping and molding a child's attitudes and behaviors over the years that he or she is entrusted to your care.* This project is deserving of your diligence, fervor, humility, and prayer.

Training your children cannot be approached in a careless or haphazard manner because, left to their own devices, children rarely gravitate toward virtuous behavior, selfless attitudes, and responsible decisions. If these are not learned at home during thousands of interactions with parents and other family members, they may never be learned at all—to the detriment of the child and everyone around him.

But you don't need to live in a state of constant anxiety, wondering whether one false move on your part will unleash a career criminal years later. The discipline of children involves an overall mind-set rather than a cookbook full of behavioral recipes ("If he does this, you should do that"). Discipline can include a variety of techniques and approaches that vary depending upon the child's age and temperament. And what brings about a desired result with one child may prove to be a dismal flop with a sibling. While you will want to have an overall plan in mind, you will have to improvise along the way.

The subject of training and discipline often raises a lot of questions, concerns, and even controversy. For example:

How do I sort out all the input and advice I get, including the impact of my own upbringing? Your approach to discipline will be influenced significantly by your own experiences as a child or adolescent. You may even overcompensate for extremes that have affected you. If you were treated harshly as a child, you may tend toward being permissive, and vice versa. You will also receive plenty of advice (some more worthwhile than others) from relatives and friends, books and magazines, sermons, radio and TV programs, child rearing classes, and your child's physician. You will have to choose wisely from these resources, separate the wheat from the chaff, and try to avoid becoming a "Method of the Month Club" parent.

Am I too rigid or too lenient? If you don't worry about this question once in a while, you may be at risk for extreme or unhealthy discipline patterns.

How early can or should discipline begin? Based on developmental milestones, you can't expect a baby under eight months of age to follow directions, although certain behaviors (such as day and night sleeping patterns) may be shaped by parents. As your baby becomes mobile, you will need to begin establishing and enforcing limits through a variety of approaches. If you haven't started some basic molding and training of your child by eighteen months, you're off to a late start.

Why is it so difficult? And why does my child keep challenging me? Sometimes (or perhaps most of the time) bringing up children seems at best loaded with uncertainty, at worst a perpetual uphill struggle. Why? Because each child is a unique creation, a person with a mind, spirit, and will of his own. Children are not built like cars or computers; they do not arrive with instruction manuals that guarantee that *B* will happen if you do *A*. Nor do they enter your life as "blank slates" whose thoughts and actions are completely determined by whatever input you provide at home. While many of their behaviors are predictable in general terms, they are not little robots who will automatically yield to your direction.

Some children who are endowed with a particularly strong will seem bent on bucking everyone who crosses their path—beginning in the delivery room. If you have been blessed with one of these children, don't panic, and don't give up. You won't be the first parent in your neighborhood to bring up a strong-willed child, and as you continue to shape that powerful will, you may well see not only an adolescent who resists peer pressure but later a young adult who has become an effective leader.

What about disciplinary spanking or other physical punishment? This question, which will be reviewed in some detail later on, has become increasingly controversial in recent years. Some parents use spanking (a form of corporal punishment) too frequently, too severely, and too long into childhood. A few parents abuse their children in the name of discipline. In response to these harmful extremes, many authors and organizations have concluded that *all* physical discipline, including disciplinary spanking, is inappropriate. But this position is also extreme. At the right time, for the right reasons, and with the right safeguards, spanking can be a useful tool in rearing young children.

EXTREMES IN DISCIPLINE: WHAT NOT TO DO

No mother or father disciplines children with absolute perfection, and like every other parent in the world, you will make mistakes. You may say or do something that you later regret, or you may neglect one or more worthwhile aspects of the training process. But parenting involves a long learning curve, and children brought up in an environment where it is clear that they are deeply loved will be resilient in the face of numerous parental errors. Nevertheless, stay away from patterns of missteps and omissions that could have a lasting negative impact on your child. If any of the following have taken root in your home, remember that it's never too late to make midcourse corrections.

Physical abuse. Punching, slapping, whipping, burning, and other horrors inflicted upon children are *not* discipline. They are abuse and have no place in the rearing of a son or daughter. They do not serve to benefit the child in any way; they do serve as unhealthy ways for a parent to vent anger. These behaviors indicate a basic defect in the parent's communication skills, the parent's lack of respect for the child's body and emotions, and a gross misunderstanding of a parent's responsibilities. If this type of violence has occurred in your home, seek counseling immediately to prevent further damage. Such help is especially important if you received this sort of treatment as a child, because abusive patterns may continue through generations unless someone has the courage to break the cycle.

Verbal thrashing. Even if you don't throw sticks and stones or break any bones, your words can hurt your children. Harsh, degrading, insulting language—"You are so stupid," "I'm disgusted with you," "You little jerk"—burns its way into the memory and emotions of a child. While physical abuse scars the body, verbal abuse scars the mind and heart, and neither is a proper exercise of parental authority. It is important to seek counseling to rein in these verbal beatings and stop the abuse.

Authoritarianism. This rigid micromanagement of childhood behavior stresses pure obedience without any understanding or internalization of principles. There may be times when you need to declare, "Because I'm the mom, that's why!" But demanding knee-jerk submission in every detail of life will wear thin as the years pass. You can probably impose this regime on your children when they are younger, but as they reach adolescence, their rebellion will be a certainty—and probably will be spectacular.

Management by yelling and screaming. Some parents arrive at the mistaken conclusion that their children will respond to them only when they raise their voices in anger. This idea usually develops over time through many repetitions of a scenario in which a parent's direction is ignored by a child—and nothing is done about it. When this pattern is fully developed, a child will have learned to gauge accurately when Mom or Dad is likely to take action.

Typically, after five or six requests or orders have been ignored, the parent's voice becomes more forceful, words are clipped, and the child's middle name is used: "John Patrick Smith, you get into that tub NOW!" The child has calculated that something unpleasant is likely to occur at this point and heads for the bathroom. The parent comes to believe that anger got the desired results, and he or she may resort to it more frequently. In fact, it wasn't the anger, but *action* (or the likelihood of it) that got the child moving.

Eventually, if action doesn't always follow the angry words, a child may learn to ignore even the most intense outbursts. This not only dilutes the effectiveness of all other communication within the family but may lead to a disaster in an emergency. (Imagine a child chasing a ball into the street unaware of the truck bearing down on him and ignoring, as always, his parent yelling at him to stop.)

Idle threats. Many parents attach threats of dire consequences to the orders they give a child: "You'd better not _____, *or else!*" But if the child repeatedly disobeys and *"or else"* never happens, she will learn that a lot of what Mom or Dad says is just hot air. This may escalate to some form of home terrorism; a frustrated parent whose warnings aren't taken seriously may increase the verbal artillery to abusive levels or become enraged to the point of finally making good on some extravagant threat. As with "management by yelling," it is action and consequences early in the game, and not threats alone, that motivate children to follow directions.

Laissez-faire parenting: little or no adult input or involvement. This occurs when one or both parents are too busy, overwhelmed, tired, or indifferent to set and enforce consistent limits. A child who is left more or less to his own devices will probably not be very relaxed and happy, but rather quite unsettled, because the boundaries that provide security are missing. Even though most kids push and shove against limits, they will become surprisingly anxious if few or none are present.

Nonstop bribery. Rewards have a definite place in training children, but parents should not haggle or make deals over every direction they give a child—especially those that are not negotiable. It would be quite inappropriate to say, "I'll give you a cookie if you get in your car seat." A child should not become used to the idea that virtue is only worthwhile if there's a prize attached. Moral values eventually need to be internalized, not merely bought and sold.

"Democratic" parenting. One of the great cultural follies of our times is the belief (often expressed with humanitarian fervor) that parents and children should have equal say in all matters and that a mother or father has no right to exert any parental authority over a child. A variation on this theme occurs when a parent is unwilling or unable to override a child's drives and desires, usually out of fear of rejection, an unwillingness to deal with conflict, or the mistaken notion that anything that causes an infant or child to become upset is terribly harmful.

But conflict is inevitable in any long-term human relationship, including the one between parent and child. Misguided attempts to keep a child from experiencing any unhappiness by routinely giving in to her every desire will ensure that she is miserable and unpleasant. Respect for a child's identity and feelings is important. But someone needs to be in charge while she is growing up, and for everyone's sake, it should not be the child.

Overt permissiveness. This is a more extreme and naive version of democratic parenting; it is assumed that children are born bundled with "virtue software." They are thus seen as innocent little "clean slates" who may even possess moral qualities their elders have lost. According to this misguided viewpoint, while they might be corrupted by a negative environment, children in a nurturing setting do not need correction. Some parents tolerate a great deal of disrespectful and destructive behavior in their young children based on the assumption that they are "getting it out of their system." Unpleasant surprises during late childhood and early adolescence await those who adopt this approach.

SIX BASIC PRINCIPLES OF DISCIPLINE

1. Balance love and limits.

Balance expressions of love—physical affection, kind words, comfort, help—with appropriate boundaries and consequences. Children cannot survive without experiencing consistent and unconditional love. From the first day of life through her journey into adulthood, your child must know that your love is rock solid, the foundation from which she can safely and confidently explore her world. This message summarizes the essence of unconditional love:

> You are loved, you are important, and you always will be, no matter what happens. I care enough about you to provide for you, stand with you, coach you, correct you, and even die for you if necessary. My commitment to you is not based on what you do or don't do, how you look, whether your body is perfect or handicapped, or how you perform in school or sports. It is based on the fact that I am your parent and you are my child, a priceless gift that God has loaned to me for a season. Eventually I will release you to live your own life, but while you are growing up, I consider caring for you an assignment of utmost importance.

Children also need, and actually fervently seek, boundaries and ground rules. Expressing love and enforcing limits are not contradictory but intimately related. Allowing a child to have her way without any restraint is not an expression of love. At the other extreme, harsh, rigid, or authoritarian treatment of children, even if it produces apparent model citizens, isn't an appropriate exercise of limit setting either.

2. Parents must assume leadership in the home.

For a variety of reasons—whether the nonstop attention required to rear infants and small children, fatigue, distractions, or one or more strong-willed children at home—it is possible for parents to find themselves struggling simply to maintain order and manage the demands of daily life. After a few or several years, the children may set the family's agenda and even drift into a general disrespect or disregard for the parents' authority. This is an unhealthy state of affairs for three reasons:

- Children lack the wisdom, knowledge, experience, and capabilities to train and nurture themselves.
- Children will not gain the skills and responsibility to live independently as adults without ongoing direction from parents who require that the children learn and do things that don't come naturally.
- Children want to know and will ask in a variety of ways, "Who's in charge here?" If the answer is "I guess I am," the result will be uncontrollable, disruptive, and generally unhappy children.

The critical importance of establishing your right to lead is central to the next two principles.

3. Distinguish among normal behavior, childish irresponsibility, and willful defiance—all of which need your guidance and correction but in different ways.

- The normal explorations of infants and toddlers should be encouraged—but in a manner that is safe for themselves and their surroundings.
- Throughout your child's years at home, you will have to deal with numerous episodes of childish irresponsibility—knocking over the milk, leaving your saw out in the rain, losing her new gloves, forgetting his lunch, not feeding the cat, leaving toys strewn all over the living room.

  These actions need correction, but they usually do not represent a direct challenge to your authority. A steady diet of rewards, consequences, and lots of patience will gradually introduce your child to responsible behavior over a period of several years.

- On specific occasions (with some children, on a regular basis), however, the issue will be willful defiance. This can begin surprisingly early (between fifteen and eighteen months of age), may continue through adolescence, or become relatively rare by the grade-school years.

  Willful defiance takes place when your child (1) knows and clearly understands what you want (or don't want) to happen, (2) is capable of doing what you want, and (3) refuses to do so.

  Whether passive or "in your face," the child's defiance is asking several questions: Do Mom and Dad really mean business? What's going to happen if I don't do what they want? Are they tough enough to make me? Who's really in charge here?

  When confronted with such a situation, act clearly and decisively, meeting the challenge head-on. Not only must your child not have his way, but his attitude about what he has done must be turned around as well. When the conflict is over, you should be on the same team once again. You don't need to be harsh or hostile, but you must not back down. If you do not establish your right to lead early in the game (by the age of two or three at the latest), your ability to influence or control your child later on will be seriously compromised.

At times it may be difficult to tell whether your child is being defiant or irresponsible. Did he hear you? Did he understand clearly what you wanted? Can he actually accomplish it? Failing to get straight A's is not defiance. But refusing to shut off the TV and sit down with the books after being told to do so probably is. When dealing with willful defiance, the child's attitude is the central issue. As Dr. James Dobson has noted in a memorable adage, "If he's looking for a fight, don't disappoint him." This doesn't refer to having a literal brawl with your child, of course, but rather to a consistent posture of standing your ground when your authority has been clearly challenged.

4. Accept the fact that conflict between parent and child is inevitable.

Whether dealing with a full-blown showdown or managing a series of minor irritations, it is impossible to avoid conflict with your child at some point. Effective, loving parenting is characterized not by the absence of conflict but by the resolution of conflicts in ways that maintain both your leadership and your child's dignity.

5. Love and concern for the child's best interests must be your final guide.

The effort required to give good discipline is a continuous expression of love, and that love may take you in some unexpected directions. It may lead you to allow a child to suffer some consequences for his irresponsibility, even when you might easily bail him out. If he repeatedly forgets to take his lunch to school, letting him feel hunger for a couple of hours (rather than running the wayward sack over to the school office every day) will change his behavior far more than reminding him sixteen times over the breakfast table. You may both hurt while the consequence is playing out, but the final outcome—a learning experience with long-term benefits—will serve his best interests.

On the other hand, love may also lead you to overlook the specifics of a child's transgression based on his intent. If he makes a mess in the kitchen while trying to fix breakfast for you, the motive of the heart should overshadow whatever has been spilled on the counter and floor. (He can, of course, be asked cheerfully to participate in the cleanup chores—another good learning experience.)

Love will also cause you to examine your own motives as you deal with different child rearing situations. Are you responding harshly to whining because you're tired or overwhelmed? Are you giving in to demands and tantrums from a two-year-old because you were the victim of excessive punishment as a child and don't want to overreact? If you're upset over her messy room, are you concerned about her attitude toward her possessions or what your relatives will think if they see it? If you feel that your motives are unclear and your actions unpredictable, spend some time with an older parent whose child rearing results you respect, or meet with your pastor or a counselor to discuss what has been taking place.

6. Stay on your knees.

If you think you've got parenting wired because your firstborn was a compliant, relentlessly pleasant child, cheer up. You will probably be blessed with a miniature tornado next time around, and whatever you did with Number One won't begin to manage Number Two. Similarly, if you've read books (including this one) and feel you've got the discipline situation figured out and reduced to a formula, brace yourself—something thoroughly humbling will probably cross your path in the near future. There is only one Parent who completely understands all sons and daughters on the face of the earth, and seeking His wisdom on a daily basis should be a priority for all who train and nurture children.

TOP TEN GROUND RULES OF DISCIPLINE

Here are some building blocks, the brick and mortar of the process of training children.

1. Keep your primary goals in mind.

If you plan to take the assignment of training children seriously, it is important to have a firm grip on your basic goals. What are you trying to accomplish? The following, listed in order of increasing sophistication, should be on your child rearing agenda.

Keeping the child safe. Many limits you place on your child, beginning as soon as he can move himself from point A to point B, will be designed to keep him from harm. Early in his explorations he will have no idea whether an object in his world is friend or foe. He should not find out primarily through painful trial and error. As the months and years pass, he should gain an increasingly sophisticated understanding of cause and effect and consequences.

Preventing harm to others.

Preventing damage to property (whether the child's or someone else's).

Teaching respect for those in legitimate positions of authority. This must begin with you, the parent, and later extend to other designated caregivers. Soon after her first birthday, your child will make clear that she wants to know who's in charge here. If you haven't established your authority and your right to lead very early, you will be in for a bumpy ride later on. Establishing your authority does not mean that you need to be harsh, vindictive, or dictatorial. Instead, you are preparing her for the reality that *everyone* at various times of life must submit to someone else.

Eventually a child's respect must encompass teachers, coaches, law-enforcement officers, employers, and so on. Ultimately, she must also learn to recognize God's authority over her life—and understand that this authority is motivated by love and a boundless desire for her (the child's) well-being. Whether you realize it or not, your child's concept of God will be affected to a significant degree by her experiences with you during her years at home.

Teaching internal controls for actions and words. The ability and willingness to delay gratification are not programmed into children, who usually want what they want when they want it, which is *now*. Learning to wait one's turn and to put off the reward until the work is done isn't merely an exercise for toddlers and grade-school children. This training received in childhood has ample application to adult life as well, in arenas as diverse as education (plowing through years of course work to earn a degree), finances (waiting to buy something until one can afford it), and sexuality (delaying the pleasure of intercourse for the wedding night).

Furthermore, what comes "out of the mouths of babes" (as well as older children) often isn't particularly delicate or thoughtful. While not enforcing a repressive notion of children being seen but not heard, one of your most important projects over the years will be teaching your child to engage the mind before putting the tongue in gear.

Teaching basic civility. Manners, politeness, and general decorum are not inborn behaviors in children. Not only should saying please, thank you, and other details of civilized life be taught at an early age and repeated until they become automatic, but as a child passes through the grade-school years, the *attitudes* of respect and selflessness that underlie the habits will become habits as well. Ideally, both the attitudes and the behaviors will be modeled consistently at home—but this does not guarantee that your example will be followed, and specific instruction will usually be necessary.

Preventing negative behavior patterns and more serious long-term consequences. Selfishness, dishonesty, disrespect, poor impulse control, aggression, and destructiveness are annoying and disruptive in a four-year-old. In a fourteen-year-old they can lead to devastating or even lethal outcomes, not only for a teenager but for his family and an ever widening circle of people who must deal with the consequences of his words and actions.

Teaching internalized values. Honesty, responsibility, compassion, perseverance, loyalty, self-discipline, courage, and faith are admirable qualities in a grade-school child. In an adult they lead to a life of productivity and service. People demonstrating these qualities often emerge as leaders in their circles of influence.

2. Discipline should be appropriate for the child's age and capabilities.

A baby under the age of seven months is unable to act in a self-conscious manner or to carry out more than a handful of specific acts. Thus, efforts to make baby "mind" at this age are futile and ill advised. If she cries or wiggles during a diaper change, there is no point in attempting to "discipline" her to do otherwise.

If she develops a world-class episode of colic, she isn't doing it to ruin your day, assert her independence, or challenge your authority. She doesn't feel right, and crying is the only way she can express that discomfort. However, some shaping of behavior (such as reversing day and night sleep patterns by stimulating her during the day) is possible at an early age, as discussed in earlier chapters of the book.

Between a baby's eighth and fifteenth months, some limit setting must begin as a baby becomes more mobile. However, *an intense desire to explore her surroundings is normal, and her fierce determination should not be interpreted as defiance.* She may crawl toward the same plant fifteen times, not because she is trying to take charge, but because it looks terribly interesting, and her memory is very short. The primary methods to utilize at this age are baby-proofing and distraction, which are preferable to a steady diet of No's! from parents and older children.

After fifteen months, episodes of true clashing of wills are likely to begin. She will not only be more mobile but increasingly capable of actions that can be annoying, damaging, or dangerous. Her improving memory prevents distraction from being effective in turning her attention away from the things you want her to avoid. And while she is also capable of understanding simple directions, overt defiance and negativism are also likely to be displayed.

During these months (up to about age three), your expectations for behavior that your child can control should focus on her safety, as well as on preventing her from harming people or damaging the world around her. Specific goals for her should include coming when called, responding to simple directions (such as not touching or manipulating things that are off-limits), and not hitting or biting anyone—including you.

On the other hand, you cannot expect a child this age to sit still for long periods of time (such as in church or at a movie), to be affectionate with someone (a visiting relative, for example) on cue, or to show much interest in formal learning activities. It is futile to force a child this age (or any other) to consume whatever food you have placed before her. Remember that you determine what kinds of food are on the plate; she determines how much she'll eat.

As your child progresses into grade school, your expectations will become more sophisticated, encompassing both moral behavior and increased levels of responsibility. Be careful, however, about imposing consequences upon a child for physical or intellectual shortcomings that are beyond her control (see sidebar).

3. Constantly praise what your child does right.

Praise and positive feedback are a critical cornerstone for training children. The positive things you say to a child should normally outnumber the negative by a wide margin. This may seem difficult when you're dealing with a toddler who is constantly into everything throughout the house or with an adolescent for whom you feel time is running short for corrective action at home. But at both ends of childhood, and in between as well, actively watch for and applaud behaviors that are praiseworthy ("I really liked the way you helped your brother put away his toys"). As part of an effort to "accentuate the positive," let him overhear you when you compliment one of his accomplishments or a virtuous behavior to a friend or relative. The well-worn advice to "praise in public, criticize in private" is particularly applicable to children, who can be profoundly affected by what they hear said about themselves in the presence of others. Remember also that saying complimentary things about his appearance ("I just love your curly hair") may be nice during a cuddle session, but this won't necessarily improve his behavior.

Rewards and special privileges are perfectly appropriate ways to bring about desirable results, especially in situations where you are trying to increase effort or responsible behavior. For example, many parents set up systems in which points are awarded for activities such as getting out of bed on time, keeping a room clean, or taking out the trash. When a certain number of points are accumulated, an appropriate reward (such as a trip to the park or a small toy) is given. A variation on the theme (especially for children with a shorter attention span) involves offering a treat that will begin as soon as one or more tasks are completed. ("When everyone's toys are picked up, the back porch is swept, the animals fed, and dishes put away, we can all go out for frozen yogurt.") Or money may be offered for completing extra work such as weeding the yard. And, yes, it's okay to offer a reasonable premium for a certain number of A's or B's on the report card, especially if this inspires a child to put forth more effort on schoolwork.

Some parents might argue that rewarding children is merely bribing them for things they should do anyway. It's true that you should not use rewards on a nonstop basis, especially for nonnegotiable behavior such as brushing teeth or coming when called. But few adults go to work every day purely out of the good-

BEHAVIORS THAT SHOULD NOT NORMALLY BE SUBJECT TO PUNISHMENT

- *Normal exploratory behavior in infants and toddlers* (as discussed in chapters 4 and 5).
- *Toilet training.* It will happen when she's ready.
- *Bed-wetting.* This is a physiological event that is not under conscious control and will rarely (if ever) respond to rewards or punishment.
- *Speech problems.* These need professional assessment, and a lot of work may be needed at home, but delayed or garbled speech is not a character-development issue.
- *Accidents.* An older child can be involved with cleanup, repair, and restitution, especially if carelessness was involved.
- *Irritability and negativity specifically related to illness or extreme fatigue.*
- *Report cards that fall short of perfection.* Children should not be punished for failing to bring home straight A's, but you can set up appropriate ground rules for the effort a child puts forth at home, such as doing homework before fun and games. If a

child's school performance is falling short of her capability, the problem may be a need for more self-discipline, but specific learning problems may be involved as well.
- *Attention deficit/hyperactivity disorder (ADHD) problems.* A child with ADHD may have a great deal of difficulty with impulse control and learning from mistakes, even when she wants to do the right thing. However, among many other things (including perhaps medication), she still needs discipline and training to make progress and survive in the world. Parenting a child with ADHD is an art and a true test of one's patience and stamina.
- *Performance in sports.* Dropping the ball in center field or failing to make a team shouldn't provoke disciplinary measures at home. In fact, parental support and encouragement at such times are extremely important.

ness of their heart, and a paycheck is as concrete a reward as anything you might concoct for your child. There is nothing wrong with allowing a child to strive toward tangible goals as long as they are not fostering overt greed or materialism.

4. Limits and expectations must be defined clearly by parents and understood by their children.

For discipline to be effective, especially during the early years, a child needs to know and understand what you want and what will happen if he doesn't comply. By the time he arrives at the preschool years or soon thereafter, he should be able to repeat back to you both the limit and the consequence of breaking it. If he misbehaves but truly appears not to have known that what he did was wrong, an explanation is more appropriate than punishment. (However, if a mess was made or damage done, he should take part in the cleanup and restoration process.)

When discussing consequences, don't make threats that are outright lies ("If you do that again, the police will come and take you away" or "If you don't stop that, the doctor will give you a shot!" A child who has been told that an immunization or any other medical treatment is a punishment is not only misinformed but may come to resent the doctor or nurse as well.) Cooperation during future visits may be jeopardized, and the child might become reluctant to say something about an important symptom for fear of being "punished" by the doctor again. Furthermore, don't issue a warning involving a consequence you are not actually willing to carry out. "If you don't stop arguing, we're going to cancel our trip to the lake!" is either an excessive or an idle threat, especially if the trip has been planned for six months, with reservations and a deposit already mailed. After several grandiose warnings that never come true, your children will catch on and not pay attention to you. But if you're truly willing to blow an entire vacation over an argument in the backseat, you need to reconsider whether your punishment really fits the crime.

How many rules and regulations you actually spell out will depend on your child. He should learn that the basic moral principles you have taught him apply to the world at large and not just to his immediate family. But you may have to make these connections explicit. For example, even if it seems self-evident to you, you may have to make it clear that the statement "Don't take things that don't belong to you" includes what is in the neighbor's garage as well as what is in his sister's toy chest.

As you begin to increase a child's responsibilities at home, your expectations will generally need to become more detailed. It probably won't occur to him to hang his shirts in the closet rather than throw them on the floor, for example, so if you want him to do this (and he's capable), he will need specific directions.

One fundamental expectation deserves special mention: Your child should learn to follow your directions whether or not you decide to give reasons and explanations. If you find yourself haggling and debating with your child every time you ask or tell him to do something, it's time to tighten the reins. Present a plain-spoken declaration of your right to lead ("I'm the parent, you're the child, and what I say goes. Period!"), along with a warning that further arguing will lead to unpleasant consequences.

Remember, however, that while you have the right to expect your child's obedience, you also have the responsibility to lead in a manner that is reasonable and has his best interests at heart. Like adults, children and adolescents care passionately about what is fair, and they become agitated when consequences seem to appear out of thin air. The New Testament warns parents not to exasperate their children, and a steady stream of arbitrary or unjust punishments will not only exasperate them but reap a bitter harvest years later.

You will need to exercise particular wisdom in situations where you really didn't give specific directions, even if you feel they shouldn't have been necessary. He might insist that "Nobody said I couldn't jump off the roof!" and you might feel justified in retorting with equal fervor (as you head for the emergency room to treat his twisted ankle), "You should have known better!" But these frustrating episodes can actually be rich opportunities to teach broad principles (looking before leaping, thinking before acting), which will be more effective than merely generating more detailed rules.

5. Consequences must occur consistently and in a timely manner.

Ideally, your child should respond to any specific direction you give ("Please pick up your toys now") without delay, distraction, or argument. In reality, many parents would faint if their child actually obeyed them right away, without some fussing or complaint. But this goal can be achieved if the following principles are put into action:

When appropriate, give a little advance notice if you intend to interrupt something your child is doing. ("Tyrone, in ten minutes I want you to head upstairs and start your bath. I'll set the buzzer so you'll know when it's time." Or "Monique, when your video is finished, I need you to set the table.") Make sure your directions are understood.

If and when your child doesn't do what you have asked, take action and explain why.
("I see you're still sitting here twenty minutes after I told you to start your bath.
Tyrone, it's very important that you do exactly as I tell you. To help you remember next time, you're going to bed a half hour early tonight." "Monique, I let you
finish your video, but you didn't set the table when it was done. I respected what
you were doing, but it's very important that you respect me by following my directions. I want you to set the table now, and to help you remember to do what
I ask, you're not going to watch any videos for a day.")

You don't have to get angry or raise your voice. You don't have to complain
or make threats. Just take appropriate action, making sure that what you do will
be meaningful but not harsh and that you will follow through with the action. If
Monique shrugs and says she isn't going to watch any videos tomorrow anyway,
extend the ban for as many days as needed to get her attention.

Make certain that your response to a child's misbehavior is *timely.* A toddler will
not remember what you were upset about an hour ago, and an older child should
not be kept in suspense all day waiting for some undefined but worrisome punishment to be delivered.

Be sure to enforce your rules and limits *consistently.* Not only should your children know that you will back up your words with action every time, but they
should also know that your response won't waver to any great degree. The same
transgression shouldn't bring about a soft reminder one night and a harsh punishment the next. On-again, off-again discipline is confusing, and it generates
disobedience and unhealthy fear. In a two-parent family, both parents should
strive to dispense consequences in a similar manner. "Wait till your father gets
home" is a phrase you should never have to use, because Mom and Dad should
deliver the goods with equal conviction.

All of these principles are important because most children become experts at the
game called "What happens if . . . ?" They spend a lot of time observing cause and
effect and can usually predict with some accuracy when parental action is likely to
occur. In many families, the odds depend upon which parent is playing the game,
what else is going on, time of day, tone of voice, and numerous other factors. If a
child hears a lot of talk about what he should or shouldn't do but little of it is
backed up with action, he will probably pay little attention (unless he is extremely
sensitive to tone of voice or verbal disapproval alone). The bottom line is that if
and when your child challenges your leadership (whether actively or passively),
respond with action—calmly, respectfully, quickly, decisively, and consistently.

6. The consequence should be appropriate for the transgression.

In most situations, **words** are all the response you will need. For toddlers and small children, **a disapproving look** and **a tone of voice** that says you mean business will often promptly change behavior or even bring tears and the need for comfort. Remember that what you say should be appropriate for the age-group. For the toddler, simple statements such as "Don't touch the stove," especially when accompanied by physically lifting him away from it, are appropriate. For older children, reaffirming the reasons for your limits is worthwhile as well. And if you make it a point to sound pleasant and relaxed most of the time, your more serious tone of voice will be far more effective when you choose to use it.

Withholding a privilege can be effective from toddlerhood through adolescence. If your toddler bangs a toy against the coffee table despite your clear direction to stop, put the toy away for a while. If you've told your first-grader to put his bike in the garage but it remains on the front lawn all night, a day without it will help remind him next time. If your adolescent has ignored specific instructions about being home by a certain hour, a week without phone or driving privileges can be a meaningful way to get her attention.

Time-out can be useful with toddlers, preschoolers, and early grade-school children, especially when emotions need to cool down. This involves isolating the child in a playpen, in his room, or simply on a chair—without toys or other entertainment—for a specified period of time. Usually one minute of time-out per year of age is appropriate, although if the child hasn't calmed down, more time may be necessary. This approach is usually effective—assuming, of course, that the child is willing to cooperate. If he refuses to stay on the chair or starts trashing his room during a time-out, more direct physical intervention may be necessary.

Restitution is an important principle of discipline that can and should be used, especially with older children and adolescents. If your child makes a mess, he cleans it up. If he causes someone else's property to be damaged or destroyed, whether directly or through passive negligence, he participates in the repair and restoration. He may have to work to repay all or part of the costs involved.

Not all acts of restitution necessarily involve property. If your daughter lies to someone, for example, she should confess to that person. If she has broken a promise or failed to honor a commitment, she will need to apologize to the person(s) involved. These acts of humility are often far more difficult—but also more character building—than enduring any time-out or loss of privilege.

Allowing consequences to play out is a potentially powerful approach to discipline, especially during the school-age years. The basic principle is this: Look at childhood mistakes as learning opportunities, and avoid rushing in to rescue your child from natural consequences (provided, of course, they are merely unpleasant and not potentially dangerous). For example:

- If he leaves his bike on the front lawn and someone steals it, don't replace it immediately. He'll be more careful with the next bicycle he owns.
- If she forgets to bring home her permission slip for the field trip, let her miss it. She won't forget the next time.
- If he plays roughly and carelessly with his new toy and breaks it, don't go straight to the store to buy a new one. Let him mourn the loss and talk with him about taking better care of his possessions in the future.
- If she dawdles every morning and then misses the school bus, let her deal with the fallout from the unexcused absence.

Your motivation should not be anger or spite, and your tone should not be "I told you so," "Now you'll listen to me," or "That'll teach you!" If anything, this process should be painful for you; you should provide emotional support and comfort while you resist the urge to bail him out. Whatever you choose to teach during one of these episodes need not come with a flood of reprimands because he has already felt the sting of wrongdoing.

Why should you and your child endure these unpleasant experiences, especially when it is often within your capability to end them quickly and easily? Because what he learns from an uncomfortable episode as a child may save him from a disastrous or even lethal miscalculation as an adolescent. A child who is allowed to become an expert on consequences will be more likely to think through the outcomes of his actions later on when the stakes are higher. Going without his lunch won't kill him, but getting involved with illegal drugs or premarital sex might. Furthermore, if he is repeatedly spared the consequences of his misbehavior throughout childhood and adolescence, he may never learn self-control or exercise good judgment as an adult.

Physical punishment (specifically, disciplinary spanking) is a tool that can be useful in specific circumstances. However, some voices in our culture condemn all spanking, based on claims that it teaches violence, perpetuates abuse, damages a child's dignity, and doesn't change behavior. These criticisms are valid for abusive forms of corporal punishment such as slapping, kicking, beating, and in cases of spanking when it is used excessively or inappropriately, such as when representing an expression of anger and frustration, causing injury.

But when utilized with appropriate guidelines, spanking can and should be neither abusive nor damaging to a child's physical or emotional well-being. With toddlers and preschoolers, a controlled swat on the behind may be appropriate to bring a confrontation to a timely conclusion. A disciplinary spanking should be administered only in response to an episode of willful defiance characterized by a clear, appropriate parental directive that the child understands and is capable of following; a direct challenge from the child, especially with a disrespectful or hostile tone; or persistent and blatant refusal to cooperate.

In such situations, attempts to reason with a hotly defiant toddler or to "share your feelings" with a disrespectful preschooler are likely to be futile. Allowing a child to call you names, spit at you, throw objects, take a swing at you, or damage your home is inappropriate and unhealthy, does not help him "get it out of his system," and virtually guarantees more of the same destructive and obnoxious behavior in the future. And if the conflict continues to boil or escalate, your anger and frustration may reach a flash point at which hurtful words or actions may result.

Any physical action you take in such circumstances should not be an outpouring of anger or an act of revenge, but rather a tactic to turn your child's behavior around and bring the rebellion to a swift conclusion. A spanking of one to three quick swats should provide a brief, superficial sting to the buttocks or the back of the upper thighs. It should be just hard enough to get the child's attention, bring on some tears, and break through the defiance.

Many parents wonder whether a disciplinary spanking should be administered with a neutral object or with the palm of a hand. One might argue that a child should not experience the touch of a parent's hand as a painful event and that a mother's or father's hands should be used exclusively for holding, caressing, or comforting. Furthermore, if a spanking is administered with a neutral object—a thin flexible switch, for example—a brief time will elapse while it is located, decreasing the likelihood of lashing out impulsively in the heat of the moment.

On the other hand (no pun intended), any object that extends more than a few inches from the hand can gain surprising momentum during a spanking, especially when the wrist is in motion at the same time. Since a neutral object, unlike the hand, cannot "feel" the force of its impact, it may be difficult to know whether a spanking is producing an appropriate superficial sting or much more severe pain.

The bottom line is this: Whether the hand or a neutral object is used in a spanking, it should not cause bruising or other damage to the skin. (You should try your method of choice on your own skin first.) Unfortunately, some misguided or abusive parents utilize fearsome hardware during spankings—razor straps, heavy belts, belt buckles, canes, or worse—that virtually guarantee injury to the child. This type of punishment, as well as face slapping, punching, hair pulling, or any other form of violence, is completely inappropriate and has no place in the rearing of a child.

A disciplinary spanking should be carried out in private, between parent and child (and not in front of the rest of the world or wide-eyed siblings). It must be followed by reconciliation, comforting, reassurance, and simple teaching about how to avoid such an episode in the future. *You may not need to take this course of action more than a few times during your child's life.* Once you have established clearly that you are in charge, many (if not most) defiant episodes can be settled using other measures such as verbal reprimands, time-outs, or restriction of privileges. If you have a particularly strong-willed child, however, more than a few disciplinary spankings may be necessary. But if you find yourself taking this type of action on a daily or weekly basis, you should reevaluate your basic approach to discipline. Perhaps you are taking too harsh a response to childish irresponsibility or not communicating clearly to the child what you expect. Or it is possible that for various reasons your child is not capable of understanding or following your directives. If spankings have become a frequent occurrence in your home, in order to prevent physical, emotional, or even spiritual damage to your child, you should consider seeking alternative approaches and other help from a counselor or pastor who shares your basic values and views on child rearing.

Disciplinary spanking should not be carried out

- if you feel extremely angry, highly stressed, or emotionally unstable;
- if you were abused as a child, unless you have worked through your past hurts (and the issue of corporal punishment of your own children) with a professional counselor;
- if you are not clear about the difference between childish irresponsibility and willful defiance, either in general or in the specific situation at hand;
- if both parents are not in agreement about its appropriate use;
- after a child reaches the age of ten. Disciplinary spanking should occur infrequently after the age of five or six;
- by anyone other than a child's parent, except under specific circumstances (such as a prolonged period of care by another person in the parent's absence) in which explicit permission and ground rules have been laid down.

*7. A unified approach to discipline, carried out regardless of who is in
charge of a child at any given time, should be a firm parental goal.*

If other caregivers are involved in your child's upbringing, they should be
brought up to speed on your viewpoint and techniques of training and discipline. If a child's mother and father are divorced, every effort should be made to
maintain the same standards in each parent's household. Without such unity,
children will learn to play one parent or caregiver against the other ("Mom said
no, so let's ask Dad").

An honest disagreement about principles and practices should not be discussed in front of the children. Under no circumstances (except an imminent
threat to a child's life or health) should one parent openly contradict or overrule
the instructions of the other. This is not only disrespectful, but it also under-
mines the other parent's authority. If necessary in the heat of the moment, parents should call a time-out and discuss their issues behind closed doors before
taking further action.

8. Don't restrict teaching of values to times of confrontation.

In many families, the only time moral principles are discussed is during corrective action resulting from an episode of wrongdoing. But this will tend to leave
children with a stunted or even repressive sense of values. Be on the lookout for
"teachable moments," those conversations during which you can give your child
a broader and deeper understanding of right and wrong.

*9. When appropriate, allow your child to make choices that will give
her a growing sense of competence and individuality.*

During the preschool years, this can involve simple decisions such as which pa-
jamas she wants to wear or which story she wants to hear at bedtime. As the years
pass, the range and significance of the options should increase—which summer
camp to attend, which musical instrument to play.

Don't offer choices or begin haggling over issues for which there should be
no negotiating: for example, sitting in the car seat, bathing, visiting the doctor.

*10. Remember that children learn a great deal about appropriate
behavior from what they see modeled by the adults in their lives.*

You can talk about virtues and work diligently to instill values in your children,
but like water seeking its own level, their moral sensibilities aren't likely to rise
above whatever goes on in front of them at home. At least for the first several

years of life, you as a parent are their authority on just about everything. Your words and actions provide hundreds of little vignettes that can teach them about responsibility, kindness, honesty, faith, and perseverance—or the opposite of these virtues. The beginning of wisdom in providing training and discipline for your children is an honest, ongoing appraisal of your own life and values. No matter how busy or tired you might feel, don't shrink from this important and worthwhile process.

Emergency Care

IF YOU DIAL 911 . . .

- Tell the dispatcher that you have a medical emergency, and then state briefly what has happened (including the age of the child), where you are, and the number from which you are calling.
- *Stay on the line* so you can answer any questions the dispatcher might ask. He or she may also give you specific instructions for emergency care prior to the arrival of emergency personnel. Do not hang up until the dispatcher indicates it is time to do so. (He or she should hang up first.)
- If it is nighttime, turn on your outside lights—especially those that illuminate your address.
- If possible, have someone stand outside to direct the emergency personnel to the victim.

THE MEDICINE CABINET

- appropriate thermometer for age. Know how to read it. (See "When your child has a fever," page 155.)
- petroleum jelly (Vaseline)
- antiseptic wipes
- Band-Aids and gauze pads with adhesive tape for cuts and scrapes
- Steri-strips or butterfly closures
- antibacterial ointment
- elastic (Ace) bandages: 2-inch width for children under 12 months; 3-inch width for

children ages 1 to 5; 4-inch
width for children over age 5
- Popsicle stick for finger
  splinting
- acetaminophen drops, liquid,
  or chewables, appropriate for
  age (Tylenol and other
  brands)
- ibuprofen liquid or tablets,
  appropriate for age
  (Children's Advil, Children's
  Motrin, and others)
- instant cold packs (small
  plastic bags that become cold
  when squeezed to mix the
  chemicals inside them)
- tweezers

FIRST

Prepare a first aid kit for each car
and a smaller version for hiking
or biking. Include the following
items:

- antiseptic wipes for cleaning cuts
- antibacterial ointment
- Band-Aids
- gauze pads and adhesive tape
  for larger scrapes
- sunblock
- instant cold pack
- elastic bandage—3-inch width
- acetaminophen (Tylenol) or
  ibuprofen (Children's Advil,
  Children's Motrin, or others)
- tweezers
- Steri-strips or butterfly
  closures
- money for a phone call

MEDICINE CABINET

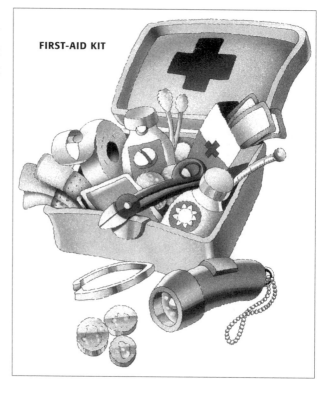

FIRST-AID KIT

CARDIOPULMONARY RESUSCITATION (CPR): YOUNG CHILD—AGES 1 TO 8

1. Check to see if the child is conscious.
   - Tap her chest or shoulder, or give her body a gentle shake.
   - Do not shake her head and neck.
   - Call out to her, "Are you OK?"

2. If there is no response, shout for help.
   - As soon as someone is available, have him or her call 911.

Tilt head back and lift chin. (See 4.)

3. Roll the child onto her back if she is not in that position already.
   - Support her head and neck, keeping them in a straight line with her back.
   - Lay the child on a firm surface.

4. Check to see if she is breathing.
   - Kneel next to her head.
   - Tilt her head back and lift her chin to open the airway.
   - Put your head near the child's mouth and nose.
   - For 5 seconds, look, listen, and feel for breathing.
     (a) Is the chest rising?
     (b) Can you hear breathing sounds?
     (c) Can you feel air moving against your face?

5. **If you can't see, hear, or feel the child breathing, you must immediately begin breathing for her (rescue breathing).**
   - Pinch her nose shut using 2 fingers.
   - With your lips make a tight seal around the child's mouth.
   - Give 2 full breaths.
     (a) Breathe into the victim for about 1 to $1\frac{1}{2}$ seconds, watching for the chest to rise.
     (b) Pause to let the air flow out, and then give another breath.

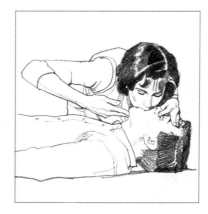

Make tight seal over victim's mouth. (See 5.)

6. Check her pulse.

- Feel for a pulse at the side of her neck for 5 to 10 seconds.
- If you feel a pulse but she is not breathing:

    (a) Give 1 breath every 5 seconds.

    (b) Recheck the pulse every 10 to 12 breaths.

    (c) Continue breathing for the child until

      —she begins to breathe without help, or

      —another rescuer takes over, or

      —you do not feel a pulse.

7. **If there is no pulse, begin CPR.**

Have someone call 911 for help, if this has not been done already.

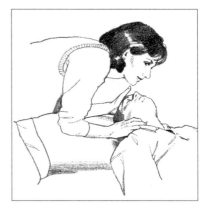

Feel for pulse at side of neck. (See 6.)

8. Position your hands on the child's chest.

- Place the middle finger of 1 hand at the lower end of the breastbone (where the lower border of the rib cage meets the breastbone).
- Place the heel of your other hand on the breastbone, 2 finger widths above the end of the breastbone (where you placed your middle finger).
- Remove your finger from the lower end of the breastbone and place the heel of that hand over the hand that is on the breastbone.
- Don't allow your fingers to rest on the child's chest.

    (a) Point your fingers upward (away from the body), or

    (b) mesh the fingers of your 2 hands.

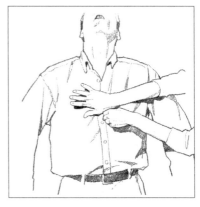

Position hands on victim's chest. (See 8.)

9. Compress the chest by pressing straight downward.

- Use your body weight, not your arm muscles.
- Keep your arms straight, with elbows locked.
- Lean with your shoulders over your hands.
- You should move straight up and down, not rock back and forth.
- The breastbone should depress 1 to 1½ inches.

- Give 5 compressions over about 4 seconds. (Count 1 and 2 and 3. . . .)

10. After you have given 5 compressions, give 1 full breath.
    - Gently tilt the child's head back.
    - Pinch her nose shut with your fingers.
    - With your lips make a tight seal around the child's mouth.
    - Give 1 full breath for 1 to 1½ seconds.
    - Check the pulse.

    If there is no pulse:

11. Repeat the cycle of 5 compressions and 1 breath for 10 cycles.
    - After 10 cycles (about 1 minute), check for a pulse.
    - If there is no pulse, continue CPR.
    - If a pulse is present, check for breathing.
      (a) Carry out rescue breathing if the child is not breathing.
    - Continue CPR or rescue breathing until
      (a) the child is breathing and has a pulse, or
      (b) another rescuer takes over.

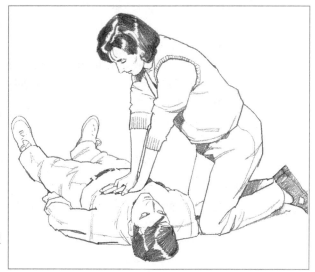

Compress chest, using body weight. (See 9.)

CARDIOPULMONARY RESUSCITATION (CPR): NEWBORN TO 1 YEAR

1. Check to see if the baby is conscious.
   - Tap his shoulder, or give his body a gentle shake.
   - Do not shake his head and neck.

2. If there is no response, shout for help.
   - As soon as someone is available, have him or her call 911.

3. Roll the baby onto his back if he is not in that position already.
   - Support his head and neck, keeping them in a straight line with his back.
   - Lay the baby on a firm surface.

4. Check to see if he is breathing.
   - Gently tilt his head back and lift his chin to open the airway.
   - Put your head near the infant's mouth and nose.
   - For 3 to 5 seconds, look, listen, and feel for breathing.
     (a) Is the chest rising?
     (b) Can you hear breathing sounds?
     (c) Can you feel air moving against your face?

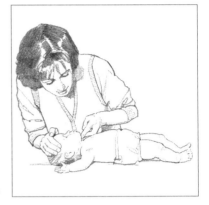

Tilt head back and lift chin. (See 4.)

5. **If you can't see, hear, or feel the infant breathing, you must immediately begin breathing for him (rescue breathing).**
   - With your lips make a tight seal around the baby's nose and mouth.
   - Give 2 slow breaths.
     (a) Breathe into the infant for about 1 to $1\frac{1}{2}$ seconds, watching for the chest to rise.
     (b) Pause to let the air flow out, and then give another breath.

6. Check his pulse.
   - With 1 hand, keep the baby's head tilted back.
   - With your other hand, check for a pulse.
     (a) Feel for 5 seconds on the inside of the baby's upper arm, between the elbow and shoulder. Also listen for a heartbeat by placing your ear next to the baby's chest.
   - If you feel a pulse but he is not breathing:
     (a) Give 1 breath every 3 seconds.
     (b) Recheck the pulse every 20 breaths (about once per minute).
     (c) Continue breathing for the infant until
       —he begins to breathe without help, or
       —another rescuer takes over, or
       —you do not feel a pulse.

Make tight seal around nose and mouth. (See 5.)

7. **If there is no pulse or heartbeat, begin CPR.**

Have someone call 911 for help, if this has not been done already.

Feel inside upper arm for pulse. (See 6.)

8. Position your fingers on the baby's chest.
   - With 1 hand, keep the baby's head tilted back.
   - Place the index finger of your other hand on the center of the breastbone, just below the level of the nipples.
   - Place your next 2 fingers (the middle and ring fingers) right next to your index finger (slightly farther down the baby's breastbone). Then lift your index finger.

9. Compress the baby's chest using your 2 fingers.
   - Push the breastbone straight down $1/2$ to 1 inch.
   - Give 5 compressions over about 3 seconds.

10. After you have given 5 compressions, give 1 full breath.
    - With your lips make a tight seal around the baby's nose and mouth.
    - Give 1 full breath for 1 to $1^1/_2$ seconds.
    - Check the pulse.

If there is no pulse:

11. Repeat the cycle of 5 compressions and 1 breath for 10 cycles.
    - After 10 cycles (about 1 minute), check for a pulse.
    - If there is no pulse, continue CPR.
    - If a pulse is present, check for breathing.
      (a) Carry out rescue breathing if the baby is not breathing.
    - Continue CPR or rescue breathing until
      (a) the baby is breathing and has a pulse, or
      (b) another rescuer takes over.

Compress chest using 2 fingers (See 9.)

Make tight seal around nose and mouth.
(See 10.)

CHOKING EMERGENCIES: ONE-YEAR-OLD TO ADULT

1. Determine if the person is choking.
   - If there is forceful coughing or the person can speak, do not interfere.
   - Ask the person if he is choking.
   - If he is unable to speak or cough, have someone call 911 and take immediate action (step 2 and following).

2. Get behind the victim and position your hands.
   - Wrap your arms around the victim's waist.
   - Make a fist with 1 hand.
   - Place the thumb side of your fist against the middle of the victim's abdomen—just above the navel but below the rib cage.
   - Grab your fist with your other hand.

Wrap arms around victim's waist. (See 2.)

3. Give abdominal thrusts.
   - Quickly pull your fist inward and upward into the abdomen.
   - **If the victim is pregnant or too big to reach around the abdomen, give chest thrusts instead.**
     (a) Place your fist against the center of the breastbone.
     (b) Grab your fist with your other hand, and give thrusts into the chest.
   - Continue thrusts until
     (a) the object is forced out of the victim's airway, or
     (b) the victim becomes unconscious.

If the victim is unconscious:

4. Have someone call 911 for help, if this has not been done already.

5. Roll the person onto his back if he is not in that position already.
   - Support his head and neck, keeping them in a straight line with his back.

- Lay the victim on a firm surface.
- Clear any material out of the mouth.
  (a) **Be careful not to push any object or food farther down.**

6. Check to see if he is breathing.
   - Kneel next to his head.
   - Tilt his head back and lift his chin to open the airway.
   - Put your head near the person's mouth and nose.
   - For 5 seconds, look, listen, and feel for breathing.
     (a) Is the chest rising?
     (b) Can you hear breathing sounds?
     (c) Can you feel air moving against your face?

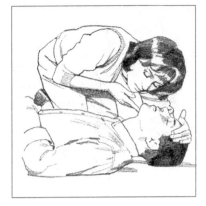

Tilt head back and lift chin. (See 6.)

7. **If you can't see, hear, or feel the victim breathing, you must immediately begin breathing for him (rescue breathing).**
   - Tilt the victim's head back.
   - Pinch his nose shut using 2 fingers.
   - With your lips make a tight seal around the victim's mouth.
   - Give 2 full breaths.
     (a) Breathe into the victim for about 1 to 1½ seconds, watching for the chest to rise.
     (b) Pause to let the air flow out, and then give another breath.

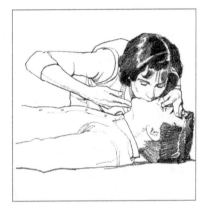

Make tight seal over victim's mouth. (See 7.)

If the breaths will not go in:

8. Tilt the head farther back, and try again.
   - Pinch his nose shut using 2 fingers.
   - With your lips make a tight seal around the victim's mouth.
   - Give 2 full breaths.

If the breaths still will not go in, the airway is probably blocked.

9. Give abdominal thrusts.
   - Straddle 1 of the victim's upper legs.

- Place the heel of your hand on the victim's abdomen, just above the navel and below the rib cage.
- Place your other hand on top of the first, and point your fingers toward the victim's head.
- Give 5 quick thrusts toward the head and into the abdomen.

10. Sweep the victim's mouth with your finger.
    - Use your fingers and thumb to grasp and lift the victim's lower jaw and tongue.
    - Slide 1 finger into the mouth, down the victim's cheek to the base of his tongue.
    - Try to hook or sweep the object out.
      (a) **Be careful not to push any object or food farther down.**

    If the person is still not breathing, repeat steps 5 through 8.
    - Tilt the head back.
    - Give 2 slow breaths.
    - Retilt the head.
    - Give 2 slow breaths.
    - Give 5 abdominal thrusts.
    - Do finger sweep.

11. Continue this sequence until the object is removed and you can inflate the victim's lungs.

12. Once you are getting air into the victim, check for breathing and pulse. (See CPR, page 201.)
    - If he is not breathing, begin rescue breathing. (See CPR, page 201.)
    - If he does not have a pulse, begin CPR. (See CPR, page 202.)

CHOKING EMERGENCIES: NEWBORN TO 1 YEAR

1. Determine if the baby is choking.
    - If there is forceful coughing or the baby can cry, do not interfere.
    - If she is unable to cry, cough, or breathe or if she is coughing very weakly, have someone call 911 and take immediate action (step 2 and following).

2. Position the baby face down on your forearm.
    - Support the baby's head and jaw as you turn her face down.
    - Position her so that her head is lower than her chest.

3. Give 4 back blows.
    - Use the heel of your free hand.
    - Strike forcefully between her shoulder blades.

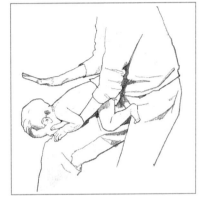

Position baby face down on forearm.
(See 2 & 3.)

4. Turn the baby onto her back.
    - Support the baby's head and jaw as you roll her over.
    - Rest her back on your thigh.

5. Give 4 thrusts to the chest.
    - Place 2 or 3 fingers in the center of her breast-bone (just below the level of the nipples).
    - Thrust downward quickly about $\frac{1}{2}$ to 1 inch.

6. Repeat steps 2 through 5.
    - Turn the baby face down.
    - Give 4 back blows.
    - Turn the baby on her back.
    - Give 4 chest thrusts.

Give chest thrusts using 2 or 3 fingers.
(See 5.)

7. Repeat this sequence until the baby begins to cough or breathe, or until she coughs up the object.

If the baby is unconscious:

8. Have someone call 911 for help, if this has not been done already.

9. Roll the baby onto her back.
   - Support her head and neck, keeping them in a straight line with her back.
   - Lay the baby on a firm surface.

10. Clear any material from the baby's mouth.
    - Use the fingers and thumb of 1 hand to grasp and lift the baby's lower jaw and tongue.
    - Use the little finger of your other hand to sweep the object or food out.
    - **(a) Be careful not to push any object or food farther down.**

Clear material from baby's mouth. (See 10.)

11. Check to see if she is breathing.
    - Gently tilt her head back and lift her chin to open the airway.
    - Put your head near the infant's mouth and nose.
    - For 3 to 5 seconds, look, listen, and feel for breathing.
      (a) Is the chest rising?
      (b) Can you hear breathing sounds?
      (c) Can you feel air moving against your face?

12. **If you can't see, hear, or feel the infant breathing, you must immediately begin breathing for her (rescue breathing).**
    - With your lips make a tight seal around the baby's nose and mouth.
    - Give 2 slow breaths.
      (a) Breathe into the infant for about 1 to $1\frac{1}{2}$ seconds, watching for the chest to rise.
      (b) Pause to let the air flow out, and then give another breath.

Check to see if baby is breathing. (See 11.)

If the breaths will not go in:

13. Tilt the head farther back, lift the chin, and try again.

If the breaths still will not go in, the airway is probably blocked.

14. Repeat the sequence of back blows and chest thrusts until the baby is breathing on her own or you are able to inflate her lungs.

- Turn the baby face down.
- Give 4 back blows.
- Turn the baby on her back.
- Give 4 chest thrusts.
- Check the mouth for any object or food.
- Tilt the head back.
- Give 2 slow breaths.
- Retilt the head.
- Give 2 more small breaths.

15. Once you are getting air into the victim, check for breathing and pulse. (See CPR, page 204.)
    - If she is not breathing, begin rescue breathing. (See CPR, page 204.)
    - If she does not have a pulse, begin CPR. (See CPR, page 204.)

Make tight seal around nose and mouth. (See 12.)

Safety—Indoors and Out

HOME SAFETY: INDOORS

- Never step away when your baby is on a high surface such as a changing table or countertop.
- Keep the sides of a baby's crib raised.
- If an infant seat is used outside the car, place it on the floor.
- Avoid infant walkers.
- Install safety gates (*not* accordion-style) to guard stairways.
- Lock doors to dangerous areas such as the basement and garage.
- Check the stability of drawers, tall furniture, and lamps before a baby becomes mobile.
- Remove tablecloths that might be within the reach of a toddler.
- Make sure any windows above the first floor of a multistory house are closed or have screens or guards that cannot be pushed out.
- Don't underestimate the climbing ability of a toddler.
- Remove or pad low furniture with sharp corners, such as coffee tables, in your child's living area.
- Place safety latches on all drawers and cupboards that are off-limits.
- Move anything dangerous—cleaning products; plumbing, gardening, painting,

refinishing, and agricultural chemicals and supplies; knives or other sharp utensils; and medicines—to high cabinets that are latched.

- Make knives off-limits to a child until he is old enough to learn (and demonstrate) how to use them correctly.
- Put covers on unused electrical outlets.
- Keep electrical cords out of the reach of children.
- Remove all poisonous plants from the home.
- Put the number of the nearest poison center on all phones. Call if a child puts something in his mouth that might be poisonous.
- Buy syrup of ipecac, but use only if directed to do so.
- Purchase all medicines in containers with safety caps.
- Do not transfer toxic substances to bottles, glasses, or jars, especially if those containers originally contained familiar liquids for drinking (such as juice).
- When leaving your children with a baby-sitter, leave emergency phone numbers, a permission slip for emergency care, and insurance information. (Or designate whom the sitter should call.) Make certain the sitter knows the address and phone number of your home, in case she needs to provide this information to emergency personnel.

FIRE AND BURN PREVENTION

- Never eat, drink, or carry anything hot near or while holding a baby or a small child.
- Don't cook when your child is at your feet. Use a playpen, high chair, or crib as a safety area for small children while you are preparing food.
- Use the rear burners on your stove, and keep the pan handles out of reach.
- Check formula, food, and drink temperatures carefully.
- Keep hot appliances and cords out of the reach of children.
- Do not allow your child to use the stove, microwave, hot curlers, curling iron, or steam iron until he or she is old enough to learn how to do so safely.
- Install and maintain smoke detectors in accordance with fire regulations in your area. If they are not wired directly into your home's electrical system, check smoke detector monthly and replace batteries annually.
- Provide nonflammable barriers around heating surfaces and fireplaces.
- Teach your child to drop and roll on the ground if his clothing catches fire.
- Have your heating system checked annually.
- If there are one or more tobacco smokers in the family, they should not be allowed to smoke inside the home.
- Keep matches and lighters out of the reach of children.
- Have a working fire extinguisher near the kitchen, but instruct your child not to play with it. However, older children and adolescents should be taught how to use it in an emergency.
- Do not permit your child to possess or play with fireworks.

SMOKE DETECTORS

Residential fires kill about 5,000 people every year in the United States, and the majority of these fatalities result not from burn injuries but from inhalation of smoke and toxic gases. Death usually occurs at night, when the victim is sleeping. Properly installed and maintained home smoke detectors could prevent many of these deaths.

SMOKE DETECTOR

Smoke detectors are considered the best and least expensive early-warning systems because they can alert people in a home *before* the fire ignites, *before* the concentration of smoke reaches a dangerous level, or *before* a fire becomes extremely intense. The risk of dying from a fire-related incident is twice as high in a home without functioning smoke detectors as in a home with them.

Smoke detectors can be wired directly into a home's electrical system, or they may be battery powered, in which case fresh batteries should be installed at least once a year. Each smoke detector should be tested regularly in accordance with the manufacturer's recommendations to ensure it is operating properly.

At least one detector should be installed on each floor of a multistory home, preferably near a bedroom so that sleeping residents will be given early warning in the event of a fire. Local fire regulations and/or building codes may specify that more smoke detectors must be installed for a particular home's floor plan.

FIRE AND DISASTER PREPARATION

Hopefully you will never have to deal with a major fire in your home, but some basic preparation can prevent confusion and panic should one occur. Cover the following details with your children:

• Using 911. (Call only after you've left the burning building.)

- Staying low to the ground when smoke is present.
- Avoiding opening any doors that are hot to the touch.
- Escaping through a window (including the use of a chain ladder in a multistory home).
- Discussing what firefighters may look like in their full gear. (Unless prepared ahead of time, children might be frightened by the bulky shapes with face masks and axes or other tools; hiding from the firefighters could be disastrous.)

FIRE ESCAPE ROUTE

- Getting help from neighbors.
- Agreeing on a meeting place if family members have different escape routes.
- Practicing family fire drills.

Make sure that your home address is clearly visible from the street. If possible, have the numbers neatly painted on the curbside as well.

While you are talking about your family's response to a fire, you should also go over contingency plans for any possible natural disaster (earthquake, flood, tornado, hurricane) that might occur where you live. Include instructions as to whom you or your children might contact in case communications are disrupted. (It may be easier to get in touch with a relative across the country, who could serve as a communication center for the family.)

WATER AND TUB SAFETY

- Turn down your water heater to 120°F or less.
- Make sure that an adult—not another child—bathes a baby.
- Remain in the room during every second of a child's bath. Have everything you'll need available at the tub before you start.
- Install strips with a roughened surface or lay a rubber mat in the bathtub to prevent slips and falls.
- Provide a barrier around any pool or spa. This should consist of a tall, hard-to-climb fence (which can be locked) extending around all four sides of a pool or an approved pool or spa cover.
- Do not leave buckets filled with water in any area where a toddler might play.

- Prohibit swimming in fast-moving water such as a creek, river, or canal.
- Permit diving *only* after the depth has been checked and your child has been taught how to dive correctly.
- Never leave your child unsupervised when he is in, on, or around water.
- Keep rescue equipment at the waterside, and take CPR training.

FIREARMS

- Any guns kept in the home should be unloaded and locked up, with ammunition locked in a separate location.
- Keeping a handgun for protection is dangerous to your family.
- Teach your children never to touch any gun they might find. If they see or hear about a gun at school, tell them they should tell an adult immediately.
- Non-gunpowder firearms (BB or pellet guns) should not be considered toys and are not recommended for children.

HOME SAFETY: OUTDOORS

- Before allowing your mobile child to explore the great outdoors around your home, take a child's-level survey of any area she might reach. If she's a skilled crawler, keep in mind how fast she can move while your attention is diverted.
- If you have a swimming pool, make sure that a childproof fence surrounds it. (Some states require this safety barrier by law.) If your yard contains a spa, it should be securely covered when not in use.
- Check the lawn for mushrooms—if you are not absolutely certain that they are nontoxic, get rid of them because anything a young child finds will likely go straight into her mouth.
- Make sure that potentially hazardous items such as garden tools, insecticides, or fertilizer are not accessible to children.
- Older children should not use garden, hand, or power tools until you teach them to use them correctly and safely. Give them detailed instructions (including demonstrations, if appropriate) and safety precautions; they should repeat back to you both directions and cautions before they are allowed to handle any potentially hazardous equipment.
- Protective eyewear must be worn if the use of any tools will produce flying debris. In addition, ear protection should be used when using loud power tools.
- Don't forget to apply sunscreen with a sun protection factor (SPF) rating of 15 or more if a child is going to be outdoors for any length of time, especially between the hours of 10 A.M. and 3 P.M.—even on a hazy or overcast day. This is particu-

E
M
E
R
G
E
N
C
Y

larly important at higher altitudes or around lakes and seashores where the sun's ultraviolet light (which provokes the burn) can reflect off of water and sand. Special caution is needed for infants, because *a baby's skin can become sunburned after as little as 15 minutes of direct exposure.* Sunscreens containing PABA shouldn't be used on a baby's skin before six months of age. If you take your baby outdoors for any length of time, keep her in the shade or use an umbrella, and make sure that her skin is covered with appropriate clothing (including a hat or bonnet) if some sun exposure is unavoidable.

WEATHER SAFETY

* Dress your child appropriately for the outing, allowing for adjustments if the weather changes.
* Carry rain gear in your car.
* Apply sunblock (SPF 15 to 45, depending on skin type) before you or your child go outside.
* Take and use hats and sunglasses.

BICYCLE SAFETY

* Make sure your child takes a bike-safety class or teach him the rules of the road yourself.
* Stick to bicycle paths whenever possible.
* Children under age six should not ride on the street.
* Make sure that the bicycle is the right size (take the child along when you buy it). When sitting on the seat with hands on the handlebars, the child should be able to touch the ground with the balls of his feet. When straddling the center bar with both feet flat on the ground, there should be at least one inch of clearance between the bar and the child's crotch.
* Do not buy a bicycle with hand brakes until the child is able to grasp with sufficient pressure to use them effectively.
* Keep the bicycle in good repair and teach your child how to fix and maintain it.
* Insist that your child wear a bicycle helmet and always wear one yourself.
* Discourage your child from riding at night. If it is necessary for him to do so, be sure that the bicycle is properly equipped with lights and reflectors and that your child wears reflective (or at least bright) clothing.

SAFETY GEAR

- Provide the protective equipment appropriate for any sport in which your child participates. Make sure it is worn at practices as well as at games.
- Your child must wear a properly fitting helmet that meets the standards of the American National Standards Institute (ANSI) or the Snell Memorial Foundation when riding a bike or when sitting in a carrier seat on your bicycle. Wear your own helmet as well, both for self-protection and to set a good example. Critical injuries to the skull and brain can occur during a bicycle accident, and a helmet can reduce the severity of damage by as much as 90 percent. As your child grows, the helmet will need to be sized upward accordingly.
- Make sure that your child uses wrist guards, elbow and knee pads, and a helmet for rollerblading and skateboarding.

PEDESTRIAN SAFETY

- Fence off and/or supervise any outside play area.
- Provide a play area that prevents balls and riding toys from rolling into the street.
- Prohibit riding of Big Wheels, tricycles, and bicycles in or near traffic or on driveways.
- Hold a young child's hand when walking around traffic.
- When crossing the street, teach and model safety measures: Stop at the curb, then look—left, right, then left again—before entering the street.
- Plan walking routes that minimize crossing heavy traffic.

MOTOR VEHICLE SAFETY

SEAT BELTS AND CAR SEATS

Over the last 20 years, widespread use of seat belts has led to a steady reduction in traffic fatalities. Proper use of seat belts and car seats decreases the risk of serious injury or death by as much as 50 percent. But in the United States, the leading cause of death in people under age thirty-five continues to be motor-vehicle-related injuries. Most of these individuals were not properly restrained by seat belts or car seats.

SAFETY ON THE ROAD

- Parents and children should wear their seat belts. *Do not start the car until everyone is secured in an infant or child seat or properly belted.*

- *Never hold a child in your lap when you are riding in a car.*
- *A child under twelve should never be placed in the front seat of an automobile with a passenger-side air bag because deployment of the bag can cause fatal injuries in a young passenger—even during a minor accident.*
- For children under 40 pounds (18 kg), use a car safety seat approved for your child's age and weight in accordance with the manufacturer's directions. (Make sure you have a safety seat for your infant's first important ride home from the hospital.) *The seat should be secured in the rear seat of the vehicle.* For an infant who weighs less than 20 pounds (9 kg), the seat should face backwards. Buy or rent the next size up as your child grows larger.
- Toddlers 40 to 60 pounds should be properly secured in a booster seat.
- When the child reaches 60 pounds, lap and shoulder belts should be used. The lap belt should be low and tight across the pelvis, not the abdomen. The shoulder harness should be placed snugly over the collarbone and breastbone, not the shoulder.
- If your child takes off his seat belt or gets out of the car seat while you are driving, pull over safely and stop the car. Do not attempt to deal with this (or any other) problem while driving.
- Insist that your child wear a seat belt, no matter whose car he rides in.
- Never leave your child unattended in a car.
- Never transport a child in a cargo area that is not properly equipped to carry passengers (specifically, the back of a station wagon, van, or pickup truck).
- Do not allow your child under age twelve to operate a motor vehicle, including a motorcycle, motorbike, trail bike, or other off-road vehicles. An adolescent should operate one of these vehicles only if he is licensed and properly trained, and has demonstrated appropriate responsibility.
- Be very cautious about allowing your child to ride as a passenger on a motorcycle, motor bike, trail bike, or off-road vehicle. Insist on a proper helmet, slow speed, and a mature, sober driver.

Index

Quick Medical Reference Sheet

Photocopy this chart for each child in your family

CHILD'S NAME _____

Birth date _____ Blood type _____

Any allergies or ongoing medical conditions _____

_____

_____

Child's physician _____

Long-term prescriptions used by the child:

    Medication _____ Prescription # _____

    Medication _____ Prescription # _____

    Medication _____ Prescription # _____

    Pharmacy phone # _____

Illness _____

    Year and month _____

    Physician treating _____

    Severity of illness/specific problems _____

    _____

    Treatment/medications used _____

    _____

Illness _____

    Year and month _____

    Physician treating _____

    Severity of illness/specific problems _____

    _____

    Treatment/medications used _____

    _____